"Faith and doubt stand in loving tension in this splendid collection. . . . With such an amazing cast of characters, it's practically impossible to go wrong. . . . This is a rich feast of accumulated wisdom."

—*Publishers Weekly* (starred review)

"This absorbing book demonstrates the many paths available to those who choose to make a positive impact on the world. The men and women interviewed here speak with conviction and passion, enabling readers to begin to understand and respect the distinct cultures, even if their beliefs are contradictory."

—*ForeWord*

"The book is a collection of essays and reflections on faith by some of the world's best-known figures and some lesser-known leaders, too."

—*Arkansas Democrat-Gazette*

"This is a feast of ideas and insights, a banquet of hard-won wisdom to which you can return time and again when your heart yearns for inspiration and your intellect for illumination."

—Bill Moyers

"A noted theologian (Paul Tillich) has said that religion is a search for the truth about our relationship with God and our fellow human beings. This book will help us in that search."

—Jimmy Carter

"Some books—almost all books, in fact—are for reading. Only occasionally is there that stately book which is so substantial and yet so open and present, that it is for being with. This is a book for being with. . . . *The Life of Meaning* is more infused with wisdom than any I have seen in many, many a year."

—Phyllis Tickle

The Life of Meaning

Reflections on Faith, Doubt, and Repairing the World

BOB ABERNETHY and WILLIAM BOLE

And the contributors to PBS's *Religion & Ethics NewsWeekly*

Foreword by Tom Brokaw

SEVEN STORIES PRESS

New York ◆ Toronto ◆ London ◆ Melbourne

Seven Stories Press
140 Watts Street
New York, NY 10013
www.sevenstories.com

In Canada: Publishers Group Canada, 559 College Street, Suite 402, Toronto, ON M6G 1A9

In the UK: Turnaround Publisher Services Ltd., Unit 3, Olympia Trading Estate, Coburg Road, Wood Green, London N22 6TZ

In Australia: Palgrave Macmillan, 15–19 Claremont Street, South Yarra, VIC 3141

College professors may order examination copies of Seven Stories Press titles for a free six-month trial period. To order, visit http://www.sevenstories.com/textbook or send a fax on school letterhead to (212) 226-1411.

Book design by Jon Gilbert

Library of Congress Cataloging-in-Publication Data

Abernethy, Bob.
  The life of meaning : reflections on faith, doubt, and repairing the world / Bob Abernethy and William Bole ; and the contributors to PBS's Religion & Ethics NewsWeekly.
     p. cm.
  ISBN: 978-1-58322-758-9 (hardcover : alk. paper)
  ISBN: 978-1-58322-829-6 (paperback : alk. paper)
  1. Spirituality. 2. Meaning (Philosophy)--Religious aspects. I. Bole, William. II. Title.

BL624.A245 2007
204--dc22

                                        2006038953

Printed in the USA.

9 8 7 6 5 4 3 2 1

For our families

Contents

Foreword

—

Who doesn't want to have a meaningful life? And who doesn't need help in determining how to accomplish that? This rich, *meaningful* book is, literally, an answer to your prayers or, if you prefer, a fascinating journey through the labyrinth of questions we all have about life, faith, God, choices and doubts.

Bob Abernethy and William Bole have done us all a great favor with this collection of reflections and observations about what constitutes a meaningful life. Some of the interview subjects are well known—Desmond Tutu, Martin Marty, Harold Kushner, Madeleine L'Engle, Jimmy Carter, and the Dalai Lama among them—and yet their insights have a fresh vitality and profoundly personal connections to the questions we're all asking.

Others here are not as well known but they're exceptionally well prepared to help steer us through this ever more challenging topography of life and its meaning.

These lessons are compelling because they mix the certain with the ambivalent, the committed with the I-am-not-so-sure. Can we be moral and spiritual without being religious? God has expectations for me? Look, I have some questions for God before we get to me. I tried prayer but God didn't answer.

Why do the Hindus have so many deities and, by the way, is the God of Evangelicals a little stricter than the God of, say, Congregationalists?

In this book you will find lives well lived and a wide-ranging congregation of men and women who through their own experiences and studies have given us fresh incentive for the pursuit of a Life of Meaning.

—Tom Brokaw

Acknowledgments

Our great thanks to all those interviewed by *Religion & Ethics NewsWeekly* over the past decade, and especially those who contributed their voices to this volume. Each time we have read and reread what they told us, we have been impressed all over again by their insight and eloquence. They remind us that the purveyors of great wisdom are alive and well in our times just as they were long ago.

Also, thanks to the Lilly Endowment for its generous support of *RENW*, and to the Corporation for Public Broadcasting, Mutual of America and all others who have helped fund the program.

At Seven Stories Press, thanks to Dan Simon, Theresa Noll and Ruth Weiner. Dan, our editor, is a great encourager as well as a kind critic, and he helped us see the value of turning raw interview transcripts into spoken essays.

Thirteen/WNET in New York is the program's producing station and the producer of this book. Thanks, also, to the Public Broadcasting System, the program's distributor, and to all the public television stations that carry the show. At Thirteen, our gratitude is to Bill Baker, Tammy Robinson, Stephen Segaller, Shari LaPayover and Catherine Cevoli.

Thanks also to Peter B. Kaufman, who connected Thirteen and Seven Stories Press.

Special thanks to Arnold Labaton, *RENW's* Executive Producer, who offered valuable comments on the manuscript, along with editors Missy Daniel and Janice D'Arcy. Daniel, who edits the program's web site, first proposed this book and drafted sample items; her edited interviews posted on the web site helped guide our work, and her suggestions were always helpful. Also, our gratitude to Anne Hobbs for research and to Janice Henderson and Alan Schwartz for technical backup.

Our final, though not fewest, thanks go to the journalists. We are especially indebted to the correspondents and producers who conducted interviews presented in this book, starting with, again, Missy Daniel, as well as *RENW* managing editor Kim Lawton, who also lent a very helpful hand with several items, especially the introductions to her interviews with Rachel Remen and Anne Lamott. We are grateful to Lucky Severson and the other reporters and producers whose interviews turn up in these pages: Judy Valente, Susan Grandis Goldstein, Chris Roberts, Kate Olson, Jeff Sheler, Anisa Mehdi, Maureen Bunyan, Richard Ostling, Menachem Daum, and Herbert Kaplow.

Additionally, we thank all the other correspondents, editors, producers, and colleagues, who have helped forge this ongoing experiment in religion journalism and public broadcasting, on the air, online and in print. They include Gerry Solomon, Marcia Henning, Judy Reynolds, Patti Jette Hanley, Ted Elbert, Deryl Davis, Oren Rudavsky, Phil O'Connor, Gail Fendley, Fred de Sam Lazaro, Saul Gonzalez, Tim O'Brien, David Anderson, Deborah Potter, Phil Jones, Paul Miller, Tanya Zebulon, Keesha Dyson, Nancy Glass, Tim Martin, Mary Schultz, Lynn Rosenbleeth, Greg Hotzenpiller, John Ryan, Amanda Brezing, Cara Beale, Kevin Eckstrom, and Liz Abernethy.

—Bob Abernethy and William Bole

Introduction

by Bob Abernethy

———

In 1998, retired South African Archbishop and Nobel Peace Prize–winner Desmond Tutu was a scholar in residence at Emory University in Atlanta, where I interviewed him for *Religion & Ethics NewsWeekly*.

We spoke about issues in that week's news and Tutu's health, as he was recovering from cancer surgery.

Then, when we finished, I asked "The Arch," as he said some of his friends refer to him, "While we are here, with the lights and the microphones and the camera, would you mind if I asked you about your spiritual life?"

Without hesitation and with great intensity, Tutu spoke about his wordless prayer, his sense of being in God's presence, which he likened to sitting near a warm stove on a cold morning.

"I don't have to do anything," he said. "The fire warms me. I just have to be there, quiet," and I think his simple description moved all of us in the room.

Typically, over the ten years since *Religion & Ethics NewsWeekly* began, the reporters and producers doing interviews for the program have encouraged our subjects to address the great questions about life and how to live it, and their insightful and eloquent comments comprise the substance of this collection.

I was a correspondent for many years for NBC News—in Washington, London, Los Angeles, and Moscow. I covered American politics, the start of the space program, the fall of communism, and many other great stories. But nothing I have done has been as personally satisfying as founding and working on *RENW*, and the main reason for that is the many opportunities the show provides for sitting down with the likes of Archbishop Tutu—extraordinary men and women who speak as naturally about their faith and doubt and spiritual practices as they do about the weather.

Here is Martin Marty, for instance, the great Protestant historian of religion, describing his "wintry spirituality"—and insisting that taking a nap can be a form of prayer.

Robert Franklin notes the African-American church's "defiant spirituality."

Rabbi Irving Greenberg, former chairman of the United States Holocaust Memorial Council, speaks of a post-Holocaust theology that can be "credible in the presence of burning children."

Eileen Durkin, a cradle Catholic in Chicago, sees the world as sacramental and all life as a gift.

Rachel Remen, a physician, writer, and teacher in northern California, speaks about the difference between healing and curing, and of responding with compassion to the pain of people "whose names we don't even know."

Madeleine L'Engle, one of whose books affirms the "hum of the universe," prompts Robert Wuthnow, the Princeton sociologist of religion, to make the qualification that, for him, the hum is in "a minor key."

Thomas Lynch, poet and funeral director, says, "Grief is the tax we pay on loving people."

Novelist Anne Lamott speaks of finding God in the "utter dailyness and mess of it all," and calls laughter "carbonated holiness."

And Thich Nhat Hanh, a Vietnamese teacher and writer, says "engaged Buddhism" means "If you hear the bombs falling, you know that you have to go out and help."

The men and women represented here are not hermits withdrawn from the world most of us know. Only a few are theologians. These are people fully engaged in teaching, writing, advocacy, ministry, healing, and other familiar careers. Most of them are associated with a particular faith tradition but some are not, describing their outlook and practices as more spiritual than religious.

Whatever their beliefs and observances, however, there is one thing most of them share and that is their sense of "Something More," as many of them put it—something or someone both beyond the material world and also part of it. Thus, our contributors would deny the claim that everything is physical and fully explainable—eventually—by science and reason alone. They fully respect the world of "stuff," but they are also open to mystery and intuition, and many of them say they live their lives in both the material and spiritual realms, even working and praying simultaneously.

There is no avoidance of the dark realities of life—of pain and disappointment and evil. Rather, with great courage, those quoted here accept both the suffering that is part of the everyday and the ultimate goodness of the "Something More." Some of them also observe that suffering strengthens faith.

In my own everyday world in Washington, D.C., the spiritual dimension of things sometimes seems distant or forgotten. So it has been deeply affecting to sit down with these honest, learned, and expressive people and hear them reveal—without preaching—the specific beliefs, practices, and points of view that define and enrich their lives. I have felt my own spiritual understanding grow steadily with exposure to their company, all of whom I now think of as friends.

There is nothing superficial about these grounded people. But neither is there anything about them that is dour or overly pious. They are just a group of informed and likable men and women with a perspective on the world that, in Martin Marty's words, "rings true to the human condition and also affirms."

Over the years at *Religion & Ethics NewsWeekly*, we never had the opportunity to give this material the full space and context it deserves, using only a fraction of it on the air and on our Web site. So, as our treasury of conversations grew, cassette on cassette, so did our frustration that these interviews, with their provocative ideas and distinctive language, were sitting, unheard and underappreciated, in our bulging videotape library.

Fortunately, Thirteen/WNET in New York, which produces *RENW*, and Seven Stories Press agreed on the need for this collection, and the gifted editor William Bole and I were given the chance to assemble and edit it.

Bill is a longtime religion writer and editor, a Roman Catholic who lives in Andover, Massachusetts. I am a member of a United Church of Christ congregation in Washington, D. C.

As Bill and I read and reread the transcripts of these interviews, we realized that they organized themselves into themes and even suggested a kind of framework or arc: finding meaning in life; seeking "the More," in William James's words, and finding ways to communicate with it; dealing with suffering and evil; being spiritual and/or part of a religious tradition; relating to other traditions; and, finally, creating extraordinarily well-lived lives. Moreover, it also became clear that some of our contributors had such valuable insights into each of our major topics that they needed to be heard several times throughout the book, suggesting an unfolding group conversation—perhaps even a kind of community—with arguments as well as agreement.

Thus, the collection as a whole became a sample of the national and global search for meaning through many traditions, and of some of the ways people hope to communicate, even unite, with the transcendent. James Wind, president of the Alban Institute in Virginia, calls this "the biggest story of them all."

Bill and I have edited and rearranged the material for readability and clarity, and so have a few of our interviewees. Our goal has been to preserve the vitality and authenticity of the words as they were spoken and at the same time present them as essays.

This book is for all those interested in finding meaning in their lives, everyone with a nagging sense that there must be "Something More," everyone who approaches faith with doubt as well as hope, and all those seeking ideas and language that can deepen the faith they already have.

Bill Bole and I hope you find what is here interesting. Maybe you will also find these words helpful, challenging, and even inspiring. As we have, too.

CHAPTER 1

The
Meaning
Makers

Long before scientists knew that we share at least 95 percent of our DNA with chimpanzees, great minds were considering our virtues as animals. And they were asking: what sort of animal are we? What's the added value of being a *human* animal?

Benjamin Franklin surmised that human beings are by nature "tool-making animals," in fact, the only tool-making animal, a thesis that eventually surrendered to experiments showing that chimpanzees, our closest kin, rustled up stones and branches to make all sorts of implements in the interests of busting open coconuts and hauling down banana bunches. Two thousand years before Franklin, Aristotle fell closer to the anthropological mark when he observed that we are "social animals," beings in relation to one another. In recent times people who contemplate such things have hit upon the notion that the human person is actually a "meaning-making" animal. We manufacture meaning out of the rawest materials—out of sickness, war, death, as well as routine events. These days, we even look to extract meaning from molecules.

In a significant universe, the diagnosis of a serious illness is not above all a medical event; it may be an invitation to become more than who you are, "to live closer to the soul," as we will hear in these pages. A war is not merely the use of deadly force; it is "a force that gives us meaning," an impulsion that speaks of myth and tragedy. The butterfly that flaps its wings in Beijing and affects the weather in New York is more than a meteorological phenomenon; it is a sign that everyone and everything influences the course of events, a concept that is "threatening and exciting." Even the dough that stirs to life has a purpose beyond the palate, because it puts the bread baker in touch with "the wonder of which I cannot see—which is indeed happening beneath my hands." These and other reflections that follow point to a reality beyond the "real world," or perhaps to a force that inhabits our world, infusing it with spirit, meaning, and purpose.

At the opening of the documentary series *Cosmos*, millions of viewers heard Carl Sagan declaim that the "cosmos is all there is or ever was or ever will be," which is a way of saying we live in a wholly material universe. But many people, religious and nonreligious, are wagering that there is more to this cosmos than matter and motion. The sociologist Robert Wuthnow and his research team at Princeton University interviewed physicists, engineers, nurses, and many others, and most felt, as he put it, that "there's got to be something more. We're not quite sure what it is, but we're certainly convinced that the mystery and the huge expanse of knowledge of the universe points us to something transcendent." Something beyond the tangible, the mundane, the merely verifiable.

Higher meanings, richer symbols, deeper values, unobservable forces are explored here by people who make their meanings in varied daily pursuits.

1.

Limning the Rites of Death

Thomas Lynch is a funeral director, essayist, and poet who reads his rhyme to audiences nationwide—and who appreciates a generous introduction. "It's always nice to hear such kind things about you in the present tense and to be vertical when you hear them," he told one audience in South Carolina. Bob spoke with him on a cold, early spring morning at his home in Milford, Michigan, across the street from the family mortuary where Lynch guesses he has arranged six thousand funerals over the past thirty years. In this 2001 interview, Lynch offers his meditations on mortality, which he calls "the signature of our species."

The etymology of the word "dismal"—the bad day, the dark day, the unlucky time—is exactly what most people feel when a death occurs in the family. So, because undertaking is directly related to a death in the family, it is the dismal trade. But that doesn't mean it's a morbid trade. When I see people at this most difficult time in their family history, I'm also seeing what's best about our species—the attachments and the affection and the faith. That's part of the great satisfaction—you are dealing with people all the time. I keep telling them that for every dead guy, there are 150 or 200 people to whom that death matters. We have the dead outnumbered at funerals, and it is the living that we spend our time with and among.

A funeral is the way we get through a death. It has not changed fundamentally since the species began doing it forty thousand years ago. The fashions have changed, but the fundamental obligation of a funeral is to bear witness to a death in the family and to initiate remembrance—that's pretty much the same. In some cultures they do that with fire, other places with graves. Some places use caskets. Some places use old doors. Some people leave their dead on the tops of mountains to be eaten by scavenger birds. Some people put them in vaults in veterans' cemeteries. Those are fashions.

But the fundamental obligation of a funeral is to provide an opportunity for the living to confront their dead and to dispose of them in a way that's other than the way we dispose of a rock or a rhododendron—that's not changed.

The funerals in my own family—the doing of them, just the large-muscled involvement in them—give us a chance to say what happened, and to whom, and how it is, and how we're going to manage. Think of the people who must be there to get a funeral going. You have to have someone who agrees to quit breathing, forever, and then you have to have someone to whom that death matters, and then you have to have someone who tries to make some sense of it. This doesn't seem to change. We have the dead guy, and we have the people to whom the death matters, and someone— shaman, rabbi, priest, a holy one, a witch, whatever it happens to be—comes in and says, "This is what happened, and this is why."

The fashions are constantly in flux, but I do think that we are returning to a time when people see their obligations to take part in these things in a way that for three or four decades we were trying to get away from. Through the 1970s and 1980s, people were getting comfortable with "disappearing" their dead and then having a memorial service or a gathering afterward— weeks, months, years afterward—to talk about it. This follows the same sort of progress with other things—with birth and sickness and age. We have, in some ways, the women of the baby-boom generation to thank for the hospice movement. They refused to see their parents die surrounded by the machinery of intensive care and said that they would, as an alternative, bring their people home where they could really take care of them. Even though the medicine had to be downsized, humanity was upsized in that transaction, and I think all to the good. In the same way, men of my generation absolutely refused—for reasons that I'm not entirely sure of—to sit out in the waiting room with a handful of cigars, waiting to be declared a parent by some health care professional. They wanted to be there. They wanted to witness it. They weren't of much use, apparently. All they said was, "Breathe, honey. Breathe." But being there was important. And in the same way, funerals are more a matter of presence and attendance and witness than they were, say, twenty years ago.

People are more serious about their own obligations to tend to these things. Anybody can get on their cell phone and get out their gold card and have their dead parent or grandparent "disappeared" from the face of the earth by someone like me. We can handle that. But, more and more, people are identifying a death in the family as a time when the object is not to get around it, but to get through it. And so they are, in a sense, reinventing funerals. They are reinventing liturgies and ceremonies and metaphors and symbols that speak in a new generation's language to this old, human predicament. Because this is the signature of our species. We die. We don't all pay taxes. We won't all sleep with another member of our species. But we will all die. The numbers are convincing on this, you know. One hundred percent. They hover there—all the time.

The Funeral as Poetry

A poem is an effort to say something by organizing the images and the icons and the symbols and the acoustics of the language. It is an effort to say something about what we reckon is unspeakable—great history, great love, great hope, great hate.

Certainly a funeral is an effort at the same thing. It's the same enterprise, to organize some response to what is unspeakable—unspeakable heartache, unspeakable helplessness, unspeakable despair, unspeakable gratitude, unspeakable faith. We try to organize that around a death in the family. And funerals operate in the same way that poems do. They operate by metaphor and icon and liturgy and symbol.

That we need symbols is, I think, constant throughout. We need a way to say unspeakable things and funerals do. So do poems.

I do believe that if we were left to our own devices, we would almost speak in poems, because most of us hear poems before we hear anything else. For me, the first one was, "Angel of God, my guardian dear, to whom God's love commits me here." I hadn't a clue what that meant. Grisly little thought, actually, when you think about it. Like "Now I lay me down to sleep. I pray the Lord my soul to keep. And if I die before I wake, I pray the Lord my soul to take." It's a grim thought when you are two or three, when we are instructed to say these things. But we are attracted to the acoustics.

"Trochee, trochee, falling: thus / Grief and meter order us."* It is the acoustic of the rhyme and the meter of those words that make us go after their meaning.

We must live in relation to our mortality. That relationship is ours to define. But we all know people who live as if they're never going to die. We may call them daredevils. And we know people who live as if they're going to be dead tomorrow. They might be hypochondriacs. But between those two extremes there are most of us who walk around feeling that kernel of our mortality in us. We know it's there, and we see it in the little losses of our lives every day, when we look in the mirror and find ourselves grayer, or balder, or blinder, or full of more aches and pains. That is our mortality beckoning from inside of us. We may take that seriously on some days, and we may let it pass on others. But I do think that living as if you're going to die does bring a certain meaning to life.

The Dead Don't Care

The instinct to preplan has been around for a long time. We like to do that with big life events: birth, death, and marriage. Ever since the pyramids, we've been preplanning things. The pharaoh noticed it could happen to him, and we've been, in a sense, prefunding funerals since we stuffed money in a mattress. Pirates used to have gold earrings to pay for their return if they should die at sea. But the preselling of funerals is a different thing, and that's based on the hopeful idea that if you've got it paid for, you've got it taken care of. And it's just not so. Even the planning doesn't take care of it any more than Planned Parenthood has made for better parents or prenuptial agreements have made for better marriages. Preplanned funerals haven't made for better funerals; they're just better planned funerals. And certainly the preselling of funerals is just abusive, as far as I'm concerned. It makes no particular sense.

It is for the heirs to do. You're leaving them everything. Why wouldn't you leave them the decisions that they have to live with? Someone asked me

---

* From Seamus Heaney's "Audenesque."

last week, "Do you trust your children to make the right decisions about your funeral?" And the answer is, "Well, if they make the wrong decisions, I trained them, and I'll get what I deserve. And whatever decisions they make, they'll live with, I won't." I'm convinced that the dead don't care about these things. I've never had someone dead say to me, "I'd rather the blue suit" or "I prefer that mahogany casket." They never do. Because our survivors have to live with decisions, they ought to have a hand in making them. The discussion between parent and child, between husband and wife, between partner and partner about these things should be ongoing. But to hold someone to a particular task—it's very narcissistic. "Here's what I want done with me when I'm dead."

I think it is my job to convey my values to my heirs. But I don't have to arrange things down to the doilies. The best example of this I ever got was a letter. I was a young funeral director, and a man brought in a letter that his father had left for him. It spelled out the things that were important to him, that he thought were valuable for a funeral. He said, "I've always thought this hymn spoke directly to the hearts of people," and he listed the hymn. He said, "I've always thought this verse had meaning" and "I've always thought this was important and that was important. And I'd like to be buried next to your mother." On and on he went in this letter. And at the bottom of the letter was a paragraph that I've always thought of as a kind of coupon. It was a disclaimer, and it said, "I've felt, furthermore, that all this is done for the living. So do whatever you want. It won't bother me one bit." So he had done both things. He had communicated his values without giving someone hoops to jump through.

I think it's important that the living see the dead. That's part of the witness of it. That's part of the "this is why it hurts, that's what's happened." I do think the presence of the dead at their funeral is very much like the presence of the baby at a baptism or the bride and groom at a wedding. They are the focal point. It is the reason we gather. And so to invite everybody but the dead guy makes no particular sense to me. My grandmother used to insist, "When I'm dead, I want a closed casket." But I explained to her that when she was dead it would be her children and grandchildren who needed to come face-to-face with that reality. And I've got to tell you, after years and years of sitting and standing with families who have waited for their dead to be returned from wars, or tragedies that happened far from home, or disasters that always turn up in the news, I know that finding what was lost is really important. It's essential. It's fundamental. It's not about whether the casket's open or closed. It's whether or not the living can conquer death.

When Choosing Flames . . .

Cremation is an ancient and honorable way of disposing of our dead. And it works. It does what it's supposed to do. It disposes of them with honor. The problem I have with it is the way we practice it in this culture. We do it devoid of all its ceremonial value. We do not see it. People typically go to a cemetery and see the grave and watch the casket lowered into the grave. But they do not go to the crematory and see the body burned. In India, where most of the dead are burned in public crematories, the family builds the pyre. The flame is brought from the home fire to ignite the fire. People sing and pray and watch. And the cremation has so much more meaning. But in our Western culture, where we have devalued fire—not least because we are all told that when we're in trouble with God, we go to hell, where we burn—we see fire as wasteful and punitive.

I make available to people the option of staying and watching the cremation. Few take it. I think that'll change, though. More and more people will do that. Again, this is partly fashion. I do ask people, when they talk about cremation, to think of what is happening. Too often we're busy talking about the urns and not about what burning represents. When a family says to me, "We want to have a cremation," I want to discuss what that means to them, because for many families it's the first one. Fire is either punitive and wasteful, or it is purifying, releasing, reuniting. It has either positive values or negative values. I just want a family to identify which values they hold.

In some ways the body is just a shell, but it's the "just a" part that I have a problem with. The emphasis there is not on what the body may or may not be. The emphasis, when you say it's "just a shell," is on the minimalization, as if it oughtn't hurt, because it's "just a shell." It is the one and only shell most of us get. It is the one and only shell that we rush to the hospital, that we've had coffee with for forty years. It is the shell that put us through college. It is the one and only body of the one we love. In the West, they don't say, "Please cremate." They say, "Just cremate. When I'm dead, just cremate me." The emphasis is not on the value of the fire. The emphasis is on minimizing what's happened. "Spare me the bother. Cremate." Whereas I think cremation should be a positive, liturgically rich event. It should be purifying, releasing, reuniting.

I'm glad to be alive. You know, every day you wake up is a bonus. I'm glad for the well-being of my family. I feel blessed. Which is not to say that I'm not like the next guy—full of doubt and wonder and worry sometimes. But the older I get, the list of things that I have to worry about is getting shorter and shorter. And if I just turn those things over to God (whoever God is these days, and she or he changes a lot for me from day to day), God seems to be taking care of them.

2.

Staring Down the Gods of War

In his book War Is a Force that Gives Us Meaning *former New York Times correspondent Chris Hedges spoke of war as a drug—which he imbibed. During a 2003 interview, Bob couldn't help but note that in pictures of him taken during the fighting in the former Yugoslavia, Hedges looks happy. The correspondent offered a clarification.*

"Happy" is not a word I would use to describe it. But I had a sense of purpose, a sense of meaning. I had a sense of ennoblement. I think we ennoble ourselves in war. There is a rush in war. And it's very hard, if not impossible, to re-create this feeling in anything else.

I have a lot of respect for those people who engage in war, even while I also recognize its very self-destructive quality. I gave a talk at West Point, and I certainly found an understanding among the older officers who teach there, many of whom had been through Vietnam. Just because you're a professional soldier doesn't mean you like war. In many ways, those who have been through war hate it in a way that only those who have been through war can hate it. Yet they know that they have a job to do.

There are times we have to wage war, when it is morally imperative for us to use violence—certainly in the cases of Kosovo, Sarajevo, Rwanda. But I think, ultimately, being in a war, while it can give you meaning, it's probably meaning that is devoid of happiness. Real happiness only comes through love—not through war. And in wartime there's hardly any love at all.

The ancient Greeks and Romans understood that war is a god and that war always begins by calling for the annihilation of the other. But left unexamined or unchecked, war always ends in self-annihilation. And in an age of apocalyptic weapons, of course, we flirt with our own destruction, especially when those arrayed against us have their hands on apocalyptic weapons.

Thucydides, Cicero, Virgil—all of these great writers deal with the same issues. Virgil and Cicero came out of a very bloody civil war that ended with the reign of Augustus. I found that a lot of the writing of Catullus, the great lyric Roman poet, just spoke to me over hundreds of years in a very powerful and moving way. I memorized a lot of Catullus's poems. And when I went to visit a friend's grave in Sarajevo, I stood over it and recited the poem that Catullus had written to his own brother who died near Troy. It gave me a kind of continuity, a clearer understanding of who I was and the age in which I live.

> By strangers' coasts and waters, many days at sea,
> I came here for the rites of your unworlding,
> Bringing for you, the dead, these last gifts of the living
> And my words—vain sounds for the man of dust.
> Alas, my brother,
> You have been taken from me. You have been taken from me
> And by cold hands turned to shadow and my pain.
> Here are the foods of the old ceremony appointed
> Long ago for the starvelings under the earth.
> Take them. Your brother's tears have made them wet. And take
> Into eternity my hail and my farewell.

Freud, in *Civilization and its Discontents*, writes about the forces of love, of Eros—those forces to preserve, to conserve—and the forces of death, of Thanatos—that aggressive instinct to destroy, even to destroy ourselves. For Freud, these two things are in constant tension, which is why Freud says war is inevitable. He doesn't believe that war will be eradicated. One of these forces is always ascendant. There's a constant tug-of-war between them.

After the Vietnam War, we asked questions about ourselves and our nation. It made us a better people. We were forced to step outside ourselves. We were forced to accept our own capacity for evil, for atrocity. We struggled, perhaps for the first time in a long time, to see ourselves as the outsider saw us. I think this was Eros. I think Eros was ascendant at the end of the Vietnam War.

But gradually, Thanatos or death, that love of power and that glorification, that myth of war, rose—we reveled in the prowess of our military and our weapons. Ever since the Persian Gulf War, it's death that's been ascendant. That's what frightens me so much now.

It's very hard to make antiwar films or write antiwar books, because even if you look at a movie like *All Quiet on the Western Front*, you may recognize how horrible war is, but at the same time, you yearn for that kind of comradeship, which is not friendship. It's very different. You yearn to be tested like that. That's part of the way the myth is sold to us, that we're not finally complete human beings until we've been through the experience of war, the maw of war.

You see that now with the way we mythologize the Second World War and forget the reality of the war. One of my uncles was destroyed by the war in the South Pacific and died as an alcoholic in a trailer. My family carried his burden from the end of the war until his death. And I don't think my family was alone. But that's not the kind of stuff we're reading about or hearing about now.

I'm not a pacifist. Wars are always tragic but probably inevitable. I supported the intervention in Bosnia. I supported the intervention in Kosovo. I feel that we failed as a nation by not intervening in Rwanda. If we've learned anything from the Holocaust, it is that when you have the capacity to stop genocide and you do not, you are culpable. You have blood on your hands, and we do for Rwanda. But I also understand what war can do, especially when you fall into the dark intoxication that war brings.

War Is Zen

I think for those who are in combat, it very swiftly can become an addiction. War is its own subculture. It can create a landscape of the grotesque that is, perhaps, unlike anything else created by human beings. There is that rush of war. In an ambush, when danger is that present, there is no past. There is no future. You are thrust into the present in a way that is like a drug. I mean, even colors are brighter. War is Zen, and that becomes a very heady way to live.

In Sarajevo, for instance—when you left, you would be sitting in Paris for four or five days, and all you did was hunger to go back. The culture of war took you over. I remember stepping outside of war zones in El Salvador or the Balkans into peaceful environments, and the familiar had a quality of what Freud calls "the uncanny." Everything that was familiar seemed strange, because everything that was strange had become familiar.

I would be in a hotel in Paris or London, and although I was there physically, I was really four paces back. You fly, and in a matter of hours, you're outside a war zone. I remember it was as if I were looking at things through a tunnel. That culture takes over; you don't function outside of it.

War is like a poison. And just as a cancer patient must at times ingest a poison to fight off a disease, so there are times in a society when we must ingest the poison of war to survive. But what we must understand is that just as the disease can kill us, so can the poison. If we don't understand what war is, how it perverts us, how it corrupts us, how it dehumanizes us, how it ultimately invites us to our own self-annihilation, then we can become the victim of war itself.

War is one of the most heady and intoxicating, addictive enterprises ever created by humankind. It has an allure, a fascination, a draw that sweeps across national lines, ethnicity, race, religion. It has perverted, corrupted, and ultimately destroyed societies and nations across the globe. The only way to guard against it is finally to understand what it does and how pernicious it is and to see past the myths and lies that we use to cover up the fact that, at its core, war is death.

In every conflict I've covered, you reach a point—and I think I reached this point certainly in El Salvador—where you feel that it's better to live for one intoxicating, empowering moment than ever to go back to that dull routine of daily life, and if your own death is the cost of that, then that's a cost you're willing to accept.

That comes right out of *The Iliad*. It comes right out of Achilles. There's a vase in the Metropolitan Museum of Art, and it shows a scene from the Trojan War where Achilles is thrusting his spear into the chest of the queen of the Amazons, Penthesilea. The legend is that as Achilles killed her, their eyes met, and he fell in love with her. What he was doing, of course, was killing love. And once love was dead, there was no hope of going back.

In *The Odyssey*, which is really a story about recovery from war, Odysseus goes down to the underworld and meets Achilles and says, "You are the greatest of the Achaeans, the hero of the Achaeans," and Achilles says, "I'd rather be up there as a slave, as a serf hacking at clods of earth than down here." There was an understanding in Homer that all of the myth and the glory that was so much a part of *The Iliad* was, in fact, after the war was over, bankrupt and empty. It's why so much of the bombastic rhetoric, so much of the way culture is infected and destroyed—in wartime, we always destroy our own culture first before we go off and destroy the culture of the other— is so forgettable and perhaps even embarrassing once the conflict is over.

War is like imbibing a drug. Once that drug is kicked, once that war is over, many decisions that are made in warfare—not only what we do to others, but also what we do to ourselves—are exposed for being not only wrong, but stupid. Ultimately, what happens is that you embrace death, because that's what war is—it is necrophilia. It is the love of death. When war begins, it looks and feels like love. It isn't love. That's the chief emotion war destroys.

When you look at the beginning of the conflict in the Balkans, people were ecstatic. They were in the street. They were waving their nationalist flags. A kind of euphoria often grips a country in wartime. And war is, of course, the very opposite of that. It is a bit like the beautiful nymph in the fairy tale that seduces you, and then when you kiss it, it exhales the vapors of the underworld. Humankind has an attraction to war. But once you're in it, it very soon takes you over. War always creates a kind of moral perversion, and that's why you see sexual perversion so interrelated with war.

Routine death becomes boring. It's why you would go into central Bosnia and see bodies crucified on the sides of barns, or why in El Salvador genitals were stuffed in people's faces—mutilation, the body as a sort of trophy, the body as a kind of performance art. This is an inevitable consequence of war. As you fall deeper and deeper into that culture, and as it becomes harder and harder to exist outside of it, what you do is finally embrace your own annihilation, because like any addiction, it creates a kind of self-destruction. There is constantly a search for that first high of war that you can never re-create.

It becomes a kind of suicide. I had a very close friend, Kurt Schork, who ended up in Sierra Leone in May of 2000. He was ambushed with another friend of mine, Miguel Gil Moreno, and it's because they couldn't let go.* They couldn't let go, and they died because of it. And they're not alone. That was a big moment for me. Kurt is irreplaceable. He was a remarkable man. I realized I had to stop. I had to get out.

The costs were tremendous. These are images, memories that I'll have to carry with me for the rest of my life. There are days when they're very, very hard to bear. I have a very hard time connecting sometimes within the society in which I live. I certainly am ultrasensitive to the notion of violence as entertainment. I took my son to see the *Lord of the Rings*, and I had to walk out. I couldn't watch it.

I did it far too long. I struggle with that kind of trauma and keep it wrapped in protective wool, but it's there. And it's hard when it surfaces.

I'm like my friends in Sarajevo. They all sat around at the end of the war, and they didn't miss the suffering and the death, but they also realized that this was probably the fullest moment in their life. There was a kind of nostalgia for that, a sense of that comradeship, a sense of that excitement. Yet that kind of lifestyle or that kind of rush can probably never be re-created.

But, at the same time, I have no desire to go to Iraq. I don't want to do this anymore. I don't feel the pull of it anymore.

Love Radiating

In every conflict I've been in, the only antidote is people who find their fulfillment, their sense of being, in love. In the Balkans, these were often couples who had mixed marriages, and therefore, they were immune from the rhetoric. To paint all Serbs as evil, or all Muslims as evil, or all Croats as evil was to denigrate the spouse, to dehumanize the spouse, which they couldn't do. These relationships are always sanctuaries—sanctuaries that I went to in wars that I covered.

---

* Schork was a Reuters correspondent, and Moreno a cameraman for Associated Press TV News.

It doesn't mean they didn't become victims. It doesn't mean they weren't eventually wiped out. But it provided a small circle of sanity in the midst of the insanity, where all of that rhetoric, all of that drive for the ruthless annihilation of the other was held at bay, always by couples, which is why, usually, when you look at people who intervene in a town or a village to help a minority under threat, it's usually couples—one of whom has that kind of moral quality and knows they have to take a moral stance, and the other who has that kind of compassion and caring that the daily maintenance of taking care of another requires.

Love is the only force that finally can counter the force of death, the death instinct. When shells would come into Sarajevo, at the most horrific moment of death, when people were literally lying in pools of their own blood dying, family members, friends, brothers, sisters, spouses would claw through the crowds looking for their loved ones. Just as death seemed to radiate out from that point, at the same time love radiated out. You can't go through an experience like that and not understand the palpable power of love, the power of that one act of reconciliation and forgiveness—the Muslim farmer who gives milk to the Serb baby for two hundred plus days, and the way he was reviled by his neighbors. Yet when I interviewed the Serb couple whose baby had been saved, they could never denigrate Muslims the way their Serb neighbors could because of that act.

What appear to be small acts of love—in those acts are seeds of hope. That little child may grow up in the Serb part of Bosnia, where to this day there's terribly racist rhetoric against Muslims. And that child must know that she is alive because of a poor Muslim farmer whom she may never meet.

We cannot underestimate these acts that often seem minimal and small in the face of war, but which I've come to understand are immensely powerful and give us hope.

3

Exposing the Spiritual Crisis of Modern Medicine

Dr. Rachel Remen believes physicians can take part in healing the spirit as well as the flesh. Her spiritual sensibilities are well accompanied by her physical surroundings in northern California, where she lives in a beautiful home atop a mountain that was shrouded in mist on the day Religion & Ethics NewsWeekly *managing editor Kim Lawton spoke with her in the fall of 2005. Kim told us the entire home has an Eastern flair, decorated with Buddha statues and Asian teapots. Interviewed in her garden, Remen spoke of mysticism as well as medicine, explaining that serious illness is an invitation to the soul, a path to becoming more than who you are. Through her project Finding Meaning in Medicine, Remen helps doctors recover from a medical malaise that, in her diagnosis, has left them detached from the innermost values that first drew them to the healing profession.*

Over time an illness can become a spiritual path. If one genuinely and unflinchingly meets the difficulties of an illness, especially a serious illness, the person you are at the end can be larger than the person you were going in, and all those around you can become larger people and live deeper lives as well. This is possible even in the absence of cure. We can't cure everything or even most things. Cure was the great hope when the age of scientific medicine burst in on us—we were going to be able to fix it all. We now know that a great many things can't be fixed, but even so, the possibility of growing beyond our limitations, of becoming able to live more deeply and passionately with greater meaning is always there, even in the absence of cure. It's possible to live a good life even though it is not an easy life.

There is a real difference between healing and curing. I think my deep interest in this difference grows out of my own life experience. I was diagnosed with Crohn's disease fifty-two years ago, and I haven't been a well person in more than half a century. When I first became sick nobody knew how to cure this disease, nobody even knew what caused it. This is still true today. Years ago I was told that I would need many surgeries and would be an invalid. I was also told that I would die by the time I was forty. But as time went on, I became aware that something hidden was growing in me, something stronger than my disease. Slowly it changed me and gave me new eyes. I looked at the world differently and found in myself capacities I did not know existed. Perhaps they did not exist before I became so sick. Eventually I no longer ran from other people in trouble. I actually became stronger as a person, much more loving, much wiser as a person. Over the years I have had eight major surgeries and live with physical limitations, but I am much more able to live because of these experiences. I am able to do a much larger work in the world because of it. I would say that I am more whole. And because of my long experience I am very aware of this potential for healing in us all.

I love the traditional Hindu greeting—*namaste*. It means, "I see and I greet the hidden wholeness in you." No matter how you appear, how weak or sick or different from me you are, I can see past that to the wholeness in you. And I bow to that in you. Because I have learned to see your potential, I can befriend it and enable it to become a little more visible in this world, a little closer to the place that you live from every day. When you see something in another person and acknowledge it, you strengthen it. And so in your presence they may experience a greater potential in themselves, maybe for the first time.

I think that's the challenge of illness. Illness is an invitation for the greatness in us to become more visible, an invitation to become more transparent and to live closer to the soul. And we who work with illness need to be able to respond to that invitation and support people in this natural process of becoming more than they are in the face of adversity, of learning to live beyond the limitations of their circumstances. We need to recognize the spiritual dimension in others and in ourselves.

My grandfather was an Orthodox rabbi and a wonderful storyteller. He was also a student of kabbalah, the mystical arm of Judaism. For my grandfather, the spirit of God was present at all times and in all places. God could talk to you in the kitchen or in the supermarket. There was no place to go to be out of relationship with the Holy One, so it just made sense to stay awake and pay attention because the mystery at the heart of life could show itself to you at any time. For Grandpa, the world was a constant dialogue, a constant learning process, a constant uncovering of the holiness.

I, too, think that life is constantly showing us the holy nature of the world. And medicine is a front-row seat on life. You get to see spirit in action. You also get to become spirit in action, no matter what your religion is. Most doctors recognize this. Few doctors have not experienced what they would call holy moments in their work, moments of awe, moments when they have known themselves to be in the presence of something larger than themselves, be it courage or love or mystery.

I often wonder if this work is actually a calling. Perhaps there is something about the way that we are made inside that has brought us to this profession. The people who do this work move toward situations that many people would avoid and pull back from. When someone is in trouble or in great need, especially someone that you do not know, a lot of people pull back or look the other way. But the people who go into medicine have a different sort of response. They are magnetized toward such situations, not because of what they know, but because of the way they are made inside. And because of this, they recognize that somehow they belong in places of need and trouble. When I teach, I often ask medical students and doctors, "How old were you when you first realized that the needs of living things— insects, plants, and animals—mattered to you? How many people were between twenty and twenty-five, how many people were between fifteen and twenty?" Over the years I have asked these same questions of many thousands of physicians and students. The great majority of those I have asked say that they were under fifteen when they first realized that they moved toward the unmet needs of living things with an intent to make a difference. So medical expertise is only the most recent set of tools with which they have responded to the needs of the life around them. And their intent to make a difference in the life around them—their service impulse—has been a way of life for them, long before they were experts, from the time that they were very young. We are in this work not because of what we know, but because of who we are.

Our stories are the container for our meaning and our values, the lineage of this difficult work. I encourage groups of doctors to meet on a monthly basis and share with one another stories about their common experiences in this work. Stories of compassion, of grace, of love, of healing, of courage, of loneliness and commitment and valor—these stories enable doctors to remember who they are and what really matters to them. Parables are a part of all the world's religions because a story is a container for what has enduring meaning and value. Stories remind us of what is important, what really matters. We carry a story not in our minds—we carry it in our heart and in our souls. A good story is like a compass which points to what is most real and reminds us of how we might live our lives. And if you go into your work carrying your stories and the stories of your community with you, you have a permission and a support to live closer to the values that have been important to you ever since you were a child, despite the pressures in your everyday work.

I believe that medicine is in a time of crisis. Most people would characterize this as an economic or a political crisis, or a crisis of patient access, that sort of crisis. But I think the real crisis in medicine is a spiritual crisis, a crisis of integrity. It has to do with a system, an infrastructure that makes it difficult for people to live by their life values, to relate to people in ways that are compassionate because of economic or time pressures and the policies that come from them. It makes people unable to practice their service according to the best they know, not just scientifically, but also spiritually. When you separate people from the values that they have held closely from their early childhood, they lose their sense of meaning, integrity, and commitment. They feel helpless. They become cynical and depressed and hostile. Our medicine is only as good as the people who practice it. In one generation it is possible to destroy the lineage of a profession that has endured for thousands of years. The lineage survives only as long as the innate values of those who practice the profession. The values of compassion and service and harmlessness and respect for life are passed on and strengthened from generation to generation.

I think that the spiritual core of medicine is at risk at this moment. We could demean this work and become biological technicians, but that's not what medicine is about; it's never been what medicine is about. Medicine is not a work of science, it is a work of service, and service is a special kind of love. The prayer of Maimonides, the great physician/rabbi of the fourteenth century says, "Inspire me with love for all of thy creatures. May I see in all who suffer only the fellow human being." Medicine is about the capacity to value human life as a holy thing, to recognize the life of total strangers as being as valuable as your own. And if anything is needed in this world today it's just that—the ability to move beyond our differences and respond with compassion to the pain and trouble of people whose names we don't even know, who share with us only the bond of a common humanity.

4.

More Than Is Dreamt of in Your Theologies

Marilynne Robinson is an acclaimed essayist and novelist. John Polkinghorne is a prominent physicist and Anglican priest. They, like many others today, are exploring the shared space of spiritual meaning and scientific understanding, and the unexpected ways in which theology rhymes with cosmology. Robinson spoke with Religion & Ethics NewsWeekly *editor Missy Daniel in 2005 and Polkinghorne with correspondent Chris Roberts in 1999.*

Marilynne Robinson . . .

It's a difficult thing to describe theology, what it means and how it disciplines thinking. Certainly, theology is the level at which the highest inquiry into meaning and ethics and beauty coincides with the largest scale imagination of the nature of reality itself. Often, when I want to read something that is as satisfying to me as theology, what I actually read is string theory or something like that—popularizations, inevitably, of scientific cosmologies—because their description of the scale of things and the intrinsic, astonishing character of reality coincides very beautifully with the most ambitious theology. It is thinking at that scale, and it is thinking that is invested with meaning in a humanly evocative form. That's theology.

I think there is a profound connection between poetry and theology in Western tradition. Both poetry and theology push conventional definitions and explore perceptions that might be ignored or passed off, but when they are pressed they yield much larger meanings, seem to be part of a much larger system of reality. The assumption behind any theology that I've ever been familiar with is that there is a profound beauty in being, simply in itself. Poetry, at least traditionally, has been an educing of the beauty of language, the beauty of experience, the beauty of the working of the mind, and so on. The pastor [a character in her novel *Gilead*] does, indeed, appreciate it. One of the things that is nice about these old pastors—they were young at the time—who went into the Middle West is that they were real humanists. They were often linguists, for example, and the schools that they established were then, as they are now, real liberal arts colleges where people studied the humanities in a very broad sense.

I think we have demythologized prematurely, that we've actually lost the vocabulary for discussing reality at its largest scales. The idea that myth is the opposite of knowledge, or the opposite of truth, is simply to disallow it. It is like saying poetry is the opposite of truth. A sermon is a form that yields a certain kind of meaning in the same way that, say, a sonnet is a form that deals with a certain kind of meaning that has to do with putting things in relation to each other. Sermons are, at their best, excursions into difficulty that are addressed to people who come there in order to hear that. The attention of the congregation is a major part of the attention that the pastor gives to his or her utterance. It's very exceptional. I don't know anyone who doesn't enjoy a good sermon. People who are completely nonreligious know a good sermon when they hear one.

A sermon is a valuable thing, in part because it's so seldom true now that you hear people speak under circumstances where they assume they are obliged to speak seriously and in good faith, and where the people who hear them are assumed to be listening seriously and in good faith. This is a kind of standard of discourse that is not characteristic of the present moment. I think that it makes a sermon, when it is a good sermon, stand out in anyone's experience.

One of the things that is wonderful about hymns is that they are a sort of universally shared poetry, at least among certain populations. There isn't much of that anymore either. There are very few poems people can recite, but there are quite a few hymns that, if you hum a few bars, people can at least come up with two verses. Many of the older hymns are very beautiful. Isaac Watts, of course, is a hymn writer in the tradition of Congregationalism who lived in the seventeenth and early eighteenth centuries. He is very interesting and important because he was also a metaphysician. He knew a great deal about what was, for him, contemporary science. He was very much influenced by Isaac Newton, for example. There are planets and meteors and so on showing up in his hymns very often. But, again, the scale of his religious imagination corresponds to a very generously scaled scientific imagination. It makes his hymns continue to have a spaciousness and resonance that locates, for me, the religious imagination in a very beautiful way.

John Polkinghorne . . .

Science is very successful and very important, and I want to take it very seriously. It's very limited also. It can tell you some things, and there are things that we need to know which science can't tell us about. Not just about religion, but many other things as well. So I quite often say to my scientific friends, "What about music?"

If you ask a scientist as a scientist to tell you all that he or she can about music, they'll say it's vibrations in the air. And they can give you quite a very complete and exact account of the form of those vibrations. But we all know that that description, which is complete in scientific terms, has missed the whole mystery of music. Music is very, very much more than vibrations in the air. And so we have to have a wider view of reality that can embrace extra dimensions of music, which science, by its own choice, is unable to speak about. Religious belief is different from scientific belief in the sense that it involves the whole person. I believe passionately in the existence of quarks and gluons as the smallest bits of matter. But that doesn't affect the way I live my life. I can't, however, believe in Jesus Christ without that affecting the way I live my life, as well as how I think about things. So, of course, religion is more overarching and more all-demanding than scientific belief can be.

Physical sciences are at least open to the idea that there might be a divine mind and purpose of some sort behind what's going on. People can't think about cosmology, the nature of the universe, I think, without asking deeper questions of whether there's a meaning and purpose behind it all. I believe that the marvelous order of the universe, the wonderful order that science discovers and rejoices in, is a reflection of a divine mind behind it.

The biologists, on the other hand, are much more hostile to religion. DNA was a truly wonderful discovery. That has led biologists to think that everything is mechanical—that DNA is mechanical, animals are mechanical, everything is mechanical. And we've always known, I think, as surely as we know anything, that we're not automatons, that we have powers of choice. It seems to me that it is perfectly consistent, logically coherent that God can act within the openness of that physical world as well. And I think that in such a world, a scientist can pray.

Religion—or rather theology—is, I think, the great integrating discipline. It takes the insights of science—doesn't tell science what to think—but it takes science's insights and understandings, it takes the insights of morality, takes the insights of aesthetics, the study of beauty. The wonderful order or pattern of the world that science discovers and rejoices in is a reflection, indeed, of the mind of the creator, whose will and purpose lie behind the world. Our moral intuitions, our intimations of God's good and perfect will, our experiences of beauty, I believe, are sharing in the joy of the creator, the creation. You can soon see the gross inadequacy of thinking that science can tell you everything that you could possibly know.

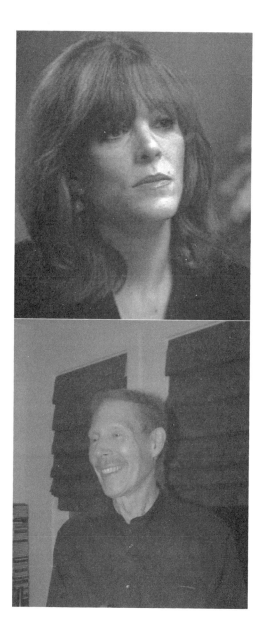

5.

Naming the Real

There are many skeptics who doubt the reality of the spiritual world, and then there is Marianne Williamson, a popular author of spiritual self-help books, who has her doubts about the "the real world." Here, she holds up a mirror to the scientific-materialist view that physical reality is the only reality, that matter is all that matters. She teaches that the spiritual is what's real, and the material—our mundane existence—is an illusion that can shrivel the soul. A very Eastern view, and not that of Tilden Edwards, an Episcopal priest and spiritual director, who sees the world, matter and all, as "just full of God." Bob interviewed Williamson in late 1997, and Edwards two years later.

———

Marianne Williamson . . .

I believe that there is a realm of thought, basically shallow thought—"like your tie," "the blue in your eyes is quite lovely," "love the wave in your hair"—which is part of the delight of life. But, it is part of the twisted nature of modern life that we spend practically all our time there.

I think that there is another dimension of thought in which it is not my physical eyes that reveal you to me. It is not even my physical ears that reveal you to me. There is an inner eye that seeks to see your innocence, which is much more important to me than your hair, an inner ear that seeks to hear what you're really trying to say, rather than just your words. Those are the domains of spirit—and to very many of us, that's the real world. It is the world that is not seen through the physical senses, but through the vision of the Holy Spirit in the Christian religion, or the *Shekinah* in the Jewish religion. All the great religious systems describe this their own way.

A Course in Miracles* posits that the love in you is what God placed there, and it is your only true eternal reality. And the love in me, which God placed there, which is an extension of him, is my only true reality. We are like waves in the same ocean, or sunbeams to the same sun. There is really no point where one wave stops and a new wave begins. So, our truth is our oneness. And this world, the physical world, much in a very kind of Eastern philosophical way, is a world of illusion in which our physical senses reveal to us a world which is not the world that God created. True reality lies in the internal domains of spirit and oneness and love.

The purpose of our lives, while living on this earth, is to develop the capacity through the grace of God to extend our perceptions beyond what the physical senses perceive. And that is what forgiveness does. Forgiveness enables me to focus on your innocence even when the physical world would speak of your guilt. And so in every moment we have a choice between an open-hearted response to each other and a closed-hearted response to each other. And every moment when I choose to bless, rather than condemn, a child of God, I am bringing the world closer to the point at which it will be a reflection on earth of what is in heaven.

Tilden Edwards . . .

I suppose you can say we have three choices. One is the material choice, that it's all material. One is a kind of spiritualized choice that kind of rejects the material and sees it as "God isn't involved with that. If you want to go to God, you get out of the material." And there's a third way that I would subscribe to, which I think is sacramental and incarnational, which says—to echo Eastern Orthodox theology—that every atom is permeated by the uncreated energies of God. The material world is an expression of God's being. It's just full of God, so to speak.

When you have eyes to see, there isn't anything ultimately separate, only relatively separate from that larger presence. And I think today there's more of a sense of this larger presence, even if you believe something is more

---

* A self-help course in spirituality popularized by Williamson.

material than spiritual and you don't know how the spiritual connects with the other. People who once were very secular are saying, "Well, I can call that spiritual. I can't call it God, maybe, but I can call it spiritual. And maybe what God is about is in this."

Sure, you have people who still have the attitude "I want to earn my money and do my job and have a good time." And my own sense is that God is just as much in their lives as in anyone else's. It's just much more invisible, and they miss out, so to speak, on the larger possibilities.

I would put it personally, theologically that the Holy Spirit is doing something in the world today. That's a new thing. The Spirit is drawing out of humanity something that belongs to our truest, best nature. And all the riches of the human religious treasury are available to help draw out the depth of that which will save us, so to speak, as a species. There's something deeper that recognizes one another as brother and sister, and makes life more full and true to who we're meant to be.

To use the phrasing of the Jesuit mystic Pierre Teilhard de Chardin: We belong to a larger reality than our own ego-self. We belong to each other on a very deep plane, where the unity is much deeper than the differences.

6.

Discovering Things Nobody Knew Before but God

Dr. Francis Collins is the medical doctor and chemist who directed the Human Genome Project of the National Institutes of Health in Bethesda, Maryland. He describes himself as a "serious Christian" for whom the discovery of the human genetic code was like seeing the mind of God. In his book The Language of God: A Scientist Presents Evidence for Belief, *Collins argues for the compatibility of scientific and religious ways of seeing the world. Bob interviewed him in 2006.*

—

The Human Genome Project was this audacious, absolutely unheard of ambitious effort to read out all of the letters of the human DNA code—all three billion of them. An enormously challenging problem. And yet, over thirteen years, we finished the job.

To be able to stand at the helm of a project which was going to reveal our own instruction book would be, for any scientist, an unbelievably remarkable experience. But for me, as a believer, it carried this additional impact of reading out the letters of the code that I believe God designed in order to bring human beings into this world, the language of God. It was seeing the evidence of his majesty and creation laid out in this remarkable digital code inherited down through millions of years, from some ancestral source that he also had planned. That, for me, was life spoken into being by God.

I think there's a common assumption that you cannot be both a rigorous, show-me-the-data scientist and a person who believes in a personal God. I would like to say that from my perspective that assumption is incorrect, that, in fact, these two areas are entirely compatible and not only can exist within the same person, but can exist in a very synthetic way, and not in a compartmentalized way.

For me, as a person who believes in a personal God, the opportunity to uncover something about us that nobody knew before but God is really a moment not to be missed. It expands the experience of discovery in ways that people who are not believers, I think, don't quite get to experience. It's an opportunity both for scientific exhilaration and actually for worship.

I don't think science can ever prove the existence of God. But there are many observations that come out of science that are actually quite intriguing and cause even atheist or agnostic cosmologists to question whether this could be just an accident.

I think the general consensus now is that the universe had a beginning, the Big Bang, somewhere around fourteen billion years ago. And in that flash of light and energy and mass everything expanded at a prodigious rate over the course of billions of years with the coalescence of stars and planets and so on.

And when you look at the improbabilities of our current universe, they are stunning. There are fifteen constants that characterize the universe—things to do with the weak and strong forces that hold nuclei together, the gravitational pull, various constants in electromagnetism. If any one of those were to have a slightly different value than it does, our universe could not support life. It would be a mass of formless gas, at best.

One does have to wonder—did the universe know we were coming or did God, who created the universe, choose those constants just so, so that complex organisms could populate what otherwise would have been a sterile universe? I find that quite compelling. The chances of our being here are infinitesimally small.

I find evidence of purpose from many directions. One is the nature of the universe, its fine-tuning to allow us to become possibilities. Another argument is this hunger that is characteristic of all humans at all times in all cultures, this hunger for something more than ourselves, the search for the spiritual. Another, and a very powerful one for me, is the moral law, the sense that we all have of good and evil, a law which causes us to do things such as sacrifice ourselves to save someone else.

I think many people are trying to find how to synthesize what we know about the natural world with a search for God. For me, that synthesis arrived gradually but in a very comforting way. And here it is. If God, who is outside space and time, chose to create a universe and populate it with creatures in his image with whom he could have fellowship, who are we to say that the process that we as scientists have uncovered—the Big Bang, the formation of stars and planets, and the mechanism of evolution—is not the way he would have done it? It's an incredibly elegant, remarkably beautiful way to conduct that marvelous act of creation. I find that enormously satisfying. Nothing that I know as a scientist is in contradiction to that. Nothing that I know as a believer is in contradiction to that. It provides this sense of harmony, of unity, where I can both worship God as the creator and use the tools of science that he has given us to explore his creation.

There is no greater flash point right now in the tensions between science and faith than evolution. Ever since Darwin's *On the Origin of Species* was published that tension has been flaring. And it seems, in my view, to be getting worse, even after all of these years. I believe that God is the greatest scientist. I believe that God gave us the abilities to explore the natural world and to appreciate the grandeur of his creation and, as Galileo once said, did not intend us to forego their use.

As a scientist who has the opportunity to explore things about the natural world, I have an opportunity to glimpse, in just a small way, God's mind. But we discover things which, in some people's view, cause difficulties in interpreting certain scriptures.

This is an area where serious believers can disagree, and what I want to say about this I also want to say with great love and understanding for my fellow believers who have a different view. But for me as a scientist, when I look at DNA, that of the human species and of all the other organisms that we now have the genomes of, the evidence that we are all descended from a common ancestor is overwhelming. Some might wish that not to be so. It is so.

Does this conflict with Genesis? I don't believe it does.

One of my greatest heartaches is that at the present time serious believers are led by some circumstances to believe that they have to defend a literal interpretation of Genesis in order to defend their faith and find themselves contradicting facts that God Almighty has given us the ability to discover.

Many believers have been attracted to the notion of intelligent design because it provides an opportunity for God or some supernatural force to be involved in evolution. Unfortunately, I think that perspective is doomed. Intelligent design basically proposes that there are certain complex structures that are too complicated for evolution alone to have designed. The problem is we are learning a lot about the examples intelligent design puts forward. And the notion that those are examples of irreducible complexity is showing serious cracks.

I do not think intelligent design is taking us to the promised land. I think this will be an argument which ultimately will not do damage to science, it will do damage to faith, as its premises are shown to be unnecessary, and science fills in the gaps.

The idea of dualism, two worlds, one material and the other spiritual, has gone on for as long as science and faith have coexisted. Do they need to keep themselves separate? Stephen J. Gould, a very prominent evolutionist, wrote about the "nonoverlapping magisteria." He said the scientific and the spiritual perspectives were both legitimate, but they should not take any chances of actually entering the same room at the same time.

I don't feel that way. I would be very uncomfortable compartmentalizing what I know as a scientist away from what I know as a believer. It seems to me the scientific and the spiritual world views are not just compatible, they're actually complementary. You learn things about each one by consideration of the other. Science allows you to ask some pretty interesting questions. Faith allows you to ask other interesting questions. They are both ways of seeking truth. They are both ways of knowing. And to decide that you have to put a wall between the two in order to avoid some discomfort just does not feel right to me at all. I am very much opposed to the dualism arguments and very much in favor of the notion that we can be complete worshippers of God and at the same time people who study his creation using science.

We are at a difficult time in our cultural history. Are we headed on a path of increasing secularism in society on the one hand? On the other hand, are we headed toward a circumstance where science is considered untrustworthy, and we move substantially more in the direction of fundamentalist views about how the world came into being and what is an acceptable perspective on that?

It seems to me those polar extremes are getting a lot of the stage. Neither of those outcomes would be good for us in the long term. We need science if we are going to survive in a complicated world and if we are going to treat terrible diseases that cry out for some form of alleviation. And we need faith if we are going to keep ourselves in perspective. Any pathway that seems to be trying to knock down one or the other is a pathway that is dangerous for our culture. So we must seek out the ways in which these world views can happily coexist. It is perhaps our strongest mandate right now if we are really concerned about our own future in this world.

Collins is a musician as well as a scientist, and he brought his guitar to the interview. When the conversation ended, he played and sang one of his favorite hymns, "When I Survey the Wondrous Cross."

7.

Waltzing with the God of Chaos

The Rev. Barbara Brown Taylor caught Bob's attention in 1995, when she was named by Baylor University as one of the twelve most effective preachers in the English-speaking world. Since then, she has given up her rural Episcopal pastorate and become a college professor and traveling guest preacher, though she still lives near the mountains of northern Georgia, where she and her husband keep a garden, sell hay, and look after three dogs, two cats, two horses, and (at the time of this interview) three llamas. Taylor is also a prolific author and columnist whose book, The Luminous Web: Essays on Science and Religion, *explores the theological consequences of contemporary science. So-called "chaos theory," in particular, has led her to embrace the image of a God who is less interested in human doings than she once believed, but who still knows her name.*

The luminous web is an image I have of the universe, the cosmos, that has people in it, but also has creatures, rocks, air, water. It's a way, for me, of combating the pyramid picture of the cosmos with human beings at the top and all these little serf animals and things below that we get to use and eat up and dig out and turn into whatever we want. So, the luminous web is my image for the interconnectedness of creation.

Where is God in this picture? God is all over the place. God is up there, down here, inside my skin and out. God is the web, the energy, the space, the light—not captured in them, as if any of those concepts were more real than what unites them—but revealed in that singular and vast net of relationship that animates everything that is. God is the web, the connection, the glue, the air between the molecules.

You've got to be careful when you start playing with images of God. But my image of God has changed terrifically. I think before the work in science,* I still had an image of God as a body. You know, God as an embodied person, somehow. I now have more of an image of God as very spread out, or very ever present. I get accused of pantheism a lot. That's close, but my sense of God is beyond that, because I also believe God is beyond creation, but certainly through creation in a way I had not imagined before.

I am so reluctant to talk about God and what God thinks and how God acts. I have such a red flag there. I go there, but when I do, I'm very reminded of Robert Capon† saying we're like oysters trying to explain ballerinas. So, I'm not much of a theologian. I'm much happier with the evidence. But, being a Christian, I believe deeply in an incarnation, which I believe is holy *enfleshment*, holy embodiment.

And, for me, that's not just human beings. That's the whole creation. So I have a strong belief in the holiness of creation.

As for God's plan? You know, whether God has a file I can break into and find out what I should be doing ten years from now? The more I learn about chaos theory, the more I favor the concept of life with God as a dance instead of a blueprint. God makes a move, humankind makes a move, then humankind makes a move based on God's move.

Scientists call it "chaos theory," and yet even they will admit that the theory's misnamed. Instead of saying that everything's essentially chaotic, chaos theory says that there are boundaries to the chaos. Take weather systems, for instance, which are delicately dependent on their initial conditions. Most people know this as the "butterfly effect." The butterfly beating its wings on the other side of the world will affect the weather in New York, because whatever is happening at the very beginning of a weather system will then multiply exponentially and bring out results that are not entirely predictable, but they won't go beyond a certain boundary. I noticed this when the hurricane was hitting the North Carolina coast last year. Forecasters knew about where it would hit, but no one could say exactly where, because of chaos theory. They didn't know the exact, initial conditions. But given what they did know, they could give parameters.

---

* Referring to her book *The Luminous Web*.
† A writer and theologian.

What troubles some religious people about this scenario is the randomness of it, but I'm comforted by the boundaries to chaos. Plus, if randomness is the way things work, and I believe in a God who created things the way they are, then that's my problem, not God's.

What I draw out of this pastorally is that however chaotic my life and the life of the world seems, there may be a boundary beyond which the chaos will not go. I won't fly off the page. Something like a .000127 percent shift in initial conditions ends up being the difference between one weather pattern and another. And what that means is: you, too, will have effect, for good or ill. No one is excused from having effect. You will affect the world. You will affect the course of events. And that, to me, is threatening and exciting.

I come out believing that all is one. I also see many different, human ways and means of interpreting that one reality. And so science seems to me like one way of measuring and interpreting reality, and religious faith seems like another. And there are many others. So, I am much more interested in the meaning made. I don't think there are multiple realities. I think there are multiple interpretations of reality. My students want to know which one's right. I always tell them there's no evidence, no evidence at all. There is this interpretation and this religious tradition. You choose, and you stake your life on your choices, but there's no evidence your choice is right—except your life.

I can't do God as a person. I think there is an absolute, a divine being so vast, so beyond comprehension that all of the cosmos can be attributed to that deity's power. And yet, that same deity has care for the individual. So I do believe in a deity, an absolute power who knows me by name and who knows every individual creature by name. But a personal God raises red flags for me, too—that sort of "me and Jesus" attitude in which "he's going to find me a parking place and be sure I'm not sad." The personal God somehow seems like a personal valet to me.

In a lot of ways, to read science is to be tempted to become a deist—to believe in a clock-maker God who sets things in motion and wishes the creatures luck. But I'm a Christian, which means I'm schooled in paradox. I'm schooled in the opposite of any truth being another great truth. And so I live in the paradox of this God who seems to have set things in motion and yet is still involved. There's some evidence that things are random to a point, and yet, I have experience of some spirit that seems to direct my feet at times. So I'm stuck with both of those, and I've somehow got to live into the paradox of that. They may not fit together, but I'm stuck with the two.

And there are days when God is definitely busy somewhere else and doesn't have time for me, so that's another part of the experience. And somehow, again, reading all this cosmology has increased my reverence. If anything, we're in a period, I think, in Christianity, where the personal God has gotten far too personal. There's a shortage of reverence around. I mean T-shirts with the crucified Christ on them and coffee cups with Jesus's face and, to me, the lack of reverence in that, the lack of respect for the deity is astounding. Thank goodness God's never let a portrait be made. But I think it's time for some backing up, some awe, and maybe a little cosmology would cure a few people of that far-too-cozy image of "me and God."

Science has given me a mental workout that I haven't gotten from theology in a while. And I have also had a renewal of wonder—wonder of creation, wonder of life, wonder of DNA, wonder of biology, wonder of cosmology. So, if anything, it's brought me to a greater appreciation of the God who is so far beyond my ken that neither I nor science will be there any time soon.

8.

The Meaning of Mud

As an author, editor, lecturer, and authority on religious books, Phyllis Tickle spends nearly half her time on the road, far beyond her backcountry home. But her sense of life and purpose radiates from the place she nicknamed "Lucy Goose Farm," where she lives, plants, feeds, bakes, sews, and grows in Lucy, Tennessee. When Bob visited her in 1997, his first words were, "Phyllis, I have come here because I want to find out why you live here."

———

We came here twenty years ago from downtown Memphis—not to escape the city, but because we felt that we were the last generation to really know how to live on the land. We have seven children, and we watched those kids try to understand life in terms of Little League and car pools, and everything was brick and concrete and asphalt in their lives. So we came out here, and all our friends thought we were crazy.

We bought this place and said, "If we have it, we're going to grow it or make it." And so we carried it to silly levels. I made their clothes. I made our bread. Sam* grew the broom corn that he made our brooms with. We had chickens, and we sold the extra eggs down at the Lucy Market. We did the whole bit. And the kids—when the calves would begin to come, they'd pick the one they thought was the best and, with Daddy, would agree that, when came a hard freeze in January, that was the one that we'd slaughter.

Out here, living this way, even though it's artificially contrived by parents who're a little weird, the first thing you learn is that we're not the measure of anything. We're never going to win out here. Do you know what I mean? Enlightenment and Western civilization in the last three hundred years has been built on the notion that man is the measure of all things. That's bull!

---

* Her physician-husband.

Man's the measure of absolutely nothing. But you forget that, when you're in the city and everything is scaled to man. Everything is to human size.

We've lived through two ice storms in our twenty years. We've had three or four tornados. We've been devastated. We lose power regularly. The well has gone out. All of those things happen, and it's life. There's a vitality here. And there is the awareness that, because we're not going to win, we don't have to. We don't have to win.

When Sam and I die, we'll be buried just on the other side of our property line, in the community cemetery. Every time I leave this farm, I pass where I will be. I have to tip my hat, so to speak, to that ground. I, who have lived on Lucy's soil, will become part of Lucy's soil—so that other people can live on it. And it's a whole way of being exposed, being surrounded entirely by story and by sheer vitality. In a city, half of what you see is inanimate. It truly is not alive. You can describe it in some way other than narrative. It has no vitality of its own. Here, everything is alive. And because it's so alive and so permanent, and because it really is going to win—it's going to bury us. Sam works seven or eight hours a day, in addition to a full medical practice, just keeping this place so it doesn't bury us. Some day, they're going to find us under mounds of kudzu.

But the truth of it is that, while all of that's happening, there's also such enormous permanence here, such a consistency of the cycles, and a magnificence of all of the growth that's happening here, that you are caught in majesty that doesn't require anything of you except just a sense of, "Yeah, it's here. And God bless me for the time I'm part of it. How wonderful to be part of it!"

The problem with a great deal of institutional religion right now in this country is that it is separated from vitality. It is separated from the sense of constant livingness. It becomes a theory, as do so many things in the city. It becomes something that you can manipulate and becomes an *object*.

Out here, nothing is an object. And the first thing you learn is that you can *colive* with these things, you can coexist with these things. You can engage them in story. You can't engage them in fact. You can engage them in terms of their changing cycles which, the more they change, are ever the same. That's basically theology. I don't think it's any accident that every great religion has begun in a Garden of Eden—it's not just Judeo-Christian tradition that began in a garden—because it is in the garden where the measure of all things is life itself. If you want to call that God, so be it. But the measure of all things is life, itself, in a garden. And the intimacy is with everything—everything I touch here is alive. Even the fence posts are in the process of rotting or being taken down by paper wasps or something. Everything is alive. Life pushes in our doors. You know, the house is full of flowers and plants and mud that gets tracked in, and all of that.

Inhabiting a "Thin Place"

The Celts call it the "thin place."* And I'm not sure that the Lucy Goose Farm is exactly a thin place, but the activities that happen here are "thin" activities. As spirituality became very important in America over the last five years, I got more bread-making books to review than you would believe,† because you can't mix bread without being in what I would call a "thin" activity. When your hands are in that dough and when you are stilled, when your attention is stilled to exactly what that yeast will and won't let you do—and it's different every time you put your hands in it—you're in the kind of activity that says, "I am manipulating, I am shaping, I am dealing with life, and it deals back." It has its own will. It has its own way of being. And it becomes a kind of prayer, because you're manipulating for the sake of your children. Your mind is stilled. Your hands are occupied. And you're aware of the wonder you cannot see—which is indeed happening beneath your hands.

There are activities one does that become a kind of physical mantra. They're repetitive things that allow the mind to be quiet and allow the soul to come out. We, in this country, are kind of fearful about letting souls come out and about dealing with our spirits. We're getting over that.

---

* Where the gap between the human and the divine is at its narrowest.
† At that time, Tickle was a contributing editor of *Publishers Weekly.*

CHAPTER 2

Evil and Suffering

In the midst of a natural or human-made disaster, the question usually comes not long after the first responders arrive: Why? Why the devastation from Hurricane Katrina in New Orleans? Why the shedding of innocent blood in Lower Manhattan on September 11, 2001? These aren't, above all, technical questions hinging on the levies of Lake Pontchartrain or the steel trusses of the Twin Towers. These are ultimate questions about the nature of evil and suffering, about the human need to make sense of it all, to square the apparent senselessness of these occurrences with the belief or hope that we live in a friendly universe, that there is, in spiritual terms, a divine force that is all-powerful and utterly good.

Within the discipline of theology, the thriving subspecialty known as "theodicy" seeks to reconcile the reality of evil with the omnipotence of God—a loving God, at that. Bracketing for a moment the existence of God, the whole effort would stall at the starting gate if there were no larger scheme in which terrible things do or can make sense. Not everyone, however, sympathizes with this search for meaning in the universe. Evolutionary biologist Richard Dawkins insists that there is, in reality, "no design, no purpose, no evil and no good, nothing but blind, pitiless indifference."

Those who appear in the following pages believe there is good, there is evil, and there is love and care in the cosmos. They are all searching, but not all of these seekers have found what is to them a satisfying, let alone ultimate, explanation of unutterable woe. Not all have let God off the hook. Those here who are religious affirm the unlimited goodness of their God, but not all of them are sure about the unlimited power or prerogative of God. The Holocaust has planted this doubt in the minds of some believers, while personal suffering has generated such thoughts in others, among them Bob's cousin, Rev. William Abernethy, a United Church of Christ minister who has struggled for over two decades with Parkinson's disease.

Besides, people who find themselves in the throes of misfortune are not always looking for "the answer," as undertaker Thomas Lynch has learned; he explains here that sometimes grievers are simply looking for the space to ask, "Why me?" And sometimes the best sense we can muster is that a world without suffering, whatever such a thing would look like, would not be our world. "Where there is no suffering, nothing happens," Madeleine L'Engle adds.

These reflections edge toward the unstoppable faith of an agnostic, Studs Terkel, and along the way we cautiously close in on hope, because—as Terkel affirms—"hope dies last."

9.

A Faith Difficult to Understand

Menachem Daum is a New York filmmaker and son of Holocaust survivors. He has struggled to understand the horrific events of World War II and the unremitting faith of his ailing Hasidic father, with whom he prayed in a Brooklyn cemetery during this report he filed for Religion & Ethics NewsWeekly *in April 2001. In the end, Daum was able to respect—though not really to understand or believe—this faith that survived as millions perished. Here is his story as he told it on the air, together with recollections by his relatives and a larger answer by the late rabbi-scholar Arthur Hertzberg.*

———

My father, a Holocaust survivor, would quote a Hasidic rebbe who said, "A God who had to limit himself to actions that we humans can understand couldn't possibly be God." Essentially that was his approach to the challenge to faith raised by the Holocaust.

My father's approach differed from that of my mother. On her tombstone we inscribed that she endured much suffering. This was our way of asking God to forgive her sins. In effect, we were saying she has already been punished for her sins in this world.

However, I don't think my mother felt a strong need for God's forgiveness. On the contrary. She told me when she is called in heavenly judgment she will turn the tables. She will demand to know why God stood by silently during the Holocaust as her large family was being destroyed. Her mother, Rachel, the daughter of Yitzhak. Two brothers and six sisters. Her first husband and the son she had before the war named Avrohom.

Just a few months after their liberation, my parents—Moshe Yosef Daum and Fela Nussbaum—were married in a displaced persons camp in occupied Germany. They named me Menachem, which means "consoler" or "comforter." Apparently, they hoped that I might restore some happiness in their lives.

Actually, the happiest time in my mother's life, she once told me, had been the years she spent as a student in Beis Yaakov, the network of religious schools for girls in prewar Poland.

My mother told me she retained the pure faith of a Beis Yaakov girl until she got off the train at Auschwitz. But she never told me what actually happened on the ramp that forever shook her faith. My mother had arrived at the camp with her sister Bluma. Many years later, my aunt Bluma revealed to me that my mother had an infant son in her arms. As they were roused out of the train, a veteran Jewish prisoner hurriedly came up to them. He knew mothers together with their young children would soon be directed to the gas chambers. He urged them to do the unthinkable.

Aunt Bluma Remembers . . .

"Give up the child. Quickly. We can't stay here too long. We know what we are doing. Give away the child. You are still young trees. You can have more fruit. Because of the child you, too, will go. Give away the child." A prisoner came from behind us and grabbed the child from Fela's arms. She felt the child being taken from her and said: "The child hasn't eaten, Bluma. Maybe we can still send food to him." I tried to calm her by telling her that today they were taking everyone separately, children, young people. I made excuses, but I knew what was happening.

At the Passover seder my mother would get annoyed as my father recited the Exodus story. If God did so many miracles during biblical times, then why had she seen no sign of God or his miracles during the Holocaust?

My father would wait quietly until she finished. He never offered any theological explanations to defend God. His only response was that we humans, with our limited minds, cannot expect to understand God's ways. We must live with faith despite our unanswered questions.

The tenacity of my father's faith has always been difficult for me to understand. It is a lot easier for me to understand survivors who abandoned religion. I can readily understand the religious defiance of my father's only surviving relative, his cousin Dora. I visited Dora and her friends at her bungalow in the Catskills.

Cousin Dora Defies God . . .

I cannot see a God who will allow a little baby to be killed for no reason at all, and I really lost my belief then. I had one sister and two brothers who were killed. I was the oldest. I'm the only survivor of my family. Why, what did they do that was so terrible that they should perish? I think that if God is so great and powerful, he could have struck Hitler down before he killed so many Jews. That is my belief.

My father was determined to rebuild the world he had been raised in. In the early 1950s, just as he was beginning to taste the American dream, he gave up a good job in upstate New York and moved us to New York City. He did so in order to send us to yeshivas and give us a religious education.

Most of my classmates were, like myself, children of survivors. Our teachers, survivors themselves, never mentioned the Holocaust. I suspect that, like my parents, they, too, had no answers to offer us.

[Turning to his father, Menachem says,] Dad, we'll pray, yes? We'll put on the prayer shawl and tefillin. Yes? We are going to put the tefillin on your hand. You continued to put on the tefillin in the Skarzisk camps? It wasn't easy, right?*

According to Jewish religious law, my father's condition exempts him from the need to put on the tefillin. However, I know how much this ritual means to him. During the Holocaust, he was also exempt from putting on the tefillin and yet in the ghettos and forced labor camps he made great sacrifices to do so. [In prayer] "Blessed art Thou, O Lord, King of the Universe, who has sanctified us through His commandments and has commanded us to put on the tefillin."

I try to continue my parents' ways, but to be honest, I do it more out of respect than out of conviction. I really don't understand my father's faith. I don't understand why he would risk his life in the camps for a God who had seemingly abandoned him, nor do I understand my mother's strange combination of faith and doubt, how she continued to observe the commanments of a God she could not forgive.

---

* Small leather boxes containing parchments with passages from the Torah.

Rabbi Hertzberg's Response . . .

That is one of the deep religious responses to the Shoah,* to defy God. To take it with indifference is not a religious response. To go and rebuild is a religious response. To defy God is a religious response. Because that is to take what happened with the utmost seriousness, as a matter of life and death, as a matter of your own life and death . . .

But there is an answer. At the end of the Book of Job, Job rebuilds his life. To me, the miracle of Jewish history as a whole is our capacity to begin after tragedy, after disaster. It is this capacity to begin over again that is for me the closest I can come to God's finger.

---

* The Holocaust.

10.

Easing the Divine Suffering

Where was God? For years, Orthodox rabbi Irving Greenberg—a theologian and former chair of the United States Holocaust Memorial Council—agonized over this question. He respects those who could not make the leap of faith after the Holocaust, those who stand on the other side of what he terms a "thin line" between belief and doubt. Greenberg's spiritual turning point came when he realized that God suffers together with humans, but he still had to make sense of why God, suffering or not, stood by as children burned. At that point, the rabbi arrived at a deeper understanding of the relationship between the human and the divine, a relationship in which humans have the power and freedom to make themselves collectively into a moloch, a god of destruction, if that is their choice. Greenberg spoke with producer Susan Grandis Goldstein in 1998.

It's hard to speak of a loving God, it's hard to speak of even being in the image of God, infinitely valuable and unique, in a world in which babies were burned alive by the Nazis and no one lifted a finger, in which people were gassed en masse. For example, there was a department of the SS that was in charge of bringing down the price of that gassing to make human life even cheaper. How do you speak, then, of a God who treasures humans or, in Christian terms, of a God who loved the world so much he would sacrifice his own son, and yet, here it is that, to save a half a penny's worth of gas, people were burned alive? The answer is, it's very difficult. And for many Jews, it has been a crisis of faith.

In the presence of burning children, how could one talk of a loving God? I once wrote that no theological statement should be made that would not be credible in the presence of burning children. What could you say about God when a child is burning alive? My answer is there's nothing to say. If there's anything you can do, jump into that pit and pull the child out. And if you can heal that child, if you can pour oil on their burns, then you are making a statement about God.

Speaking personally, my first emotional encounter with the Holocaust overwhelmed me. As an Orthodox rabbi, it was totally unexpected and devastating. There were days when I would say the words that we pray daily as Orthodox Jews, and I felt, how can I say them? It would be almost like a mockery of the children to speak of the God who—as we do in our central prayer—redeems the children and saves them for the sake of his great name. How could you say that in a generation where there was no liberation?

It's one of those devastating things you live with for the rest of your life. For those who have lost their faith because of it, I can only say I came to respect that. Even for the most devout people, there are moments when the ashes and the smoke of Auschwitz choke off any contact with God or heaven. Therefore, I came to see that the line between the believer and the doubter is much thinner than I once thought.

The answer is you live torn. At one point, the way I put it was that my faith is shattered, but then I was reminded of a famous line of Rabbi Nachman's, the great Hasidic rebbe of Breslov, who once said, "No heart is so whole as a broken heart." So, I came to believe that maybe "no faith is so whole as a broken faith," and I could, in a sense, admire people who responded to the Holocaust by losing their faith, because their passion, their love of God and of people made it impossible to say empty words about God. I felt more sympathy for them than I did for people who went on praying as if nothing had ever changed, as if one could talk complacently and confidently about a God who exists self-evidently, as if that's true. It just couldn't be.

My first overwhelming experience of the Holocaust took place when I was on a Fulbright scholarship visiting Israel with my wife and our newly born child. I think I shall never forget the incredible contradiction—the living witness of death in the Holocaust, on the one hand, and Israel coming to life and this newborn child coming to life. Here were the two contradictions. The Holocaust told me that there's no hope and that death wins out. There's no redeemer. And Israel told me the opposite—that the prophets had promised that thousands of years later, after the exile, the Jews would come back to Israel, Jerusalem would be bursting with the sound of children and of brides and grooms and dancing and joy, and that would be the proof that there is a God. Every day I was living both these contradictions. Tell me both can't be right, and my answer is, "You're right, too."

But you have to live in the contradiction. And I did. I think, personally, it was a combination of the two for many years. I would constantly torment myself, "Where was God? Where was God?" Then one day it hit me very powerfully that, if I was suffering this way and I hadn't been in the Holocaust, how much more in a certain sense was God suffering? If a human felt this pain, what did an infinite consciousness feel? I think that it was a turning point in my personal religious development, because I suddenly felt a certain sense, if I can say so, of compassion or maybe even pity for God, and an overwhelming sense, suddenly, that this God had not stopped the Holocaust maybe because this God was suffering and wanted me to stop the Holocaust. As a Jew, I always hesitate to use language of God suffering, because it seems to be a Christian patent. But it's not so. I came to see this has been a central belief of the Jewish people—that God shares our pain. Indeed, Christianity was never more Jewish than when it expressed it in those terms—that God suffers with humans.

I said to myself I'd asked the wrong question when I asked where was God? The answer was obvious: where else would God be, but suffering with God's people?

The real question was, why hadn't God stopped it? There, as a believer at least, I came to believe that God was asking me to stop it, that in some sense, the divine message was that the human partner was supposed to have stopped this. I must say I've thought many times, what if the Jewish people had all been Zionists in the nineteenth century and built Israel as an escape for those Jews before the Holocaust? What if the world had met its moral responsibility to stop Hitler in 1935, when it could have? What if America and the allies had bombed Auschwitz in 1944 and stopped the trains?

I came to see that this is truly a part of the covenant idea. And I came to believe that the God of the Bible who saved the Jews at the Red Sea had self-limited. That's what covenant's about—God calling humans to full partnership. That had not stopped the Romans from destroying the temple. But the Jewish people, in a sense, stepped up and took on more responsibility. I came to a conclusion that in our lifetime God had again self-limited and asked Jews—really, all humans—to take full responsibility for the covenant. In a certain sense, perfecting the world, then, means not only liberating humans, but liberating God. It means not only stopping human suffering, but stopping the infinite suffering of the divine. That's what religion's about.

How you apply this concept varies widely. Yes, in biblical times even rabbis believed that since God is moving history, when the Jews suffer, it must be a punishment for their sins. And in the twentieth century, there were those who out of faith or, I feel, a mistaken attempt to uphold the tradition argued that somehow the Holocaust must be God's punishment on the Jewish people.

I find that outrageous. It's a classic case where taking an idea to its logical conclusion makes the idea absolutely wrong. I don't believe that any sin could justify the kind of pain and suffering that was inflicted upon Jews. If one really could convince me that this was a God who did this deliberately, who had children burned alive for the sake of punishment because we were assimilating, I would say such a God would be [one] to reject, to spit at. I certainly could not respect a God who does that. I came to feel that this would be the ultimate outrage. What could you do to people after you have isolated them and hungered them and tortured them and gassed them or burned them alive? What more could you do that would be any worse? The answer is to stand there and tell them that this was done because of their sins. So the theologian would be adding the ultimate insult to this horrible injury.

The God Who Could Not

One has to come to see the other possibilities—that this was a God who either chose not to stop it or could not stop it. I came to believe this was

God's self-limitation, and it was the human responsibility to hear that message and to respond appropriately.

But then I began to wrestle. What do we mean when we speak of God in history? My answer again is that the ultimate, divine dream was of a perfect world, but humans were called into partnership. We always thought that this partnership was guaranteed, that God was going to step in and save us from our worst sins or our worst errors, that there was a guaranteed happy ending, and God was almost our ace in the hole, so to speak, against our worst mistakes. I now have come to believe that God truly believes in freedom and has given us that freedom—which means, yes, that, as Elie Wiesel once said, if Hitler had come to power twenty years later with a hydrogen bomb in his possession, he could have wiped out the whole world, not just six million Jews. I've come to believe that God has given us that kind of freedom—that we could ultimately defeat, as it were, the divine purpose if we choose to use our power for evil. And we still have the power to wipe out the world, to wipe out thousands of species, to become a *moloch*, a god of murder and death, rather than a god of life. So that is the danger.

That, to me, brings us back to the question of covenant. I've come to see that that's the whole point of partnership. When we speak of humans taking full responsibility, in what way am I different from a secularist who says that humans are totally in charge? My answer is that, as a religious person, I understand that at this moment God will not step in and save me. It does not mean that I'm not accountable to God, that God is not present to judge me, to love me and give me strength to carry out my responsibility, to criticize and warn me and judge me when I have misbehaved, to forgive me when I repent. That is the difference, I think, between arrogance and partnership. When a person is totally in charge, I think you see the arrogance. We wipe out thousands of species—that's acting like we own the world, like we are God. I think covenant makes all the difference in the world. Covenant is mistakenly believed to mean that God will do it for us. Correctly understood, I think, God is there to call us, instruct us, enable us, judge us, love us, but no longer available as the fairy-tale prince who will come and put us over the rainbow.

To put it another way, I still believe deeply in the messiah and the need for a messianic age, for an age of total transformation. But I do not believe that that messiah will come to save us from our sins. I believe that that messiah will only come when we are able, ready, and willing to bring the messiah. Elie Wiesel, again, once suggested that the messiah, the all-powerful, deus ex machina God who saves us against our own will and ability—if that kind of messiah would come again now, it would be an outrage. It's too late for such a messiah to come. It would have been a moral monster that could have come to save those children or to save those people and didn't come. But a messiah who wanted to come, but who could not come because he did not have the power and because humans failed to bring such a messiah, I think, would not only be credible—it would be a messiah that one would gladly work with and follow.

In a sense, to me, that's the starkest, ultimate outcome. The fairy tale, the God of the white beard in heaven, all's well with the world, the one who does it all for us, I think, is no longer credible, no longer possible. But a mature understanding of a God who loves us in our freedom, who has called us to responsibility, who is with us at every moment—I think such a God is, if anything, more present and more close, and maybe, having suffered together and having shared our pain infinitely, is more beloved and maybe more inspiring to follow.

11.

Evil Acts, Sacred Places

Auschwitz, Pearl Harbor, Gettysburg, the World Trade Center, the Murrah Federal Building of Oklahoma City—all of these belong to the annals of evil and suffering in modern history. But could it be that these are also sacred places, which demand a response that is scaled to their sacredness, to their transcendent claims on human memory, meaning, and ritual? Historian and religion scholar Edward Linenthal spoke with Kim Lawton, Religion & Ethics NewsWeekly *managing editor, a year after the terrorist attacks of September 11, 2001, and shortly after his visit to the tiny borough of Shanksville, Pennsylvania. There, United Airlines Flight 93 had crashed into an empty field, breaking apart and scattering into an adjacent grove of trees.*

—

Shanksville is now part of a national historic landscape, and it will never, ever again be what it was—just as Gettysburg not so far up the road will never again be a quiet, idyllic farming community. It is an incredibly eloquent place, maybe because I was unprepared for the power of that grove of trees where the debris field was—an extremely compelling place that had not yet been framed by the media. At the World Trade Center, you know what to expect before you get there, because it's part of the visual spectacle. Television had never captured well the eloquence of that field in Shanksville, and I was simply stunned by it. The townspeople in Shanksville see themselves, I think, as moral stewards of this site and feel very strongly that they have to preserve, protect, and guard it for the family members of the victims, because they'll be hosting them for years and years to come.

Memorial issues are almost, by definition, razor's-edge issues. What do we mean when we call a place "sacred ground"? What happens to a site when 92 percent of the human remains that were on that plane will never be recovered? How do you deal with that? What about the landowners? What about zoning regulations to keep out commercialization? Do you open the site to the public? Should people other than family members be allowed to walk in the area where there will always be human remains? Or must the public be kept away a little bit? Who's supposed to take part in the memorial process? Who's enfranchised to think about how to represent what happened there to the wider public? There are questions of ownership—real ownership, symbolic ownership—at all of the 9/11 sites, including Shanksville.

The wider national community believes that they, in a sense, "own" these sites, too. There are logistical questions when you have hundreds of thousands of people coming for major anniversaries. We can think about the first, the fifth, the tenth, twenty-fifth, fiftieth. These are signal anniversaries that we know from other historic sites. What's a small community to do? What about roads? Bathrooms? Directions? Where do people stay? There are compelling issues, both symbolically and logistically, that people in Shanksville will struggle with for a very long time.

When I went to the site on a cold afternoon in December, there was no snow on the ground. I hadn't realized the extent of the debris field, and I hadn't realized that so much of the human remains were simply vaporized. This beautiful grove of trees was quiet and compelling, and the wind was blowing through them. The natural beauty of the site was such a contrast with the horror that had happened there. It made it difficult for me to put together the event and the site and took me back in many ways to some of the beautiful places I had been at in Poland—killing fields that made the act of remembering even more difficult.

Sometimes we expect horrific events at sites that are ugly; the site will give us a kind of moral clue from nature as to the event. That doesn't happen often, and it didn't in Shanksville. It's a beautiful, beautiful area. It became clear to me immediately that this was going be a very volatile area and that this was sacred ground, intimate ground, a burial place for people, and yet part of the national landscape.

One thinks about disaster often when one thinks about big cities. We think about apocalyptic fantasies and disaster fiction and all that. Even after the Oklahoma City bombing, people said, "This could happen in LA or this could happen in New York, but not in Oklahoma City, in the nation's heartland." The Pentagon is certainly a military site and, while unexpected in a most horrific way, it at least is a logical target for terrorism.

Shanksville is a rural area. It's peaceful. It's serene. It is a different kind of American story that has been largely overshadowed by the spectacle of what happened in New York City. Some of it has to do with the numbers of people killed. Some of it has to do with the fact that in New York City you have the playing out of apocalyptic fantasies. The fact that we call the site "ground zero" is very revealing. "Ground zero" is language taken from apocalyptic sensibilities at the beginning of the nuclear age. It's what we called Trinity Site* in New Mexico. There have been apocalyptic nightmares about nuclear attacks on New York. In his 1949 book *Here is New York*, E. B. White wrote breathtakingly about one such scenario, imagining the destruction of New York City by a power from the air.

You also had in New York, if not the death of the skyscraper, at least what some people saw as the wounding of the idea of human achievement by building higher and higher, and maybe this is the end of that kind of work. You had the destruction of an American icon of capitalism. You had a sense of a big city brought to its knees, almost three thousand people killed. All of that lent a particular intensity to New York City and, frankly, a visual spectacle that you didn't have anywhere else.

In Washington you had the moving pictures of the wounded Pentagon building. But in Shanksville, all you had was a hole in the ground, and a hole in the ground that was filled in very quickly. There was a more subtle power—the power in the debris field, in the grove of trees—that doesn't lend itself to the kind of visual spectacle of the images of the World Trade Center with the planes flying in and their destruction and people running away. You don't have that kind of visual imagery at either of the other sites.

I was struck, regarding Oklahoma City, with the similarity to September 11 in how immediately we respond to these events. We construct immediately, because of the horror of these atrocities, a way of making sense of them—what I call a narrative of civic renewal. "Yes, it was horrible, but . . ." "Yes, it was horrible, but this will bring us together." "Yes, it was horrible,

---

* Location of the world's first atomic detonation.

but what about the heroism and sacrifice and courage of rescue workers, firefighters, police, people who ran back into the building to save fellow workers and bring them back out?"

We have to celebrate that, because they're the points of light in these horrific events. But it seems to me that there was a kind of unsettling collective effervescence after these events, because they subvert our bedrock convictions about good and evil, about justice, about the meaning of life, about how death is supposed to take place, and about the meaninglessness of violence. Often we fixate on how these catastrophes bring us together when, in fact, they bring us together and tear us apart at the same time.

You have communities that are brought together, and we must honor those stories. You also have communities that are torn apart by memorial hierarchies: Who gets remembered? How do they get remembered? Who gets remembered more intensely? How much money do certain people get? What kinds of memorials should we make? These are the questions that tear people apart.

Conspiracy theories arise, and the toxic impact of these kinds of events on the minds and spirits and the bodies of so many people lead these events to be unfinished for so long. There were psychological effects on children who, in Oklahoma City, watching TV alone in the first days after the bombing, saw over and over again the recycled images of the destroyed Murrah building. And to this day, child psychiatrists in Oklahoma City have told me these children will kick the walls of new buildings before they go into them to see that they're not going to fall down.

I've heard the same things are beginning to emerge in New York City, because children watched that recycled image of the plane flying over and over again into the World Trade Center. We aren't going to know for decades how this impacted the hopes, the fears, the sense of vulnerability, the sense of good and evil, the sense of justice of children.

The Indignities of Closure

Religious narratives and resources are mobilized to help people make sense of this. This was very clearly the case in Oklahoma City and certainly in

Shanksville and other communities after September 11. They are a way to try to put events like these—Hannah Arendt once talked about them as the "unbearable sequence of sheer happenings"—into some kind of meaningful framework.

I understand the power of these religious narratives and how important they are in the restructuring of life. I remain skeptical myself that healthy human communities can be built on piles of murdered bodies. I think the corrosive effects of these events, the toxic impact of these events are enduring. September 11 will be unfinished for so many people, and we delude ourselves in creating a dishonest and disrespectful narrative when we try to use quasireligious, pop psychology terms like "closure" and "healing process." What breathtaking disrespect to go up to the mother of a murdered child in Oklahoma City and say, "Well, it's now ten years later," or in a few years it will be. "Have you reached closure?" What could that possibly mean? That says something about our unwillingness to live with these events.

Someone once said that Americans want these events to be resolved and not endured, and I think that's very revealing. What does it mean to talk about a "healing process," as if there's this regular set of steps through which people move? This was not the case at all with family members and survivors in Oklahoma City. The event coils back on itself and erupts in different ways. People then move away from it; but a smell, a sight, a sound will bring it back. People live in an ordinary world, but then there's this other world that erupts.

Healing takes place for some people as they incorporate events like these into what people in Oklahoma City call "the new normal." If we know anything about the impact of violence, it is that there's no old self to put back together. There is only a new self to be reconstituted out of the resources that a person brings, and there is the impact of the event itself. A person brings them together. That's rebirth, that's creativity—when people practice active grief, when they rebel against being labeled as sick, as victims of post-traumatic stress syndrome, as patients. People reacted against that by working for a victims' rights movement, by working for or against the death penalty for Timothy McVeigh and Terry Nichols, by working for habeas corpus reform, by entering into the work of the memorial process. They were practicing a kind of active grief.

There's a long history of people marking sites of violent death with artifacts. I went through lots of the material at the Oklahoma City fence, and how revealing it was to see what people left there—spontaneous leavings, planned leavings, individual leavings, corporate leavings. There, as in Shanksville, a tremendous amount of religious material was left. Why? Lots of reasons, and certainly among them is that religious symbols are part of who we are. To leave a crucifix or a Native American dream catcher or the prayer of St. Francis or a Buddhist text are ways of mobilizing religious resources to make a commemorative statement and to link one's own personal convictions with a larger story—maybe to sacralize the site itself, to remove the toxic impact of violence. So it's no surprise that in Shanksville we see a tremendous amount of memorial leaving and also in that leaving, a tremendous amount of formally religious material. Religious resources are things that people turn to almost instinctively to try and contain the power of these events.

We look for the sacred in lots of places now. We consider ourselves a secularized culture, and the word "secular" makes some sense if you think of institutions not controlled by an organizational church. But I don't think there's been a secularization of consciousness at all. Everything from our fascination with certain sacred sites or relics, with the apocalyptic, with that which is beyond the immediate, graspable, or material says that the religious sensibilities in the culture are very, very, very strong. They may be located outside of organizational frameworks, but the religiosity of Americans—be it in traditional faiths, in civil religion, in a patriotic orthodoxy, or a fascination with making sense of current events in the light of apocalyptic events—is very strong and, I think, belies the notion that religiosity is fading in the culture, both for better and worse, I would say.

My definition of a sacred place is a very simple one. Any place that's capable of being defiled is by definition sacred. You can't defile ordinary space. Any place that for a group of people is so special that a certain way of being there would be an act of disrespect means that that place is charged with a particular kind of meaning.

I tell my students, if they were sitting in the parking lot at K-Mart with a boom box, no one's going to really care. They might be irritated that the noise is too loud. But if they had a boom box at Gettysburg or in the grove of trees at Shanksville or in a church, a mosque, or a temple, it would be considered an act of defilement.

When we talk about sacred space, do we mean humanizing space? Do we mean space that is charged in a way that enlarges our moral circle of "we"? Do we mean a space that is nurturing? Do we mean a positive, constructive space? What about the death camps in Poland? What about a place like Auschwitz? Are these places sacred, or are they charged with a kind of toxic, negative sacrality that is important and that transforms them, but that is a different kind of space?

The World Trade Center site is very complex. I have no great insight into what should be done there, but I have an appreciation for the complex nature of the interests that are there. In Oklahoma City you had one building—although other buildings were damaged, certainly, for blocks and blocks around. But the Murrah building was terminally wounded. You had several people killed across the street, but the Murrah building was the focus. There were three sets of remains in the building that couldn't be brought out for five weeks. Then the building was imploded. At that point, that ground ceases to be an open grave—a particular kind of sacred place—and becomes amenable to transformation to a historic site, a memorial site.

At the World Trade Center, you do not have that kind of opportunity, where all the human remains could be found. The people were vaporized, cremated, so there will be the symbolic presence, the real presence of infinitesimal amounts of human remains there, always. To my mind, this changes the nature of the site. Given the economic imperative, the cultural imperative, the transportation imperatives that are at work there, it seems clear that the whole sixteen acres are not going to be venerated and left in whatever ways we would do that, maybe, at the field in Shanksville, where nearly all of the human remains will be in that grove of trees and, I think, will alter the terms of what can be done there and who can go there.

At the World Trade Center you have a complex sacred site and some family members who feel very strongly that the whole sixteen acres should be left as sacred ground. The first sentence of that argument would be, "An unprecedented act of terrorism on American soil calls for an unprecedented use of some of the most valuable real estate in the world." That would be the opening statement for someone who wanted to make the radical argument that all sixteen acres should be left as memorial space.

What seems more likely is that there will be power points within that sixteen acres—perhaps the footprints of the World Trade Center towers themselves. But even then, what do you do with the space around it? How does rebuilding pay its own architectural respect to the power of the events that happened there?

Memorializing in the Midst

Memorials certainly do sacralize space and try to freeze in time the meaning of the event for the generation that is putting the memorial up. And memorials tell us an awful lot about the people who shape them—usually more than they tell us about the event or the person being memorialized. Any memorial is already, by its very nature, a statement about the fear of forgetfulness—"This cannot be consigned to oblivion, and so we're going to freeze the message."

Memorials also can give a sense of who really counts in these stories. Whom do the memorials memorialize? The Vietnam Veterans Memorial is one of the most eloquent memorials in our culture, because it allows people to occupy that space and think about the names on that wall across a diverse ideological spectrum. It's not a memorial that preaches at you. It's not a memorial that offers a single, totalitarian message about what you should believe about the site. It's a memorial that has, I think, accelerated the process by which we focus on names.

Perhaps there is a way these memorials are an act of protest against the anonymity of mass death in our time. We want to focus on faces, names, and stories—to read the names on the wall, to go to Oklahoma City and read the names on the chairs, to go to the USS *Arizona* shrine room and look at the names of those who were killed in the attack on Pearl Harbor, to read the public eulogies in the *New York Times* of those killed in the World Trade Center.

I've thought about the relationship between the Oklahoma City memorial process and the September 11 sites. I don't think Oklahoma City is an exact template, of course, for September 11. But when I was in Shanksville with several friends from Oklahoma City at a town meeting on memorialization last December, it really became clear to me that what Oklahoma City has to offer is a very clear example of how people who wanted to memorialize this event struggled and engaged with a process almost immediately and moved in a really majestic manner.

When I first came into the memorial process, people would say, "I was there to argue for a particular kind of memorial, because I thought only that could really do justice to the memory of my loved one." "I want an angel," "I want a crucifix," "I want an eternal flame," "I want a grove of trees," "I want a reflecting pool," "I want a flagpole with the United States flag a thousand feet above the site."

And through the agonizing process of coming together, I must say, over a period of some years, they moved from these individualized versions of a memorial—these competing memorial ideas—to a larger civic sense of what this memorial means to our nation. What is the larger civic function of memorialization? That evolution, I think, was powerful.

Whatever is done with these sites, whatever kinds of memorial architecture are negotiated at these sites, I would hope not only that these memorials are going to be our first in-place interpretation of the meaning of September 11 and the loss that we suffered, but also that they will lead people to a more profound engagement with issues of violent death and sensitize people to that, working out of this event but moving beyond it. That, to me, would be a successful memorial process.

I wonder sometimes about the tremendous acceleration of our desire to memorialize so quickly—this compression of time between event and memorialization of event. I wonder if these events are so threatening to so many of our bedrock convictions that memorializing them is an illusory way of saying, "It's over. It's contained. We've memorialized it. We've understood it. We've drawn"—and here's this troublesome word—"lessons from it. Now we can put it away. We can put it on the memorial bookshelf and move on to something else."

I think there is a kind of psychic consolation in thinking about memorials as being the period in the tremendous agony that we suffer thinking about these things. If we can put it away and say it's over, it's very consoling. But we don't know whether it's over or not. And so, in a sense, we're memorializing in the midst. Oklahoma City was one event. It was contained. There were not lots of other large-scale terrorist attacks on government buildings. One can think about the Oklahoma City bombing and the memorial that emerges as an intense remembering of a single event.

We don't know yet what we are in the midst of or whether we have, in fact, absorbed the largest blow. And hence, memorialization is coming very, very quickly, and it may provide us with a much-too-illusory comfort that this is, in fact, over.

12

Like Living in the Book of Job

Like his father before him, Thomas Lynch is the undertaker of Milford, Michigan. In 2001, he spoke with Bob about incomprehensible suffering.

I think, in a very real sense, grief is the tax we pay on loving people. And in this business you see abject, acute grief a lot. You are constantly presented with questions for which there are no answers. The best you can hope to provide is a venue in which they can utter the questions without fear and shame. It's like constantly being in the Book of Job.

The woman who dies at a hundred is not old enough, for her son and daughter, to die. Every death troubles. I think my father and my mother had this feeling—more so my father, because he was at this day after day. He really was concerned that God might take a day off on occasion. You get to worry about your children's well-being, because you see bad things happen to children. Life changes too fast. You know, there is no rhyme or reason to the deaths that happen, and in some ways, that makes life scary. In other ways, it makes it very precious. I see how much of a difference people make to one another.

We've buried men and women who left mad at their spouse or mad at their teenager and didn't come home to say, "I'm sorry" or "I'm kidding." We see the baggage left afterward. So, you try to settle those scores sooner. You don't hold grudges very long.

The Hardest Part

The death of a child really calls our faith into question. As a younger person, I often used to shake my fist in God's face when there was a death of a child and say, "What'd you have in mind here, God?" I think the shaking of the fist is probably something that most parents do when this happens. I don't want to know how that feels. I've said that to parents who have buried their children: "I don't know how you feel and I don't want to know how you feel." And I don't.

I don't have an answer for those who ask, "Why me?" You tell them, "I can't fix this, but I can be with you through this." When most people ask that question, they are not asking for an answer. They want to be able to voice the question out loud, without shame and without guilt and without someone saying, "Well, here's why . . ." They're not looking for *the* answer. They're simply looking for a space in which to either shout, or whisper, or sing that question. The question's there, for sure: "Why me?" Why not?

I think the only antidote is faith. Being an undertaker has given me a heavy reliance on faith and a greater appreciation for the language that our religions bring to this human predicament of a death in the family. I don't know how people would do it without faith. We can get through the baptisms and weddings pretty easily. That's a cakewalk compared to a death in the family. But a death in the family really grabs us by the throat and says, "What do you have faith in?" or "Do you have faith? And, if so, in what?" Not only my work as a funeral director, but also the deaths of my parents and friends and people I care about have made me more reliant on faith.

It's like in the Book of Job, when Job keeps saying, "Well, I've done what I was told to do. What's going wrong here? I'm losing everything." And God comes to him at some point and says, "Must I be wrong for you to be right? Are you accusing me? I'm the one who speaks with thunder, not you." It's quite all right as an act of faith to voice doubt and to voice wonder and to question God. I see those as articles of faith. I see people's anger and despair and hurt and wonder as part of the same pilgrimage to understand God's purpose and will.

Toward the end of the interview, Lynch referred to the occasional days when he is not sure God exists. "On such days," Bob asked, "what do you do?" Lynch burst out laughing and said, "I pray."

13.

Damning the Disease, Not (Ultimately) the Deity

Bob admitted to a personal interest in a Religion & Ethics NewsWeekly *report aired in July 2002 on the debate over embryonic stem-cell research. The subject of the story, a man who wants so much to be healed, is Bob's cousin, Rev. William Abernethy, a retired United Church of Christ minister in Beverly, Massachusetts. Abernethy had been suffering from Parkinson's disease for twenty years, and during that time he had some disquieting conversations with his God, until accepting what he took as an explanation from on high—simply, "I wish I could have done better for you, Bill." Correspondent Lucky Severson began the interview by asking Abernethy, "What goes through the mind of a religious man when he discovers he has a disease like Parkinson's?"*

———

I don't think being religious makes any difference when you go through a realization that you have Parkinson's. You are scared, frightened, challenged, excited, anxious, furious, all of the above.

It makes me furious to have that disease. To wake up in the morning and find yourself shaking so you can't do what you want to do. To find yourself adjusting to a new inability to work and walk and talk and laugh. And just as you get used to that, to be forced to face a new level of inability after that. It's a pain in the neck, at least.

It is a profoundly moving experience to go through a chronic illness. I guess I was unprepared for how significant that going-through was until I went through deep brain-stimulation surgery almost two years ago. Most people have some success with that operation. I was not one of those people. I came through that with a feeling of anger at God. I think that is hard for anybody. It may have been particularly hard on me as a minister, I don't know. What I found myself saying in spite of myself was, "God, if you can heal me, why don't you? You have had an abundance of opportunities. I have been sick for eighteen years. You talk about how you are a God of healing, so why don't you make healing possible?" And that anger was very difficult for me to deal with for several months. For the most part that is now lifted. It's almost as though God would say things to me in a tone of voice that was immensely compassionate. And that's been very important to me. It doesn't make me feel better than anyone else; it makes me feel deeply a part of God's love. So whatever happens in the next few years, stem cells or whatever, I will celebrate it. I hope.

I can't point to any rational route as to how I got there, to this feeling of God's love. But it has felt real in the last couple of years.

To worship God is to open oneself to the power of healing; to talk about salvation is to talk directly about healing. My son, who is a minister, does healing services as part of the worship menu that they offer to people in the community. He has always found it a definite part of who he is. Healing is one of the ways we are sensitive to another person's spirit. It doesn't mean that healing is always a possibility. Praying for healing is one of the things Jesus required or called us to do. But expecting that healing would automatically result is not.

I feel that God must at least be responding, "I wish I could have done better for you, Bill." And I could see God saying that without violating God's omnipotence or whatever other words medieval theologians would have used. God would be saying, "I consider myself voluntarily limited by the limits of human understanding. And people don't know yet how to do stem cells, so I have to wait a bit."

I would say I'm a better person because of this disease, but I would also say God could have found a less drastic way of making me a better person. I'm not sure God had to do Parkinsonian treatment on me to make me the better person I am.

One of the questions I ask myself is, "What do I want to say to someone who first discovers he has Parkinson's?" Or multiple sclerosis or Huntington's or whatever. I think the first thing I want to say is, "I'm sorry. It's painful, and I know you are going to go through the pain. I hope that my sorrow can somehow speak to you at points in your life when you need it." Second, I would say, "It's not the end of your life." I had a counselor once who said to me, "Parkinson's may be a part of you, but it doesn't define you." And I think that's part of what I would like to say. Third, I would like to say, "It can make you a better person. It's not the quickest or the cheapest or the easiest route to get to that, but it is a route and it will get you there, if you let it." And fourth, I think I would say, "Be open to what God is doing through that. And if that's not language that is comfortable to you, try to find some language that allows a deeper power to work through you. Maybe, just maybe, that would open possibilities that you can't see right now."

One of the things I learned through Parkinson's is how to get in touch with my own anger. I think anger is important as a part of human life. That doesn't mean that I want to act on the anger or want the anger to be destructive. I don't. But to get in touch with who I am and what I have and what it has done to me is to get in touch with anger.

I planned I-don't-know-how-many trips around the world when we retired. My wife reaches the age of retirement in a few years. I do, too. And I don't think we are going on too many trips. It doesn't mean that we won't find other things that will be important to us and fun and that we can't have a good life right here. But it does mean that when ten of our friends go off on a cruise, we are not going.

Damn it.

14.

Smells Like Hope

The writer Madeleine L'Engle, who died in September 2007, was versed in suffering. Best known for her 1962 children's classic, A Wrinkle in Time, *L'Engle wrote about her mother's death in her memoir,* The Summer of the Great-Grandmother, *and about her late husband, actor Hugh Franklin, in another book,* Two-Part Invention. *Her son, Bion, died at Christmastime in 1999, and when Bob interviewed L'Engle in her Manhattan apartment, it was Christmastime again, one year later, and she spoke of plans to bury Bion's ashes. She was suffering, and yet she could say, "I've never stopped laughing for more than forty-eight hours. And when I do, you might as well bury me." During the interview, Bob asked her about a scene at the end of* The Summer of the Great-Grandmother *when she is putting her granddaughters, Charlotte and Lena, to bed. Charlotte asked for a song.*

She wanted a long song, and I started with "Barbara Allen." And she said, "Gran, you know that's a bad one."

And I said, "Why, Charlotte? Because everyone dies?"

And she said, "No, Gran. Nobody loved anybody."

And then it was the next night, putting them to bed, that Lena just looked at me cosmically and said, "Gran, is it all right?" She didn't mean anything in particular. She meant the *whole* thing. "Is it all right?"

And I swallowed my heart and my everything and said, "Yes, Lena, it's all right."

And I'm sure it's all right with my heart. I'm not sure it's all right with my mind. What do you suppose the kids in the concentration camp felt when everybody they knew was killed? How could they say, "It's all right?" It's *not* all right. So how do you get the all-rightness out of it? I don't know. I just know it happens. And I know that where there is no suffering, nothing happens.

One time, my godmother went to visit my mother, who was her best friend, and something awful had happened. I don't know what. And she burst into tears instead of offering comfort and said, "I envy you. I envy you. You've had a terrible life, but you've *lived*."

Things may not be all right, but they're at least full of hope. I was writing in my journal yesterday and ended a paragraph with, "I think it smells like hope." And we have to hang onto that. We have to hang onto it most firmly when things are worst. It's easy to believe and have hope when things are going well.

It's when everything is awful that we really need faith.

Several weeks or months after Hugh died, in the medicine cabinet was the new shaving brush I'd given him—just sitting there unused. Never been used. And I was very sad. It's the little things that do that.

We're going up to the country to dump my son's ashes. Maybe it'll be real to me then. I don't know. It's not real to me yet. Reality is often very slow in coming. We'll see.

I'm very grateful that I have a journal and that I can write, because that helps me to objectify things that might just mess me around emotionally, otherwise. It gives them a pattern. A young poet went to Colette* and complained that he was unhappy. And she said, "Who asked you to be happy? Write!" And I think that's very good advice. Journaling defuses things. It objectifies, and I can no longer look at this and weep and feel sorry for myself.

Ultimately, [the death of my son] will be in a nonfiction book. And probably, ultimately, it'll be in a fiction book disguised, because that's the best way to do it. What we write as the truth is often very far from the fact. And one of the worst things that we do in this society is confuse fact and truth, so if it is not factual, we don't believe it. Well, mostly what I believe in is *not* factual—friendship, beauty.

I find death a lot less frightening—I don't know why—than annihilation. I think that's our major fear. I'm afraid, but I don't spend time on it now. There's too much else. I don't have to know what's next, or if anything's

* The French writer Sidonie-Gabrielle Colette.

next, or if nothing is next. I just try to get on with what I'm doing, which is writing a book about aging.

We should be busy enough with the business of living not to brood over dying. Now, that doesn't mean not being realistic about it. I know. I'm nearly eighty-two. I'm toward the end. And I hope I've learned from those first eighty-two years. I hope I've learned tolerance and understanding even of the people I despise. And I hope I will always enjoy going out to dinner, talking. One of the things I really enjoy now is when I go downstairs to Henry's [restaurant] for dinner. I'm in a wheelchair at that point, because it's easier. Well, somebody has to jump up and open the door for me. You know, I love that! Maybe it's a small pleasure, but it's a pleasure. And I think enjoying small pleasures is important. The big ones are so big, we don't have time to enjoy them.

I've never stopped laughing for more than forty-eight hours. And when I do, you might as well bury me. I hope it's not going to happen. Somehow, some of the most poignantly beautiful times have been holding somebody's hand as something bad is happening. And that—just simply the gesture of holding hands—is an affirmation of love. And as long as we have that, we can make anything.

Now, I don't know if I could *say* that if I were a survivor of a concentration camp and everybody I knew had been killed. I don't know. I had tea with Elie Wiesel, and as you know, he's still struggling with the concentration camp and everybody he knew being killed. And I can only see that second-hand, not first—I don't know how I would be firsthand. I can't make those brave statements.

And I remember standing by my desk in my apartment on Tenth Street right after the war and wondering if I would've been brave enough to speak to the Jewish professor and his wife down the hall, knowing that I might then be shoved off into a concentration camp myself. And I hadn't had to be tested on that. But I didn't know whether I'd pass the test or not. I still don't. I think we are, in times of angst, given strength we didn't know we had. So I think we should not undercut ourselves, because often the strength will come. You see it with athletes. They push and push over the line to win the race. We all have more strength than we know we have. And if we had it all of the time, it would shatter us. And so it comes only when we really need it.

In times when we're not particularly suffering we don't have enough time for God. We're too busy with other things. Then the intense suffering comes, and we can't be busy with other things. And then God comes into the equation—"Help!" We should never be afraid of crying out, "I need all the help I can get!"

15.

Redeeming the Devil

As chair of South Africa's Truth and Reconciliation Commission, Archbishop Desmond Tutu did more than anyone else to unearth the horrible secrets of apartheid, the system in which a white minority regime had subjugated the entire black population. But the Nobel Peace Prize winner also did more than anyone else to place the nation's suffering within a spiritual frame of forgiveness and hope. In this 1998 interview, the depth of his personal conviction was revealed when Bob, alluding to Tutu's recent cancer surgery, asked him, "How are you feeling?" But first, the archbishop spoke about the finding of the Truth and Reconciliation Commission that had the starkest emotional effect upon him.

I was shocked when we heard about the chemical and biological warfare program of the previous government. I think that, for me, was the most shocking, most diabolical in that it was so methodical, so clinical—something they did that shattered us.

Some of it was reducing the fertility of black women. Some of it was looking for toxins that would affect only black people. They were trying also to poison Nelson Mandela so that his brain would be affected, and when he came out of prison he would not survive for too long.

You know, anyone who expected that the revelations would make people suddenly embrace each other and love each other was totally unrealistic. When you are a mother and you hear that your child was abducted and that they shot him in the head and they burned his body, and as they were burning his body, they were having a barbecue on the side, if that mother were to say I love the people who did this, she would be crazy. People would say she was abnormal. And so it wasn't surprising that the revelations shocked people.

I learned that we have the capacity for the greatest possible evil, all of us, but more exhilarating, we have the capacity for the greatest possible good. Human beings are an incredible creation.

I am saying the grace of God is an extraordinary thing, and I believe in something that the church doesn't quite accept. It was taught by a great African who has never been canonized, Origen,* and he taught something called universalism that says that ultimately even the devil is not going to be able to resist the love of God and that ultimately even the devil will be redeemed.

Now, the church, I don't think, has been able to accept that. I have a sneaking suspicion that it will, eventually. The God that I worship is the God who cries. God weeps looking over a Jerusalem that has rejected him, and when he lifts up his arms across Israel, it's a cosmic embrace. I want to embrace everything so that God will be all involved. That is the God that I worship.

And I'm Feeling . . .

Wonderful. I think it's a good thing to have had cancer because it's a wonderful indication of your mortality and it actually makes you become more grateful, more appreciative of things that you used to take for granted, like the laughter of your children.

Of course, I always tell myself that for the Christian, since Jesus overcame death, death can't be this ghastly enemy, though of course I don't want to be tested, as it were. I mean, I believe in the resurrection, and I know that death is not the last word. I would like to continue to live. There are so many good things that one would like to appreciate. But I also realize that death is the gateway to a fuller life. To know that the everlasting arms are there, to know that Jesus is there is to know that it is not just a void and that I will not be separated in the final ultimate sense from the ones that I love.

Now, when I attend a funeral and I see the coffin descend into the grave, I think: one day it's going to be me. Serious illness does give a new intensity

---

* A third-century theologian who lived in Alexandria and was one of the great "early fathers" or scholars of the Christian church.

to your living. It gives a new quality to relationships. When I look at a rose with dew on its petals, I see a new intensity to its beauty, because I may not be seeing this for a very, very long time.

I am very blessed in the deep sense of knowing I belong in a body [that is, the body of Christ, the church] and that I am upheld by the love and the prayers and the caring of so many and that it is not Desmond against all the powers of evil. I am just one in an incredible, wonderful body.

16.

Hope Dies Last

Studs Terkel was ninety-one years old when his book Hope Dies Last: Keeping the Faith in Troubled Times *was published and when* Religion & Ethics NewsWeekly *editor Missy Daniel had a conversation with him in December 2003 about his conversations with hopeful people. In a sense, all of Terkel's classic, oral-history-style works have been about hope, his hope, because he believes in the American people enough to let them speak for themselves. He begins here by disentangling hope from mere optimism.*

━

Hope is more of a tightrope. You can hope and still feel guardedly, even a little, pessimistic: "I hope it will be better tomorrow than it is today." We use the word "hope" perhaps more often than any other word in the vocabulary: "I hope it's a nice day." "Hopefully, you're doing well." "So how are things going along? Pretty good. Going to be good tomorrow? Hope so." With optimism, you look upon the sunny side of things. People say, "Studs, you're an optimist." I never said I was an optimist. I have hope because what's the alternative to hope? Despair? If you have despair, you might as well put your head in the oven.

"Hope dies last" was a phrase used by Jessie de la Cruz, one of the first women to work for César Chávez in organizing the farm workers union. Very few women were involved in the beginning. She is one of the few. She said, "Whenever things are bleak and seem hopeless, we have a saying in Spanish: '*La esperanza muere al último.*' Hope dies last." I thought, if ever there were a time to write a book about hope, it's now.

Through history, there always have been certain kinds of people who had a hope. They did stuff they shouldn't have done. They discommoded themselves. They could have led nice lives. I want to pay tribute to people who have hope, who have always been kind of a minority, who are called "activists." "Activist" means what? Someone who does an act. In a democratic society, you're supposed to be an activist; that is, you participate. It could be a letter written to an editor. It could be fighting for stoplights on a certain corner where kids cross. And it could be something for peace, or for civil rights, or for human rights. But once you become active in something, something happens to you. You get excited and suddenly you realize you count.

I want to pay tribute to people like Virginia and Clifford Durr, who lived in the South and were well-off. He was from a top family in Montgomery, Alabama. Her father was a clergyman. He was a member of the Federal Communications Commission under Franklin D. Roosevelt when World War II was going on. He's the one who wrote that the airwaves belong to the public and that the public has the right to all variety of programs. Then came the Cold War and Joe McCarthy. President Truman said to Clifford Durr, "Your people have to sign a loyalty oath." He said, "I don't believe in it. I won't. Under no circumstances will I allow my people to be demeaned by doing this." And he resigned.

And Virginia Durr—I first heard of her in 1944 at a big anti–poll tax gathering in Chicago. The poll tax was aimed primarily against blacks and poor whites.* They couldn't vote, especially African Americans in the South. So Virginia was campaigning against the poll tax in the company of Dr. Mary McLeod Bethune, an eminent African-American educator. This big symphony hall in Chicago was jammed! Dr. Bethune was good, but Virginia Durr—this lanky forty-year-old white woman—set the house on fire. So I go backstage with a number of us to shake her hand. As I put forth my hand, she says, "Thank you, dear," and she puts forth her hand. In her hand are a hundred leaflets. She says, "Now, dear, you hurry outside and you pass out those leaflets, because Dr. Bethune and I are due to speak at the Abyssinian Baptist Church in a couple of hours. Hurry, dear!"

Virginia and Cliff Durr were ostracized by their community. They suffered a great deal. They were under investigation by Senator James Eastland of Mississippi, who was very segregationist and very antiblack. He said the group the Durrs belonged to, the Southern Conference for Human Welfare,

---

* Poll taxes imposed in Southern states "had the effect of disenfranchising many blacks as well as poor whites, because payment of the tax was a prerequisite for voting," according to the *Columbia Encyclopedia*.

was subversive because it was antilynching, anti–poll tax, and for integration. The Durrs got themselves in big trouble. Virginia's seamstress was a woman named Rosa Parks. She encouraged Rosa Parks to go to a school that was teaching organizers, the Highlander Folk School in Tennessee, with Myles Horton, a great teacher. Rosa Parks went to school there and so did Dr. Martin Luther King and others. But the school was under attack. These people, few in number and way outnumbered, were fighting way back then. I want to celebrate the ones who are doing this sort of work today.

Religion obviously has played a role in these lives. You happen to be talking to an agnostic. You know what an agnostic is? A cowardly atheist. Nonetheless, do I have respect for people who believe in the hereafter? Of course I do. I might add, perhaps even a touch of envy, too, because of the solace. If solace is any sort of succor to someone, that is sufficient. I believe in the faith of people, whatever faith they may have.

It turns out that there are a great many Catholics in the book. There's a priest at the very beginning of the book, Father Bob Oldershaw, and his brother, who is a neurosurgeon. Father Oldershaw had a parish. His altar boy, a Mexican kid, Mario Ramos, was part of a gang, and he shot Andrew Young, son of Steven and Maurine Young, a nice kid. It was a mistake, because he thought Andrew Young was a member of another gang. Here is Father Oldershaw: "That was my altar boy who did the killing. At first, I said to myself, No way! Then I started thinking about what made him do it, where he comes from. Then I had to go see the couple," who are not members of his parish, but he was praying for them. It was pretty tough. Finally, he did see them, and they got together. That couple, in a sense, have adopted as theirs the boy who killed their son. The one who arranged the whole thing was Bob Oldershaw himself.

Praying for the Corn

Kathy Kelly heads a group called Voices in the Wilderness. These are people who bear witness, as Dorothy Day did. Dorothy Day* got in trouble and was arrested many times. Why did she do this when she could lead a nice, easy

---

* Cofounder of the Catholic Worker movement.

life and mind her own business? Dorothy Day said—and I'm sure that Kathy Kelly would say the same thing—"I'm working toward a world in which it will be easier for people to behave decently." Now, think about that: a world in which it will be easier for people to behave decently. Kathy Kelly has borne witness in Basra and Baghdad to the innocent victims of war. She's been mentioned for the Nobel Peace Prize several times. She has shadowed some of the thousands of missile sites we have. Many people may not think they have seen any, but they have driven by them in the Midwest. It's like a little hill, but it just ruins the corn country around it. Corn can't be planted. One day Kathy Kelly cut through the barbed wire at one of the missile silos. There she was—all eighty-five pounds of her—on this missile site. She starts planting some corn next to it. Of course, she put up a sign. She wanted people in the passing cars to see the sign: "Beat your swords into plowshares and study war no more," from Isaiah, the Old Testament prophet.

She called up the authorities to be arrested, because obviously she violated security. Here comes a big truck with machine guns and everything. The commander says, "Get off the site with your hands raised and kneel to be handcuffed." And she does. Just then, a young soldier, a kid of about nineteen, comes off the truck toward her with a gun pointed at her head. He's trembling, because here's the enemy. It's Kathy Kelly. He's told she's a terrorist. He's trembling, but he's got a gun on her head. She looks at the boy and says, "Do you know why I'm kneeling now? Do you know why I'm here?" He says, "Why, ma'am?" "Because I'm praying for the corn to grow." Then she looks at him and senses he's a country boy. She says, "Wouldn't you like the corn to grow?" "Yes, ma'am." "Will you pray with me for the corn to grow?" He says, "Yes, ma'am." And he thought of a prayer for the corn to grow. Then the kid says—he's still got the gun to her head—"Ma'am, are you thirsty?" "Oh, yes." It was a broiling hot day. He puts his gun down, which I'm sure is a violation, and he opens his canteen and says, "Ma'am, will you lean your head back a little?" and he pours some of the water into her mouth.

The judge was kind, but she's not going to recant or say she's sorry and that she's never going to do it again. Of course not. She got a year in the federal pen. But she saw that boy in court. He was supposed to testify, and he was trembling, because he thought she might tell the story. She said no, she just winked at him, and then she said, "If he reads this book, I hope he'll forgive me for telling you the story." So that is Kathy Kelly. And there is faith. And there is hope.

I think it's realistic to have hope. One can be a perverse idealist and say the easiest thing: "I despair. The world's no good." That's a perverse idealist. It's practical to hope, because the hope is for us to survive as a human species. That's very realistic. Why are we born? We're born eventually to die, of course. But what happens between the time we're born and we die? We're born to live. One is a realist if one hopes.

My mother ran a rooming house. My family was Jewish but not religious. My mother went through the rituals, my father didn't. He was a freethinker. What made me was the hotel where I was raised. My father died and my mother ran it. Before that, it was a rooming house. In that hotel, there were these guys arguing. There were the old-time union guys and there were nonunion guys. There were what we called Wobblies, the IWW,* and the guys who were anti-them would say, "I Won't Work, that's what IWW means." They argued. That's what we're missing. We're missing argument. We're missing debate. We're missing colloquy. We're missing all sorts of things. Instead, we're accepting.

I've always felt that there's a deep decency in the American people and a native intelligence—providing they have the facts, providing they have the information. The September 11 assault was horrendous. But there's another assault that's taking place. It's an assault upon our intelligence. It's an assault upon our sense of decency as well as upon our faiths, too, I believe. We are the most powerful nation in the world, but we're not the only nation in the world. We are not the only people in the world. We are an important people, the wealthiest, the most powerful, and to a great extent, generous. But we are part of the world.

I am hopeful. The most amazing thing is that there are so many groups. I don't understand the Internet real well. I'm very bad technologically. I can't drive a car. I fall off a bicycle. I goof up the tape recorder. I'm just learning to use an electric typewriter—that's my big advance. I'm not up on the

---

* Industrial Workers of the World.

Internet, but I hear that is a democratic possibility. People can connect with each other. I think people are ready for something, but there is no leadership to offer it to them. People are ready to say, "Yes, we are part of a world." I feel hopeful in that sense.

I feel a little worried because of the nature of technology. Technology works in two ways. I'm ninety-one years old, thanks to technology—a quintuple bypass. It was the skilled hands of a surgeon, but there were also all these medical advances and the machinery that helped me. At the same time, we have the technology of destruction since Hiroshima and beyond—technology that can destroy the world.

So here we are. We have a choice to make. I'm merely paraphrasing Bertrand Russell and Albert Einstein. I always love to quote Albert Einstein because nobody dares contradict him. Einstein and Russell together issued a joint statement, and they said, roughly: "We have a chance right now to live in a new world with so many possibilities. With labor-saving devices, people can learn new ways of earning their living, new ways of following what they want to do. Or we can engage in mutual destruction." They both spoke of that back in 1955. It's more than half a century later, and what they said is even more italicized.

I read somewhere that health improves when a person takes part in community action. Something happens to him or to her biologically. It's like a tonic. When you become part of something, in some way you count. It could be a march, it could be a rally, even a brief one. You're part of something, and you suddenly realize you count. To count is very important. People say, "I'm helpless." Of course you feel that way, if you're alone. There are so many groups—environmental groups, other groups—but there is no one umbrella.

I hope for peace and sanity—it's the same thing. I want a language that speaks the truth. I want people to talk with one another no matter what their difference of opinion might be. I want, of course, peace, grace, and beauty.

And I hope that memory is valued—that we do not lose memory.

CHAPTER 3

Prayer and Meditation

Sooner or later, one way or another, nearly everyone prays.

It's the way billions of us over the centuries have learned to connect the tangible, material world with the "Something More"—the transcendent spiritual reality so many people insist is there. In our time, neither philosophy nor science nor catastrophic events has eliminated the tendency to pray.

Religion & Ethics NewsWeekly and other media outlets have commissioned national polls asking Americans about prayer. Almost all say they pray sometimes. About 60 percent say they pray every day, and nearly half of all those pollsters called "seculars"—atheists and agnostics—say they pray every day, too!

With so many different people in so many different cultures seeking a relationship with the divine over the centuries, it's no wonder that there are so many different kinds of prayer. They range from everyday petitions asking for things—"God, help me on this exam"—to simple praise, to quiet, mystical, often wordless awareness of divine presence.

There are extemporaneous, made-up prayers and set, memorized prayers, like the Lord's Prayer and the many mealtime graces. There are also traditional, written prayers of worship, such as those in Jewish services and the Episcopal Book of Common Prayer.

Prayers are mumbled and proclaimed, chanted and danced, said once in a while, at fixed hours throughout the day, or constantly, as a mantra.

Prayers are uttered by individuals, by families, by congregations, and by nations.

People direct prayers to a God who is distant, beyond our comprehension, completely separate from ourselves, and also to a presence they say is within them, in their hearts or deep in the unconscious, as close as breath.

Prayer can be active or passive, asking for something we want—petitionary prayer—or trying to discern what God wants. Often, say many who pray, prayers become conversations.

Experts say the desire to pray is often most intense in times of suffering and compassion. It also frequently accompanies feelings of awe—of nature and music and poetry.

The selections here are from prayer authorities—scholars, clergy, well-known writers. These "prayer pros" may be exceptionally experienced or learned, and they may have very different styles of prayer. But it is our sense that what they say and do, every day, is not unique. As we said, nearly everyone prays.

17.

The World's Prayers

Carol and Philip Zaleski are the authors of the much-acclaimed Prayer: A History. *She is a professor of religion at Smith College. He is the editor of* The Best American Spiritual Writing *series and a senior editor at* Parabola *magazine. Phil is a cradle Catholic who was also drawn to Asian religions. Carol was raised in a nonreligious Jewish family and converted to Catholicism. They have two young children. Bob spoke with them in Northampton, Massachusetts, in 2003.*

—

PHILIP: Prayer is communication between the human realm and the transcendent realm, which for most people means trying to communicate with a personal God, coming into contact with a person who cares about them and loves them and can help them out. And, hopefully, this communication becomes a two-way street, and God speaks back.

And this makes people happy, which tells us that prayer is something essential to our nature, as if it were hardwired in us. It's something that we need to do, and something that feels good when we do it. Even in the midst of suffering, prayer is, if not a release from suffering, a way to find meaning in suffering.

CAROL: I think that prayer is a communication in which we, the people who pray, take on the role, you might say, of a child. The basic stance is one of humility. And it usually involves a request of some kind, but also can just be an effort to come into a deeper relationship with the divine.

Essentially, prayer is an attitude of thankfulness, a sense of awe, a sense of feeling thrown into this life, and a sense of a continual miracle. And prayer is just a response to that continual miracle which is always unfolding. In my family, every time I look at my children, every time I take a step and don't fall into an abyss, I have something to be thankful for. And that comes first. And then asking for things comes after that. It comes from that sense that I've been showered with blessings and one of those blessings is the ability to ask for help.

I think there's prayer embedded in a lot of our thinking and behavior, whether or not we think of ourselves as religious. For instance, you're thinking to yourself, "Please, let me pass that exam," or "Please, let me be okay with these medical tests." And it may be something that occurs spontaneously in people who have either rejected the idea of religion or a belief in God, or have never really given it much thought. It seems to grow on all kinds of soil, even in the less-promising soil of an atheist.

PHILIP: I try to pray on and off throughout the day. When I wake up, it's a very brief prayer. And I find my prayers become more important and more intense as the day goes on, perhaps because the difficulties of the day throw me on my knees before God, even if it's an easy day.

I find that all forms of prayer help—silent prayer, saying set prayers, like the Lord's Prayer or the Hail Mary. The most important type of prayer is petitionary prayer, because I believe it's by far the most common. People often contrast petitionary prayer with contemplative prayer, which is a form of prayer where you just sit still and erase your thoughts and feelings as much as you can, and just open yourself to the presence of God.

CAROL: Traditional prayer involves the attitude of humility and conformity to the will of God, which means that the first thing you're praying for is for God's will to be done. And you may not know exactly where that will lie. You try to be on the right side of each issue, but the final issue is in God's hands.

PHILIP: Many people discover prayer in times of suffering. People can go for thirty, forty, fifty years without ever praying. Perhaps they had a taste of prayer in childhood, and then it vanished. And all of a sudden, they're faced with a terrible crisis—an illness or death in their family, and they feel bereft. They need help, and they can't find help on the human plane.

And then they realize there's an opportunity to turn somewhere else, and they get on their knees—literally or figuratively—and they pray to God.

Stopping throughout the day for prayer is very important, and one finds it in many different religions, the most famous example being Muslims, who stop five times a day, each time for a series of prayers and ritual prostrations and ablutions.

The idea is that throughout the day, we tend to get lost. We wander away, and every time we stop and are called back to prayer and to God, we return to what really matters. It's like a baseball player coming home or anyone coming home, coming back to the center of life.

CAROL: Free will is an extremely important idea in many religious traditions and certainly in Judaism and Christianity. When you pray, you're asking God to step in, but you're not necessarily asking God to overrule your free will. In fact, if you had a sense that everything was completely predestined, if you had a fatalistic sense of things, then there would, perhaps, be less reason to pray. And that may be one of the answers to the problem of unanswered prayer. If God answered all our prayers, that would mean that he was acting like a puppet master.

It may be greater that we have free will and can abuse it than it would be if we were hardwired always to choose the good, like robots.

It's very hard to try to give a pat answer to the problem of unanswered prayers. In a sense, it's the great problem of religious belief, generally. The standard answer in theological circles is that God has answered your prayer, one way. It's just a matter of how you understand that answer. Very often, it's not in our best interest to get the answer that we had in mind. There are other factors that could be at work, and only God would have the whole picture.

But that's a hard thing to say to someone who has a very sick child and is praying and is asking for the prayers of others. I think that really takes us into the realm of mystery and of God's presence with the person who is suffering, and not just God as the person who hands out favors or withholds them.

PHILIP: It may be that God answers in a way we can't see. It may be that God simply has decided that the prayer is inadequate or inappropriate. These are simple answers to a very difficult question. And when you run up against a question like the Holocaust—what happened in the Holocaust, and why were the prayers of so many millions of people seemingly unanswered—all we can say is that it's a mystery. That may be a lame answer, but it's the only one we have.

We just don't know. And here we have to admit that everything about prayer is, in a sense, a mystery. We're dealing with the mystery of God and the mystery of the human heart and the mystery of the relationship between the two. So, all we can do sometimes is stand in front of mystery and bow our head and pray some more.

CAROL: I think we should recognize the magical aspect of prayer. The danger is that we will think of prayer in a very mechanistic way, as an effort to make God do what we want, to make things happen. And that is not a prayerful attitude. It lacks that sense of humility and confession and contrition, which is characteristic of prayer.

Prayer does have a dimension that we may as well call magical, for want of a better word. And the indicators of that are that prayer involves the use of strange words, of musical words, sometimes of nonsense words. Very often, archaic language is used. Repetition is used. There's a strong sense of the inherent power of the words and particularly of names. Where divine names are used, there's a sense that those names contain the essence of God. So when you use them, you are, in a sense, invoking God, almost, one might say, conjuring God—if that's not too strong a word. And that aspect of prayer runs through all religious traditions. And whenever efforts are made to remove it completely, there's a loss in the power and intensity of prayer.

PHILIP: There's another kind of prayer which is tremendously important. These are composed prayers, the most famous being the Lord's Prayer, which Jesus himself composed.

Whenever you have a composed prayer, you have a prayer which seeks to get to the heart of the human being and to turn that human being toward God. And beauty and precision and eloquence all come and play a part, and that means the skills of poetry come into play in composed prayers.

I think the most interesting experiments involving prayer have been attempts by poets to create poems that bring the person who reads the poem into a state of prayer. There's the famous Japanese poet, Matsuo Basho, who developed the whole style of poetry known as hokku, in the 17th century. At its best, Basho's work, like that of lesser poets, brings a realization of the evanescent and unfathomable nature of all things, this awareness of the mysterious inner core of things.

And in the West, we have Gerard Manley Hopkins, a Catholic priest who, through the use of extraordinarily explosive imagery and alliteration and digging into the very sound of language, tried to get beyond language itself, to use language's magical qualities to get into the mystery of God.

CAROL: Right now, the prayer poems, you might call them, of Rumi, are extremely popular. And they embody some of the ecstatic, mystical quality of Rumi's Islamic mysticism, Sufism. They are the verbal counterpart to the experience of the whirling dervishes, who enact the movements of the planets and the orbiting of the soul around the soul's beloved. And he captures that same experience in words, in prayers, in sounds.

Rumi is the best-selling poet in the United States today, which tells us a great deal about the extent to which poetry and religious longing and religious quest are linked in our contemporary experience.

Gandhi made use of Christian prayers, and one of his favorites was John Henry Newman's "Lead Kindly, Light." That prayer has this wonderful quality of conveying a sense of security in the face of mystery: I don't need to see everything in the future, I just need to see enough light to take the next step.* Gandhi loved that prayer so much that he arranged for it to be sung in his ashram every Friday night at seven o'clock. Friends around the world would know it was being sung then, and they would sing it also. So it had that aspect of a communal affirmation that we can trust in God even if we can't see. Even if we're walking into a dark and dangerous situation, we can still trust in that light.

There are particular prayers that may have a special resonance, and among them is the prayer of Lancelot Andrewes, who was one of the trans-

---

* Newman's words are, "I do not ask to see / The distant scene—one step enough for me."

lators of the King James Bible, that has this quality that I call the "360-degree prayer." And he is suggesting in this prayer the sense of being surrounded by divine protection and grace with every step we take. "Be, Lord, within me to strengthen me, without me to preserve, over me to shelter, beneath to support, before me to direct, behind me to bring back, 'round about me to fortify." So that's the complete 360-degree circuit of divine Providence that he's asking for.

PHILIP: It's just astonishing what people have used for prayer. All of us are familiar with prayer beads. We know that people use drums, and we've heard about Tibetan prayer flags and that sort of thing.

And it seems right, because all these things are understood, all of the material world is understood, to somehow be given to us to use to make us closer to God. These things aren't alien to us. They're part of the gifts of God, and we can use them in return to go back to God.

CAROL: I think there's a body language in prayer, as well as a verbal language in prayer. So, for example, kneeling or prostration suggest and elicit in the person who's doing it a sense of humility, of surrender, of obeisance—but not of servile humility. If you were kneeling and prostrating yourself that way before a human tyrant, you would be ground down by it. But kneeling and prostrating yourself before the divine is uplifting.

PHILIP: There was a monk named Brother Lawrence of the Resurrection who talked about the practice of the presence of God. He was a cook in a monastery, and he was rather famous for dropping his pans in the middle of fixing a soufflé to pray to God and to feel the presence of God. And he would do this at any given moment of the day or night, and eventually it became a sort of a continuous practice with him. So it ties into the idea of continuous or never-ending prayer.

I learned to pray as a child. I was raised Catholic and learned the rote prayers of the church, the Our Father and the Hail Mary. And then as a young adult, I put all that behind me and explored Eastern forms of prayer, meditation, and contemplative prayer in various modes.

And now, as I get older and pray with my children, I find that, for one thing, I'm returning to the rote prayers, because they're prayers that a child can learn and can enjoy and can use. And I find I get new meaning and strength out of them. I still do some contemplative prayer, but I find that beyond both those things, prayer for me now, above all, is just talking to God. I just talk to God, sometimes on my knees. I don't know if God answers, but I have a sense that he's listening.

I also have a sense of adoring this magnificent, inconceivable person who's given life to this whole world, and in that mixed rush of adoration and gratitude and thankfulness, I find the finest and best moments in my prayer.

CAROL: As a child, I didn't know much about praying. I grew up in a family that didn't practice religion. My heritage is Jewish, and I still consider myself Jewish and Christian. I had to learn about religion from books, and I have to say I'm grateful for that, actually.

That's why I'm a religion professor, because I was looking for religion. And the only way I knew how to look was through books. But I still didn't really know how to put these things into practice. For a long time, I was studying and learning about monastic life in the Middle Ages, and I thought, "How wonderful if this sort of thing were still going on, if people were actually praying seven times a day and meditating and all of that. Too bad it's not still going on." Then I discovered that it is still going on. I had only to look.

18.

Through the Valley of the Shadow

Rabbi Harold Kushner is the author of such popular works as When Bad Things Happen to Good People *and* The Lord Is My Shepherd. *During this 2004 conversation with producer Susan Grandis Goldstein, the rabbi parsed the words of a psalm he has prayed often during difficult times.*

—

For the thirty-five or so years that I was a congregational rabbi, I knew I had this magic weapon: no matter how grievous a funeral was, no matter how tragic a memorial service was, if I just started to recite the familiar words of the twenty-third psalm—"The Lord is my shepherd, I shall not want. He makes me to lie down in green pastures . . ."—it tranquilized the congregation. It just made people feel calm. I never understood why. And then, right after 9/11, after that horrifying attack on the Pentagon and the World Trade Center in New York, when everybody was asking me, "Where was God that Tuesday, how could God have let such a thing happen?" the answer I found myself giving was: "You know, God's promise was never that life would be fair. God's promise was, when it's your turn to confront the unfairness of life, no matter how hard it is, you'll be able to handle it, because He'll be on your side. He will give you the strength you need to find your way through."

I was merely paraphrasing the twenty-third psalm: "Though I walk through the valley of the shadow of death, I will fear no evil, for Thou art with me." The psalmist is not saying, "I'll fear no evil because there's no such thing as evil in the world, everything happens for a reason." He is not saying, "I will fear no evil because evil happens only to people who deserve it." He's saying, "This is a scary, out-of-control world, but it doesn't scare me, because I know that God is on my side, not on the side of the hijacker. God is on my side, not on the side of the illness, or the accident, or the terrible thing that happened. And that's enough to give me confidence." The

123

twenty-third psalm is the answer to the question, "How do you live in a dangerous, unpredictable, frightening world?"

The psalmist starts out living in a perfect world, a world of sunshine and green pastures and still waters and everything in place. He thinks it's going to continue that way for the rest of his life. And then something happens. We don't know what. It could be a serious illness. It could be the death of someone he cares about. It could be a rejection, a betrayal, a business failure. Whatever it is, he is cast from this world of sunshine and green pastures into "the valley of the shadow of death." At first, he thinks that God has abandoned him, because the God who took care of him, the God who made everything turn out right—"The Lord is my shepherd"—wasn't taking care of him. But it's in "the valley of the shadow" that he learns what God is really all about. Not a God who guarantees happy endings, but a God who says, "Even if the ending isn't happy, I will give you the capacity, the resilience, the courage, the strength, the faith to get through it." It's a much more mature understanding of God, a much more realistic one. It doesn't depend on hiding your eyes from all the unfairness and all the tragedy and the dangers in the world. It's a matter of confronting them, staring them down, and not letting them scare you.

The psalm tells us you're going to find yourself in darkness, you're going to find yourself in the "valley of the shadow." You will feel abandoned, but you're never abandoned. That's where you will discover the reality of God.

"Though I Walk Through the Valley of the Shadow of Death"

It's such a brilliant insight by the psalmist that it's not the experience of death that scares a person. By then, it's too late. It's the apprehension of death, the knowledge of our own vulnerability, or maybe it's the death of somebody else that casts a shadow over our lives. In Kahlil Gibran's little book *The Prophet*, there's a wonderful line I've always enjoyed about people who turn their backs on the sun: "And what is the sun to them but a caster of shadows?" In other words, the only time you see shadows is if the sun is shining some place else behind you. All you have to do is turn around, and you're in the sunshine again. But people who have been hurt by life get stuck in "the valley of the shadow," and they don't know how to find their way out. And that's the role of God. The role of God is not to explain and not to justify, but to comfort, to find people when they are living in darkness, take them by the hand, and show them how to find their way into the sunlight again.

All the years I was a congregational rabbi, I would meet people to whom something really unfortunate had happened—bereavement, divorce, rejection, crippling injury. They would find themselves in the "valley of the shadow," and they'd get stuck there. That's why, I've come to suspect, maybe the single most important word in the entire psalm is one we tend to slur over when we're reciting it. It's the word "through"—"through the valley of the shadow"—to make sure you don't get stuck there.

Why do people let themselves get stuck? Sometimes, I think, they feel guilty that they're still alive, and somebody they love has died. Sometimes, I suspect, they're afraid. They're afraid that if they ever permitted themselves to recover, then they would lose the person, not only physically, but emotionally as well. And as a rabbi, I would try to explain to them, "No, that's not how it works. When you have loved somebody, they have entered so intimately into the fabric of your soul that neither death nor time can ever take them out. They are always with you. You don't have to feel you are leaving them behind. If you go back into the sunlight and pick your life up and enjoy being alive again, you are taking them with you."

"Thou Anointest My Head with Oil"

When the psalmist says, "Thou anointest my head with oil," I think that's a hard line for a modern person to understand. It sounds like something that happens at a beauty parlor. The ancient biblical person would have known the suggestion at once, what the psalmist was talking about. To anoint with oil means to designate a person as special. The word "messiah" is the Hebrew term for "anointed with oil." The name "Christ" means, literally, "the anointed one." When the psalmist says, "Thou anointest my head with oil," I hear him say, "God, when you found me in the valley of the shadow and assured me that I was not abandoned there, that I was not alone, and you took me by the hand and led me into the sunlight again, you made me feel I was special. You cared about me. You cared about whether I was happy or whether I was suffering. And, God, I owe you something in return. I have to do something with this *specialness*, and this something is to make your world a little bit better for all the other people. I want to be the one who introduces all these other people to the healing power of God."

"My Cup Runneth Over"

Two words in Hebrew, "*kosi revayah,*" four words in English, "my cup runneth over." It's gratitude. All the time he was living in a perfect world of sunshine and green pastures and still waters, it never occurs to the psalmist to say, "Thank you." It's only after he's been through "the valley of the shadow," only after he has learned how vulnerable, how fragile all of those blessings are—only then does it occur to him to say, "Thank you."

"And I Shall Dwell in the House of the Lord Forever"

Of the thousands of people I've spoken to about my book since it was published, I've run across three people who did not like the twenty-third psalm and all for the same reason. They all said the same thing—"I don't like this psalm because it says, 'The Lord is my shepherd.' And if the Lord is my shepherd, that means I'm a sheep, and I don't like being told I'm a sheep." The first time I heard this, I didn't know what to say. By the second time, I had an answer ready. I said, "First of all, this is a poem. Give me a break. You don't take a poem literally. It's images, it's metaphors. More than that, though, the psalmist's first line is 'The Lord is my shepherd.' That is, I am scared and vulnerable, and God is there to take care of me. But that's only the beginning, the first line. Look at the last line: 'I shall dwell in the house of the Lord forever.' All his life experiences, all the times he's found himself in 'the valley of the shadow' and was able to find his way out have taught him something about God and about his relationship to God. It's no longer an abstract relationship, a theological matter of speculation. It's no longer this passive, childlike dependence on God. It's a reciprocal relationship: God does things for me, and I do things for God. And I am welcome in the house of the Lord. I'm not the sheep. I am the house guest. I am friends with God. He reaches out to me, I respond to him."

The psalm talks about a man whose understanding of God has changed and matured as he went through life, from the person who thinks, "God takes care of me, so everything will be perfect," to the person who says, "Why didn't God take care of me?" to the person who realizes, "God is taking care of me. He can't guard me. He can't protect me from unfairness. He can give me the strength, the resiliency, and the courage to cope with the unfairness." There is a world out there full of threats and full of danger and full of uncertainty. I could be so scared of that world that I would stay home, but I'm not going to do that. I'm going to go out and live my life. I'm going to get on airplanes, despite the terrorist threats. And I'm going to go out shopping, despite the flu. And I'm not going to let this world inhibit me, because even if something bad happens to me, life experience has taught me that it's not the end. I can survive the worst that life has to deal me, "for thou art with me."

God becomes real at a time like that.

19

The Former President on Unanswered Prayer

Former president Jimmy Carter knows something about prayer, especially unanswered prayer or prayer that is answered a little late. Carter says he prayed fervently in 1980 for the release of the American hostages in Iran. Eventually, as he told Bob in 1998, they did come home, safe and free. But only after Ronald Reagan had been elected president.

———

I prayed more when I was president than any other four years of my life. I prayed more during the year that the hostages were held than any other year that I was in office. I prayed that I would have the patience to accomplish the goals that I established at the very beginning.

I had two goals. One was to preserve the integrity of my nation and not do anything to embarrass my country. And the second one was to bring every hostage home safe and free. And I asked God to help me with those commitments.

I could have launched a very popular military strike on Iran. I could have destroyed Iran—and in the process killed thousands of innocent Iranians, which would also have resulted maybe in the assassination or killing of American hostages. I was advised to do that. I decided not to. I guess I felt that God would answer my prayer.

Well, I never did embarrass my nation or violate its principles. Every hostage came home safe and free. So my prayer was answered. God answered my prayer later than I wanted. If my prayer had been answered a week before the election of 1980, I would have been a two-term president. But I understand that God answers prayers in different ways. Sometimes he answers "yes," sometimes he answers "no." Sometimes he answers late, and sometimes he answers, "You've got to be kidding." I don't think there's any doubt that, had I not had religious faith, I would not have been so patient.

My wife and I read the Bible aloud every night. We never fail. We both speak a little Spanish, so at this time we're going through the New Testament in Spanish. Last night, I read a chapter aloud to Rosalynn. Tonight, she'll read the next chapter to me aloud in Spanish. So that is another facet of the more formal experience that I have in religion.

I pray often for guidance. I pray often during the day. And I teach in my Sunday school classes that people should pray constantly. I can't say that I do that, but I think as we get in the habit of praying, there is a subconscious realization that we are in the presence of the Holy Spirit, that our standards of life should be those espoused and demonstrated by Christ, with a realization that when we make mistakes we can be forgiven by a loving God. Those are the things that permeate my consciousness almost in a subliminal way.

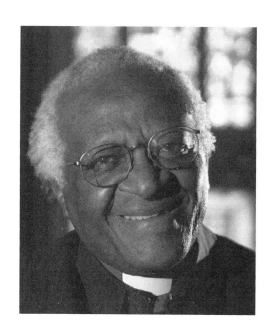

20.

Warming Oneself Before the Glow of God

Nobel Peace Prize–winner and retired Anglican archbishop Desmond Tutu was a visiting professor at Emory University in Atlanta in 1998 when Bob interviewed him. They spoke about Tutu's work in helping to end apartheid in South Africa and about current issues. Then Bob asked about Tutu's prayers.

I have come to realize more and more that prayer is just being in the presence of one who loves you deeply, who loves with a love that will not let you go, and so when I get up in the morning I try to spend as much time as I can in the sense of being quiet in the presence of this love. It's like I'm sitting in front of a warm fire on a cold day. I don't have to do anything. All I have to do is be there. And after a while, I may have the qualities of the fire change me so I have the warmth of the fire. I may have the glow of the fire, and it is so also with me and God. I just have to be there, quiet.

It's as if we're trying to engage the heart, and sometimes you may say in the heart, deep in the heart, "Jesus, I love you. Jesus, have mercy." Or just, "Jesus." And that, as the Russians used to say, becomes your spiritual heartbeat. It is something that you have within you. Or one other of the great teachers of the spiritual life would say you have a kind of spiritual nosegay, you know, something that you take away from your praying time that will be with you like a scent, a perfume that suffuses you.

Then, I will probably go off to do my walking, and I tend to have a kind of map of the world in my head because at that time I am bringing all of these countries and friends into God's presence. So I will have the map of the United States, and I have people sort of dotted all over the place, and I bring them into the gracious presence of God. I don't tell God what to do with them. I mean, God knows what is best for them.

21.

Talking to God Straight and Angry

By any measure, Stanley Hauerwas is one of the best and best-known theologians in America. He must also be the most profane. Hauerwas is a professor at the Duke Divinity School, a United Methodist turned Episcopalian, with deep respect for Catholicism. He is a native Texan, the son of a bricklayer, and a fierce critic of American secular culture, much U.S. government policy, and all casual Christianity. But for all his belief in hard-core faith and practice, Hauerwas admitted to Bob, in 1998, that he finds it difficult to pray.

I'm not a natural pray-er. I mean, I'm just not pious in that way. My wife asked me if I prayed before class, and I said "no." She said, "You should."

So I said, "Okay." I spend about thirty minutes every morning trying to write a goddamned prayer. I've done it now for, I guess, seven or eight years. And students started asking me for copies of these prayers. I thought, "This is weird, you know?"

I think it's because I don't try to assume a persona when I pray. I speak to God the way I am. And I never try to protect God. I figure God can take it.

They asked me to publish the prayers, and for a long time I resisted it. But I finally decided to do it because I am a grandfather, and I wanted to give them to my grandson.

I prayed a prayer this morning that said, "I'm angry. I'm one angry son of a bitch." I said, "I'm angry, God. I think I'm angry because I have such great hope. I hope my anger is of you. And so save me from that unrighteous anger which is petty, but don't take my anger from me. Because my anger is born of your love. And we need to remember that you are an angry God."

You're not supposed to be angry in prayer. But read the Psalms. I don't think I say anything that's any different than the Psalms, and the Psalms are tough. You know, "Smite my enemy and my enemy's children."

I try to pray that way. Just with that kind of straightforwardness and non-apologetically.

22.

On Wintry Spirituality and Napping

It's been said that if mainline Protestants had been able to elect a pope, over the last few decades that man almost certainly would have been Martin Marty. He is an energetic, wise historian of religion, retired from the University of Chicago Divinity School; a Lutheran pastor; author of more than fifty books; and, unbeknownst to many, a man who keeps himself centered by, among other practices, taking a nap wherever he is, usually several times a day. He lies down, puts his wristwatch on his forehead, and sleeps for seven minutes. When Kate Olson interviewed Marty in 1998, she discovered he considers napping not only restorative, but a form of prayer.

When I used to try to keep too many worlds together, I learned that I needed a way to break stress, and I taught myself to nap, invented a little technique. I decided that what keeps people awake is they're thinking about yesterday and they're guilty, and they're thinking about tomorrow and they're worrying, and so I have to invent some techniques to live in the present. It's as if you're on a high without drugs, and you soon learn just to let go of everything, and a few minutes later a timer goes off, and I wake up refreshed.

I believe very much that to the degree that we carry the burden of the past, which is always full of failures and frustrations, to that degree we're not free for the present moment. Whether waking or sleeping, if we can find the present moment, we're better off. I've always been moved by the heart of the Lord's Prayer. It says give us this day our daily bread, and the Sermon on the Mount says don't take thought for tomorrow. These are part of the announcements of the kingdom, they're announcements that tell us that the one who created us doesn't take care of everything that will ever happen to us, but we get strength for the day we're in, and a nap frees me for that.

A nap is a form of praying. I have never believed that prayer has to be something you are uttering all the time. I think it's a way of life, it's a conversation with God, it's a conversation with reality around you, and this is one of the modes in which you surrender. You're not in control, you're not trying to be in control, and I think that is very much what happens in good prayer.

My practices are really quite simple. Gathering over the bread and wine on Sunday in a little tiny church, waking up every morning and reminding myself that, in our language, I have been baptized, I have been turned over to God—I'm free for the day. I wake up, and I make the sign of the cross for the day as a reminder of that, and that frees me and liberates me. Most of the time, what other people would call Bible reading, for me would be Bible study, and that usually happens if I am going to preach, which isn't every Sunday. So I can't say I'm a daily Bible reader or a daily student of the Bible, though I'm immersed in it, and it flips through my brain all the time.

The disciplines of prayer, for me, are much more in the context of community than in the context of individuality. I describe myself spiritually as a hitchhiker on the spirituality of others. That is, just as in music there are Mozarts and in art there are Rembrandts, so in the spiritual life there are profound people, medieval mystics, many of them women. Many of them have written about this so profoundly, and I will open a page of that and let it work on me, and that's, for me, a much better way of rising or going deeper than if I just try to sit there and think blankly about inner space.

In our own time, interesting for me, because I'm a Protestant, have been Catholics like Dorothy Day, because she carried her piety into action, and Thomas Merton, who, though he was part of the time a hermit, had the Vietnam War and civil rights in the front of his mind and taught us a great deal of it. Also Abraham Joshua Heschel, a great Jewish student of scripture and a philosopher. I suppose, again, among the contemporaries, the one who did the most for me was Dietrich Bonhoeffer,* because we're of the same theological lineage. He writes books about things I would be reading anyhow and then goes to what we call guilty martyrdom, that is, he was in on a plot on Hitler's life and then had to give his own life up for it.

Then, most of all, I guess, the Psalms. I wrote a book after my first wife's death, *Cry of Absence*, which is entirely a reflection on the Psalms, and I think they're inexhaustible.

---

* The German Lutheran theologian who was hung in a Nazi concentration camp on April 9, 1945.

During long, long sessions of chemotherapy, my wife had midnight medication. It was palliative, it was to make the effects of the chemotherapy less terrible, and she would wake for that, and in the starkness of the night, we thought, "You can't just take medication, we want to do something that will get us back to sleep," so we decided to have a reading of a psalm at midnight. I would do the even numbers, she would do the odd, and when we reached Psalm 88—which I would commend to anybody who thinks the Bible is only about good cheer, it's about being alone, being in the pit, being abandoned by friends, by God, it's really down there—well, I just slid over, and she said, "Why did we get off, why didn't you read 88?" I said, "I didn't think you could take it." And she, with that early feminist tinge of saying, who do you think you are that you think you know what I can take, said, "No, we need those down ones, we need those dark ones, too. Otherwise the joyful ones, the hallelujahs, won't touch our lives." I have learned in dealing with people that a spiritual life devoted entirely to highs and happiness and "praise the Lord" simply doesn't do justice to reality, including biblical reality, and the most profound Jewish and Christian spirituality.

I believe by disposition I'm sunny. I'm not an optimist, but I'm a hoper. I also believe in every life, there is disappointment every day, for everybody. I don't care who it is—the highest and the mightiest and the richest and the smartest have disappointments—and if you identify God with nothing but the one who makes everything come out right, you're not ready.

What strikes me is that the people who have been the affirmers in the world, the ones who say, "yes," the ones who then carry it out into action, have been people, Martin Luther King style, who have forebodings. I think it was Albert Schweitzer who said that if he's told that every morning you jump out of bed and you're nothing but happy, you're not ready for what you're going to see as the day goes on. So, I have always found that it is in the impression of the absence of God where his presence is most felt, that in the wintry spirituality one sees more clearly. You see the structure of the tree when the leaves are gone, you'll see the whole horizon when all the bushes are down. In winter you see a very clear outline, and I think that's what I look for. It rings true to the human condition, and it also affirms.

23

Praise Every Three Hours

Phyllis Tickle, the Lucy, Tennessee, editor and writer, has been observing the ancient practice of fixed-hour prayer for more than forty years. She has an alarm on her wristwatch that she sets to go off every three hours, every day, and when it rings she stops whatever she is doing to go to a quiet place and read, often out loud, the psalms and prayers designated by religious leaders for that hour. Once, such fixed-hour prayer was required primarily for Catholic monks and priests. Now, Tickle says, it is becoming common enough to have created a market for her revisions of the traditional breviary, The Divine Hours, *along with its evening complement,* The Night Offices. *Bob profiled her in 1997.*

———

The divine office is a set of prayers, almost always ones of praise, based on the Psalms, that is offered by many Christians at a fixed hour seven times a day.

It is the work of God. It's the only work of God I know how to do. I do it five times a day.

I do this because we're told in Christianity that there must be constant prayer in our lives and also that there should be a constant cascade of prayer offered before the throne of God. On the appointed hour, in my time zone, I offer my daily office for whatever time of day it is at that point, and when I finish that, I pass it on to my fellow Christians in the next time zone. It becomes continuous and uninterrupted. It's not petitionary, unlike much prayer. It doesn't ask for anything. It simply glorifies God and acknowledges him.

It's also a way, I think, of remembering who it is I'm not and how very little I matter.

Certainly it roots me. It makes me part of a much larger communion. It removes the individuality that is so much a problem for contemporary Christians. There is no individuality in the divine office. There's no inventing of prayers yourself. These are fixed prayers that have been used for thousands of years, so that you know that you are part of a continuous stream of the word of God. You enter it, swim in it, swim back out into your other life, and then you go back in three hours later.

I can't imagine *not* doing it. Can't imagine what life would be if I had to go more than three hours without approaching the throne of God.

Does it do something for me? Perhaps. But what it really does is give me something I can do for God. This is the context in which I am. This is what I understand the Christian life to be.

Discipline is growing a muscle. And this is discipline. It's the growing of the spiritual muscle. It's the discipline that allows you even to check out, sometimes, when you're in the middle of a meeting, for instance, or in the middle of a high-pressure conversation and that watch beeps.

I drop back, and I'm doing two things at once. It's a kind of schizophrenia. I'm praying. If I cannot get away from the physical situation, I'm praying and talking at the same time. So you never escape. Once you put that harness on in the morning at six o'clock, you never take it off 'til you lay it down at ten o'clock that night. It is there. And like every good workhorse, you know, you belong to the man who put the yoke on. And it is to be yoked. It is to be yoked to the chariot of God.

Keeping the offices—fixed-hour prayer—was originally a practice of all Christians in the first century. They all did this. They did it because they were Jews. And Jews were taught to do this. Every little town in the Roman Empire had a forum bell. And it was the duty of the bell keeper to ring at six o'clock in the morning, which was the beginning of the working day; to ring at nine o'clock, which for us would be a coffee break, but for them meant that they could cool it for a while; at twelve o'clock, which was lunch and a siesta; and at three o'clock, when you went back to work; and at six o'clock, when you closed the shops. This was secular timing.

Well, the first thing you know, by the second century, fixed-hour prayer in the emerging Christian church has become six o'clock, nine o'clock, twelve o'clock, three o'clock. The nine o'clock hour is terce. It's the third hour. Twelve o'clock lunch is sext, the sixth hour, and three o'clock in the afternoon is none, the ninth hour. It's a great story of secular time taking on a whole new life as liturgical time.

There are many effects of the divine office, one of which, of course, is the constant awareness of the presence of God.

Regardless of how I perceive myself, and of the mistakes I make, and the evil that I see in myself—greed, lust, all of those things—I've still got this core. I've still got, in the middle of my day, in the middle of all of my consciousness this one place that connects me with the divine that's there, that's solid, that says, "Are you distressed by all these things you are? Are you heartbroken about all these things you have just done? It's all right. Come here." When I'm standing in that one place that is the divine office, I know God's in his heaven and that I'm part of that heaven.

24.

The Jesus Prayer and Praying with Icons

Frederica Mathewes-Green converted to Eastern Orthodoxy together with her husband, Father Gregory, pastor of Holy Cross Antiochian Orthodox Church in Linthicum, Maryland, a Baltimore suburb. She is the author of Facing East *and other books about Orthodoxy. In 1999, Chris Roberts interviewed Mathewes-Green in her living room, where the walls of one corner are covered from floor to ceiling with icons. That corner is one of the places she prays.*

I pray four times a day—at morning, noon, sunset, and right before I go to sleep. Not always in this corner. If it happens to be noon and I'm driving, I'll pray in the car. But whenever I can, I come to the icon corner to pray. It's a short, perhaps two minutes' worth of prayers—the Our Father, some familiar prayers, and usually a prayer just for that time of day.

I also get up in the middle of the night—most people don't do this—and say the Jesus Prayer for about an hour. And it's very different from praying with icons.

The Jesus Prayer is just repeating over and over, "Lord Jesus Christ, have mercy on me, a sinner," and trying to stay away from other thoughts or images. It is having just that one thought and facing the Lord and asking forgiveness and receiving his mercy.

The Jesus Prayer actually goes back to the beginning, probably the second or third century. The question was, "How do we do what Saint Paul advises, where he says to pray constantly? How do you pray constantly?" They began with just saying the name of Jesus over and over again. As you know, in both the Hebrew and the Christian tradition, the holy name is important, is significant, and has power. So just repeating the name of Jesus over and over gradually expanded just a little bit: "Lord Jesus Christ, have mercy on me, a sinner."

The idea is that you say a word with each beat of your heart: "Lord . . . Jesus . . . Christ . . . have mercy . . . on me . . . a sinner." Six beats. You try to tune it to your own heartbeat.

It's no longer a prayer you're saying in your mind, but it's one that your heart is praying inside you. You're face-to-face with the Lord Jesus, and you're looking at his beauty. You're thinking about how much he suffered for you and how much he loves you. You're not necessarily saying, "I'm such a horrible person. How could you care about me?" You're saying, "Your mercy is flowing over me, Lord. You're giving me your mercy. Go on giving me your mercy. Have mercy on me. I know I don't deserve this. I know I'm just a sinner. Thank you for how much you've already done. Lord Jesus Christ, have mercy on me."

Hopefully, you get in the habit of doing this. You set aside maybe fifteen minutes at first, maybe less, maybe more. Then you'll find during the day it sort of strikes up like a spring rising in your heart. You'll find you're stand-ing in the line at the grocery store, driving down the highway, and this prayer will just begin all the time—like background music. It's just going on in your heart all the time whatever you're doing. When you reach that point, then you've developed a humility about yourself, and you're sharing in God's love for others that can bear you through all situations. Now, I'm cer-tainly not there personally, but that's what I hope some day to be able to cultivate in my own heart.

One of the things that took some getting used to when I became Ortho-dox is that in Eastern Christianity we don't really have the division that's so familiar in the West between head and heart. That is, at one moment you're doing theology, and it's very logical. Then, on the other hand, you're doing something sentimental that's sort of very soft and very heart driven.

In the East, what there is, is everyday mysticism. We're pursuing a genuine change in our very beings as we come into the presence of God, and his light, his fire catches fire within us. We are transformed like a piece of coal. A piece of coal doesn't have any merit on its own, but it's made to burn.

So in that same way, as we come to the icons, we are actually being

changed from the inside out. It isn't merely intellectual. Anything we understand intellectually is only a servant, only a handmaiden of approaching
union with God, such that in Orthodoxy, a theologian is not a person who's
skilled at theological logic. A theologian is someone who has seen the light
of God and been transformed by it. Not that he's grasped principles, but
that he's been grasped by the deity, himself.

The classic definition of an icon is that it's a window into heaven. What it
means is that you don't stop with the object itself—the wood, the paint—but
that you use it to go through, to enter the heavenly realms, and to let them
touch you and affect you, as well. So an icon is not an idol. It is a passageway.

In confronting icons, I found something heavenly, something beyond
myself and beyond my own emotions and my own sentiments, and something that was challenging but profoundly moving. I found that with icons,
although they remain somewhat austere, there is something in them that
is healing to me. It knows the truth about me, about my failures and my
sinfulness and the things I try to ignore, and it has the answer, just like hard
medicine. The icons know the beauty and the grace and the power of God,
and I can begin my healing there.

The Orthodox definitely believe that when you start bringing icons into
your home, they'll start changing you.

People will find that not only are they looking at the icon, the icon's looking at them, and that it begins to assert itself. Pretty soon, you find that you
start buying more icons and putting more icons around. They speak to you.
The seriousness, the gravity, the beauty, and the holiness of the presence of
these icons will begin to change you.

My husband, the pastor of our church, received a phone call not too long
ago from a man who said he was a college professor, a secular humanist
who had never had much interest in religious things, and someone had
given him a copy of this icon. He said, "Ever since I've had it, it's been making me think things I never thought before. As I look at it, I feel like it's
been looking at me. I feel like this icon is looking into my soul." And he
said, "I—I never thought I had a soul before."

25

The Hum of the Universe, in a Minor Key

Robert Wuthnow of Princeton University is one of the country's great sociologists of religion. He asks Americans, "Tell me about your spiritual journey." In 2001, Bob spoke with him about trends and findings in American spirituality and then asked him, "Tell us about your spiritual journey." And he did.

The people who are really trying to get closer to God and are working at it and are spending a lot of time in serious spiritual activities probably make up 5 to 10 percent at most of the American public. The people who are sort of interested in spirituality—enough that they maybe listen to a religious song once in a while, attend a religious service once in a while, think about God once in a while—are the vast majority. Maybe 50 or 60 percent of the public is in that category.

Most people who get serious about their spirituality start by praying and meditating—usually on a regular, daily basis. They may spend forty-five minutes to an hour in the morning or in the evening, and sometimes both, consciously learning how to pray more effectively. Not necessarily just saying a lot of words, but many times putting themselves in a meditative state, where they can consciously block out all the distractions from the day, quieting their heart, listening to God. Some people use icons, some people will play religious music. Some people may have an object.

I usually choose topics to study because I'm curious. Often I'm curious because I don't feel I'm doing so well in those areas. I have not been very good at practicing prayer or meditation or spiritual reading on a regular basis. I'm learning more about how to do that. I'm finding that music at this point in my life, for whatever reason, is probably the most helpful way to get into a practice like that. Music focuses my attention on God, or puts me in an attitude of worship or of devotion, and quiets my thoughts.

I usually do this in the evening. I find music, such as many of the things that John Rutter has done—his *Requiem* includes a wonderful arrangement of the twenty-third psalm—very meaningful. I've found that John Taverner's "Song of Athene," which was played at Princess Diana's funeral, is a very meditative form of music for me, because it's quiet, it's virtually without words. Yet it moves me from a place of quiet to a place of exaltation, of praise, of worship.

I don't actually see anything. Some people do. I'm one of those people who responds more at a kind of holistic level, where I'll have an emotional surge, sometimes, that I can't describe very well other than the fact that I do feel uplifted. Or sometimes I feel saddened.

I was raised in Protestant traditions that emphasized the dark side as well as the light side, that taught me that there are evil forces or realities in this world, and that also taught me there is an austere side to God, that God is all-righteous and transcendent and beyond human comprehension. So that training, coupled with experiences over the course of my lifetime of losing loved ones or being removed from the community in which I was raised, has, I think, reinforced a sense that—despite the joys and the happiness that I associate with spirituality—there is also a kind of troubling part of it, what Martin Marty refers to as "wintry" spirituality.

I have been especially taken by Madeleine L'Engle's fiction writings, because she also sometimes describes that sense of things not being quite what we would like them to be. I think that in one of her books she talks about a kind of humming in the universe. When I think of that humming, and sometimes I feel I can almost hear it myself, it's often in a minor key, a slight discordance. Sometimes I think of this as the cosmic sadness, the reality that we die, that our loved ones die, that we experience illness and tragedies and loss. So, for me, that's a part of it, too. Spirituality, then, is coming to terms in some slight way, not to say, "No, that's not the reality," but to say, "Yes, that is the reality, but that's also something that I can accept and live with."

26.

Finding God's Presence in Darkness

The late Father Ellwood "Bud" Kieser was a huge (6'6"), gregarious Paulist priest in Los Angeles whose vocation was to encourage Hollywood to produce movies and TV programs that celebrate the full human condition and possibility. He made several movies himself and also founded the Humanitas Prize for screenwriting that probes the meaning of life. Bob interviewed Father Kieser in 1999 about his work and his spiritual life.

I usually get up at 6:10. I live in a Paulist community in Westwood in Los Angeles. We have a chapel in the rectory, so by ten of seven I'm in the chapel. I have a big sixteen-ounce glass of orange juice before I go in to meditate because I find that it gives me a tremendous surge of energy. And then I meditate from ten of seven to ten of eight.

Originally prayer and meditation for me was talking to God as somebody out there. That has evolved rather radically so that now prayer and meditation for me is becoming aware of God living within me and God being involved in my life and God communicating himself to me through the people I love and through people who don't love me. So I just bring myself into the presence of God, and then it goes where it goes.

I use the classic techniques of meditation. I sit down. I have my spine straight. I breathe deeply. I try to let go and let God, who's the ground of my being, draw me deeper, deeper, and deeper. And the deeper you get, the more God is present. He's present in darkness and sometimes in loneliness, but he's there. Then we commune with each other, and he shares himself with me and I share myself with him and I tell him where I am and what I'm struggling with and I get his ideas, and so anything that concerns me, it's part of meditation. I don't distinguish between meditation and prayer. They both come together for me.

I look at the human unconscious as a lake and floating on the surface of the lake is some garbage. So this particular morning I might have to go through some anger toward somebody. I might have to go through erotic images. So you go through those things, and the way you go through them is not to say I don't want that—you just ignore them and go deeper. Let God draw you in.

The advantage of doing it the first thing in the morning is that your unconscious is very open. You're not all distracted with the concerns of the day. You let him draw you into your unconscious, and at the pit of your unconscious is where we meet God. So the deeper you get into yourself, the closer you get to God.

In a certain way you're stripped. Which doesn't mean you stop loving the crucial people in your life. But it does mean that you don't cling to anything, you've got to let it all go, and that's why the narrow tunnel is a good image. Because there's not even any room for your clothes to get through this narrow space.

You're in a dark place, which requires an adjustment for your eyes, but as your eyes adjust, you're able to see much farther. When the sun is out you can't see too far, but in the middle of the night when the sun is down you can see the stars. So there's perspective and there's vision seeing through that darkness.

In many ways it's like walking across the desert all alone in the middle of the night, where you can see the stars. It's dark, but that's okay.

See, I think we have to let go of that desire for light. Let God give us the light when he wants to. There are no leaves on the trees. It's desolate. But you keep going. You're moving toward the face-to-face vision of God, and you're buoyed by that hope.

I used to think of God as pure being, something like that. A concept. God is more than any concept. He's more than any idea. He surpasses those things in every way. That immensity of God and the transcendence of God are very powerful. But God is not only transcendent out there and beyond everything—he's also in me. He's in everybody around me. He's in the love that joins us together. And he's in the creative process. Many writers say that at a certain point in writing they just get out of the way and let God and that creative energy, insight, love flow into them and through them onto the printed page and ultimately out to their viewers.

What meditation and prayer do is open me up and enable me to tap into the love energy of God. When you open up this way God kind of flows in, and you give him permission to permeate your being. And when he moves in, he moves in as love, as Father. He speaks his word in me. And his word in me is Jesus, and then I have to make a choice: let him take over or not. Let him be Lord. Let him be Savior.

Savior is somebody who heals. I need healing. I need to be put together. I need to be integrated. Well, if I surrender my life to God in this way, he does that healing.

In meditation I also tune into a symphony that resonates through the whole universe and has God as its author. Part of my job in meditation is to attune myself to that symphony, vibrate with that symphony, dance to that music.

We talk about wintry, we talk about the dark night, but I don't want to detract from the joy. There's a very deep joy here, and it's awful nice. There may be a lot of pain on the surface or anxiety on the surface, but deep down there is that place of joy where you live, and that's what keeps us going.

I just try to become aware of God's presence and tune into him and what's on his mind, what's on my mind. If I'm torn up about this decision or that decision, okay, what do you think here? So I make my decisions in consultation with him. I have a pretty good advisor.

We're good friends. We talk, and he tells me where he is and I tell him where I am and we share concerns and then we make decisions. All my big decisions happen in that hour, and some of my best creative ideas happen there.

I say I make my big decisions there, but then I run them by three or four or five people whose judgment I really respect. Plus I have to ask myself, does this contribute to more loving relationships? Does this make me a more whole, more integrated, more loving human being? If it is ego, then it will not. I'll be thinking about number one, and I won't be contributing to other people. On the other hand, you can't be so hung up on something not being egotistical that you don't do anything.

The biggest sin is to sit on your fanny and do nothing.

The French philosopher Jacques Maritain said, "The important thing is not success. The important thing is to be in history bearing witness."

I need to be faithful to the vocation God has called me to, to be a priest, to be a Paulist, to carry the sacred into the secular. But also to be faithful to the particular vocation he has given me, which is a vocation within show business. I think he called me to this.

So this is what he's gotten. Dante says, "In Thy will, O Lord, we find our peace." I think this has been the will of God for me. It's been a good life. I'm happy with it.

Father Kieser died on September 16, 2000. He was seventy-one years old.

CHAPTER 4

"I'm Spiritual, Not Religious"

In an episode of the prime-time television drama *Grey's Anatomy*, there's a scene in which a female intern makes what is for her a vexing discovery—that her bedmate, a surgeon at the hospital where they work, has a spiritual side. A professed atheist, she tells him that she had thought their relationship, explored largely on a stretcher in the medical supply room, was based on science. When the intern demands an explanation as to how a man of medicine could be religious, the surgeon replies, a little indignantly, "I'm *spiritual*, not religious. There's a difference." She doesn't buy it.

The line was hardly original, but it points to a social phenomenon, to a way in which growing numbers of people are framing their quest for a sense of meaning and purpose in life. Regardless of their answers, individuals have been forging their own meanings, perhaps in response to the many scientific and philosophical challenges to organized religion. That would seem true of the religious as well as nonreligious. In a 2002 poll, *Religion & Ethics NewsWeekly* asked people whether they think belief or individual spiritual experience is the most important part of religion. Almost 70 percent of Christians said individual experience.

The word "spirituality" itself has been linked far more often to the individual than to the communal search for meaning and the divine. And interest in spirituality has grown phenomenally: in just fourteen years, between 1984 and 1998, the percentage of Americans who said they felt the need for greater spiritual growth leaped from 56 percent to 82 percent, according to polling by Gallup.

Among the seekers have been those who see eye-to-eye with the surgeon on *Grey's Anatomy*, holding that in the spiritual search, religious belief or fellowship is optional at best. In this chapter, we look at the I'm-spiritual-but-not-religious sensibility, hearing from those who feel that this quest, apart from church, mosque, and synagogue, is both meaningful and sufficient. We also hear from those, avowedly religious, whose spiritual quests have led them to loosen their attachments to religious institutions in one way or another. And we note the critics who say that personal spiritual exploration can be self-centered, shallow, and unconcerned about the needs of others, that—in the words of a bumper sticker quoted by Martin Marty—"spirituality doesn't make hospice calls."

Finally, we bring ethics into this conversation, with the message that people do not need to be either spiritual or religious in order to live the ethical life.

27.

On the Altar of Consciousness

To explore the spiritual-but-not-religious phenomenon, correspondent Lucky Severson traveled to the Pacific Northwest, the most un-churched region of the United States, and visited Marilyn McGuire at her home on the San Juan Islands in Washington State. At one time a churchgoing housewife who chaired the Nixon for President Campaign in Alabama, McGuire is now a prominent author as well as a distributor of books heralding "the new consciousness." But don't call her "New Age," she told Lucky in 2002.

—

I was raising my children, and I was in a kind of high society town where you had to dress up a lot and go places a lot, and I remember saying, "I'm tired of spending money I don't have to buy things I don't want to impress people I don't like."

People would do things, it seemed to me, for the wrong reasons. Since I was a little girl, I felt like I was getting the wrong information on just about everything. I didn't think people were intentionally lying to me. I just thought, "That's not right." Whatever it was they were saying, whether it be my parents, or my teachers, or the ministers in the church, I thought, "There's better information than this."

I remember one day, years later, I heard the worst sound I had ever heard in my life, the most hideous screaming noise. It was like someone being murdered, and I went running out to my backyard, and there was this stench that I couldn't believe. I went running toward what appeared to be a chair on fire, one house removed from mine, and it was a neighbor who had poured gasoline over her head and had ignited her body. It was the most terrifying thing I had ever experienced. And in dealing with the aftermath of that, I realized that I lived two doors down from someone who was in such despair that she took her life in that way, and I didn't know it. It was heartbreaking for me, and I began to review my life. I just felt that I get up every morning, and it's like being on stage. I get dressed and I go about this business of taking my kids to school and going to the meetings, but it was something that wasn't real. That was a big wake-up call for me to examine my life and ask: where am I going, what am I doing, what do I believe, what's true, what has meaning, and what doesn't?

My children were the most important things in the world to me, and divorce was never something I had considered. My parents said nice people don't do that, and I thought I was a nice person, but in 1974, when my children were twelve, fourteen, and sixteen, I got a divorce. I changed my life a lot. I went to work, instead of doing volunteer work, which I had done. I went to work for a bank. I joined a yoga class, and I started studying a bit of Eastern philosophy. It wasn't with intent that I started doing this, but my yoga teacher was very steeped in Eastern philosophy, so she would teach us a lot of the breathing and some of the philosophy, but I was most impressed with how my body began to feel as a result of doing these exercises and in particular the breathing that went along with it. I noticed that getting out of the marriage, getting out of the society that I grew up in, going to work with regular people, and doing this yoga and breathing—there was some sort of consciousness that was evolving in me, some sort of attunement and some sort of awareness.

I wasn't thinking, "Now I am searching." It wasn't that deliberate, it was almost like something was pulling me toward it. I knew there was more to the meaning of life, more to relationships, more to everything.

In the Middle of It All . . .

I had an out of body experience. I was out of my body, and at the same time I was still on this quest in terms of looking, exploring life, and examining my own life. I went to a family reunion, and I came back with meningitis and it was dreadful. I experienced something that seems to me like part of a dream now, but it was real and it did happen.

I had a temperature of 107. I was very sick. I was coming in and out of consciousness. I just know my family thought I was not going to make it. I guess the doctors thought that I wasn't going to make it. They gave me fifty million units of penicillin every hour for about ten days. It's a wonder I'm alive to tell that story. But one of the things that I remember is being out on a table with some sort of a gown, and I would see these friendly pigs. I thought, "Aren't these friendly pigs?" They were caring for me. As I came more into consciousness, I realized they were human beings with masks on. My parents, the doctors, everyone—but in my fevered state, they looked to me like pigs.

Then another time, I had a horrible headache, terrible, terrible pain with this meningitis. At one point I was out of my body looking down at my body. I was up in a corner of the room, and I don't know what, it was just an awareness. It wasn't me in my body. I just remember an awareness of looking down at my body. It was a strange thing, and it was a very peaceful sensation I felt. It would have been really okay to have just gone, because it was total peace. And somehow, I was able not to leave. I don't think I was receiving any kind of special message from the universe. It just simply happened to me as I came so close to dying. Suddenly, life took on more importance to me. The way I lived my life became even more important, not that I was of value, but that life itself is sacred.

I think that if we are aware and conscious, messages are everywhere. You watch a flower open from a bud or a baby being born. They are messages, and we are receptors. The messages are for all of us to see. It's just the miracle of life. There is more than we think there is to our being,

I think that in the state of consciousness, the altar is kind of in the mind, in the consciousness. The sacredness of life is with everything we do. It's not just part of some ceremony that happens once a week. It isn't something that happens just on Sunday morning from ten to eleven o'clock. It is something that—every second of my waking consciousness—requires me to be what I know I can be, become all that I can become. And the priesthood is not necessary. There doesn't need to be someone talking about this or that teaching. The state of consciousness is a way of life, a way of valuing all of life, the sacredness of life. Although I really do enjoy getting together with a group of people, I don't feel that it is necessary for me to belong to a group.

I think that service to humanity is very important, whether it be to the old or the infirm or whatever. But I think that it is not necessarily a requirement. It is something that one would naturally become involved in doing more of. I have had volunteer jobs all of my life, taking care of less fortunate people and doing good works. I think one of the things that the new consciousness, if you want to call it that, or the people who have this consciousness are very concerned about is the sustainability of our planet, the place that we all share in common. If we don't take care of our planet, we are not going to have a place to live.

I was a very devout churchgoer. I call myself a recovering Episcopalian in this moment. I still love the Episcopal Church. But I don't think it matters whether the people come back into the churches or not. I think people have become disenchanted with the churches. We could discuss the Catholic Church and some of the things that are going on with priests.* I don't think that they have a monopoly on those problems in the churches, and I'm not saying that's all that churches are about, but when churches are so undisciplined and when the ministers themselves are the ones who are carrying out some of the activities when they are supposed to be setting examples of behavior—it doesn't make the church a particularly appealing place for someone who wants to find joy in the miracle of life.

I live on a little island, and there are not a lot of options. I get a little lonely here, and I think that I would become a part of more groups if there were something available here. I think if I lived in a big city, or certainly a bigger city than here, I would probably join a group or attend or participate in a group once or twice a week, just for fellowship.

A group of people who have prayer and meditation, who get together to revere their lives and reexamine—I think I would definitely be a part of that. I believe it when the Bible says that when two or more gather, there is an energy that comes about that feels really good. It feels good to have people who are kind of looking out after you. I'm not saying there's anything wrong with that, but the church? I don't know.

Last summer, I went to visit my children and grandchildren in Georgia.

---

* Referring to the sexual abuse of minors by clergy.

They have a beautiful home on a lake, and they were there with another family. We spent the whole weekend taking care of the children and the dogs and just having fellowship together. We said blessings before meals, we went walking in the woods, and we were all in a state of love and kindness toward one another. On Sunday morning, we got in the boat to go to boat church. You ever hear of boat church? I hadn't heard of boat church either. We threw on our jeans and got in the boat and went. A beautiful mist was coming off the water. We were heading up to boat church. And I'm surprised. There's Ted Turner's kids, on this same lake, and they're waving to us and we are waving back. All the boats gather up and people have their dogs and their kids, and I'm thinking, oh, how wonderful. Here's the preacher on his float boat, here's the choir and they're singing, and the first thing the preacher says to everyone is, "You're all sinners. Every one of you is a sinner." He sat and told everyone how bad they were, and I thought, this is why I don't go to church. This man has probably been up drinking all night. I don't know who he is talking about, but it's not about me, and I felt very protective of my children and my grandchildren and the two dogs sitting there. I thought, I'm sure God's not here.

Another Path to God

Yoga is, in fact, a whole philosophy. Yoga is a vast system of practices that leads a person to something called *samadhi*, which is the cessation of the thought waves of the mind—stopping the thoughts, bringing the mind to the still place. So the yoga postures are one of the ways to get to *samadhi*, or peace.

If you're being taught yoga, you need to be taught the breath that goes with it. The inhalation and the exhalation and the autonomic nervous system of the body will get that breathing in. It literally puts more oxygen into the brain, and the breathing of the body and the motion of the body bring the mind to a place where it can choose to be still. My mind might choose to be still because I'm agitated, because I've had coffee, because I've been sitting in an airplane all day. You can't hear God, you can't hear the voice if your mind is so busy with its own thoughts. So if you want to hear the voice of God or whatever one wants to call this higher power, it's important to listen, to be still and know.

There's a lot going on in our world—there's the dishwasher going and the disposal going and the traffic and the airplanes—and it's hard. We learn to tune out or we'd go nuts, so we learn to close ourselves down, and we don't hear the noise and we stay sane, but we also don't hear the things that might make us whole. We don't hear the wind blowing, the bird singing, the baby crying. So, you've got to make the effort to still the mind.

Don't call me New Age. I do know people, they drive me nuts. Everything's a symbol, everything's a sign, everything's an "Oh, wow, that crow just cawed. That must mean he's affirming my . . ." and I'm going, "I don't think so. He cawed because he's a crow." They're so involved. They're the people who have just begun, who have just awakened to the thought of themselves as a spiritual being without the help of a minister. I think that in the early stages, in the infancy of someone's spiritual growth, you see a lot of that. I think that New Age is an infant thing. I don't feel like it's a grown-up thing, and everybody's like, "Look at this. *Wowee!*" And then you have to get beyond that, or you can't be part of the world, because the world is not a well place. There's all this love and light, but there are also people flying planes into buildings.

The new consciousness is not all about "me, me, me," but the only person we are really responsible for is ourselves. The ministers of the church are trying to take care of you and me and a whole flock of people, but it's got to begin here. I quote the Bible because I love the Bible: "You can't worry about the splinter in your neighbor's eye, it's the beam in your own." Unless we can be responsible for ourselves and keep all of our dials adjusted so that we're not irritating someone else—it needs to be about "me" on that level.

28.

Unlearning Religion

Marianne Williamson began spiritual seeking as a child of the 1960s. What she eventually found was A Course in Miracles, a self-study curriculum scribed by the late Columbia University psychologist Helen Schucman through a process of "inner dictation" that she identified with the voice of Jesus. Herself a Jew, Williamson was drawn to the course's universal spiritual themes, and she popularized the course in her 1994 bestseller, A Return to Love. Since then her books and tapes have made her a spiritual celebrity and inspired millions of seekers, especially those of her generation. Here, Williamson speaks of the "mystical heart" that lies within all religions—and to which organized religion, in her view, is often oblivious. Bob spoke with her in 1997.

I had been a student of comparative religion and philosophy in school, and I was always fascinated by the academic Western philosophical traditions. But at the same time I was interested in the more esoteric, spiritual paths, as in Eastern philosophy. So when I first saw *A Course in Miracles* in the mid-1970s, what fascinated me was that it was not a religion, but rather it deals with universal spiritual themes. That's what my enthusiasm was then and remains to this day. I think specific religious traditions play an important role, of course. But I also think there is a yearning felt by millions of people to discover the underlying mystical unity that is the love of God itself.

The word "religio"* means to bind back; we are binding our consciousness back to God. And the theological principal in *A Course in Miracles*, which by the way is in all great religious systems, is that as we find our closer connection to God, we naturally discover our enthusiasm and our

---

* The Latin root of "religion."

desire for service to others. So when you turn your attention toward God, you by definition turn your attention to loving people more deeply.

A mystical theological perspective does not posit or believe in a judgmental God. As I once heard someone say, we are not punished *for* our sins, we are punished *by* our sins. No one should have to apologize for our belief in a nonjudgmental God; it's hardly a theological deficiency. To say that God is not judgmental is not to remove the mooring of his spirit. His power is simply in love, not fear. You do not have to fear God's judgments to feel just as compelled as anyone else to go back to him in every moment, ask his guidance in every moment, and to atone to him when you have made an error. Seeing God as judgmental is not necessary for a deeply religious perspective and experience of life.

I believe that God is an impersonal force, but that our relationship to him is personal. I think God is the ground of all being. I recently heard a physicist give a talk in which he spoke of an all-nourishing abyss. I think of God as First Principle, and that First Principle is love.

I think that ultimately it is not our belief in God that matters, but our experience of God that matters. In fact, there is a line in *A Course in Miracles* which says some people conspire with God who do not yet believe in him. Just saying you believe in God—it may or may not mean a whole lot. To be willing to forgive other people, to reach out to other people, to bless other people, to see the innocence in other people, to love other people—that to me is the experience of God, and it's clearly what we need most on the planet. I think that that is what God asks of each of us, not as a theory, but as a practice in our everyday lives.

It is the mystical heart at the center of all the great religions that fascinates me, that calls to me. In my own personal religious journey, Christ is there. Now, I almost hesitate to say this on television because there are Jews who roll their eyes and there are Christians who roll their eyes as well. The Jews are like, "Oy!" And the Christians are like, "We need this?" You know, I understand that, but there are millions of us who feel that we simply have to honor where our hearts have gone. As far as being a Jew is concerned, you are born a Jew, you die a Jew. It is my religious identification, although obviously there are some principles that I embrace that are not traditionally

Jewish. I cannot in my heart, nor do I wish to, deny either my Judaism or Jesus. And I do want to say, this is not in any way Jews for Jesus. Jews for Jesus is a basically fundamentalist Christian organization, and that is nothing close to what I am.

I feel there is a deep place within you and me and every human being that is the essence and truth of who we really are. It is an indestructible core created by God himself. It is not just something in you that is identical to something in me. It is that which binds us together. It is literally our oneness. And *one* of the names for that oneness—not the only name, by the way—is Jesus.

I think we're living in one of the most significant historical moments ever. We are living at a time in which we must recognize both the limits and the opportunities of the modern world view. The modern world view, particularly in the past hundred years or so, has lured the Western mind away from its spirit. Our attention has been diverted away from the inner domains, the realms of true religion and spirituality, to the outer world. The technological world view, a scientifically based world view, a rational world view has become the dominant ethos of our times. Many people feel that far too often organized religions, particularly in this country, have in fact been a little too seduced by that materialistic focus. Many people have felt that in our churches and in our synagogues, we've found more talk, more attention paid to the external aspects of life, to the hierarchy of a religion, or to the rules of the outer world, than to the inner experience of religion itself.

Not only do we feel this overexternalized focus in religion, we feel it across the board everywhere. Look at the holistic revolution which has occurred in medicine the last two or three decades. From Harvard to Duke University to the Stanford Research Institute, our most prestigious academic institutions have verified that attention paid to the mind and spiritual consciousness of a patient is an effective factor in physical healing. Prayer, forgiveness, et cetera, are spiritual medicines that augment and complement physical medicine. The spiritual revolution affects everything, even business. Corporate moguls hire expensive consultants to talk to them about making the workplace a sanctuary for the soul.

There is within each of us a divine ambassador of God's grace. Its name, in the Christian religion, is the Holy Spirit. In the Jewish religion, it is called the *Shekinah*. All religions speak of some bridge between us and God; in Buddhism, it is compassion itself. *A Course in Miracles* contains a workbook of prayer and meditation exercises, one for each day. There it says that five minutes given to God in the morning guarantees he will be in charge of your thought forms throughout the day. As we meditate and pray in the morning and the evening, we develop a spiritual musculature, the mental discipline to perceive more lovingly. We need this discipline in a world where the thought system is 180 degrees away from the thought system of God's love. The world has taught us a thought system of judgment, defensiveness, attack, and condemnation. And it is that which needs to change.

So spiritual growth is not about learning; it is about unlearning. We unlearn a destructive point of view as we sit in quiet, in meditation, and prayer. That is the action of God's spirit within us. That is where we find grace. That is why the ultimate prayer is: "Make my mind Your mind / have me think only what You would have me think / may my mind be filled with love."

And then, not only do we pray and meditate, but to the best of our ability in every situation and in every moment—not that any of us are enlightened masters—we seek to see the love in each other, to make our only purpose in any situation to serve the *unfolding* of that love on earth. In the moments when we achieve it, unbelievable breakthroughs occur. Miracles occur naturally. And the moments when we don't achieve it? Well, hey, we're human; one of our prayers is for God to correct us when we get off the path.

29.

Blessing the Doubters

An Episcopal priest and popular guest preacher, Rev. Barbara Brown Taylor left the pastorate some years ago. In a 2000 interview with Bob, she shared her misgivings about organized religion and Christianity in particular, the sort of disquiet that has led many to explore their spiritual options.

———

I'm on the edge of Christianity, and I expect to get a letter telling me I've been kicked out any day now. But my choice at this point in my life is to practice the religion *of* Jesus instead of the religion *about* Jesus. I take the gospels historically, critically as stories about Jesus. When in those stories I listen to Jesus preach about the kind of behavior he wants, I see no sectarianism. I see him ministering to a Syrophoenician woman. I hear him telling stories about people outside of Israel whom God loves as much as people in Israel. That's Jesus' religion, my take on it, anyhow. So I am at this point in my life focused on the religion of Jesus instead of the religion about him. That helps me some.

I seem to appeal to people who have left the church or who are uneasily in the church. Somehow in my books they find someone who might understand their reluctance or their distance. So I hear from a number of people who just want a religious person to bless their doubt, to bless their skepticism, to say, "It's all right. What you're asking is good to ask."

Having been brought up with a definition of faith as "adherence to a set of beliefs," I have more and more begun to turn instead toward a definition of faith as "openness to truth, whatever truth may turn out to be." So it seems to me very faithful to be jettisoning old beliefs and moving into new places.

I've spent thirty years in the church. That's not a long time, but enough time to have questions about what we do as Christians. I look at ways in which our institutionalization of the religion about Jesus has caused bloodshed, caused terrific division, caused incredible cruelty to other people in the name of evangelism or preaching the gospel, so that I'm in a very humble space around the faith that I practice now. I'm in a very small, humble space and doing my best to see the things in it that I think would displease Jesus, that would shame him, that would break his heart, and seeing how, theologically, I can deal with those things without giving up Christianity.

You and I talked earlier about "I am the way, the truth, and the life"* and the kind of violence that can do to people of other faiths. I don't want any part of that, and so I have to figure out how I live with a church that reveres that scripture and a church that says in the creed that Jesus is the only son of God, and there is no other way. I have to decide how to live with that creed and love my neighbor. So there is another paradox: Jesus taught me to love my neighbor, and my neighbor may not love Jesus. So, again, I don't find any problem with that day by day, but theologically, if you sit down and give me a questionnaire on the creed, there are probably some phrases in it I'd hold my breath through.

I would go back into parish ministry. This is my dream. I would go back because I miss leading worship, I miss baptisms, and I miss funerals. I miss hospital calls, and I miss nursing homes. I really miss that a lot. But I think my dream would be to find a group of people who would sign on the dotted line that they intend never to become an institution. They never want to pay me, they never want to own a building, they never want to have a budget. They want to give money, but it will all go beyond our community. They want to pray regularly, but they promise we will never become an institution.

That's a total pipe dream, but that kind of parish ministry is very appealing to me. Would it ever be possible? We would also pass around the duties. We might have to break the law, but we'd take turns preaching, and we would take turns celebrating the Eucharist and baptizing babies. But it would be a community of priests, and we would operate on the wing.

I'd go back for that. But I wouldn't take pay. I hope I would never take

---

* As Jesus is rendered as saying in the Gospel of John.

pay again to do that, because it felt too much like being paid to love. And you know what that is, when you get paid to love. I know there are people who can keep their pay separate from their love, but too much of parish ministry seemed to me as if I were being paid to love people. Then my heart got very confused about my job.

In 2006, Taylor came out with her book Leaving Church: A Memoir of Faith, *which told of the burnout and the doubts that led to her decision to leave her pastorate in rural Georgia. Taylor said she came to believe that she could be closer to the "Really Real"—could be more fully human—away from the pastorate than in it.*

30

With or Without Religion

Popular spirituality is too sweet for Phyllis Tickle's taste—"like eating too much icing," says the Episcopal writer, editor, and authority on religious books. Even so, her own spiritual search has often led her beyond the parish door and into "a different kind of communion," as she told Bob in 1997.

⟶

Spirituality is that part of the subjective life which we all experience, regardless of the culture, regardless of the faith to which we adhere. It's the interior world that we all have.

The spiritual world can be psychological. It can be emotional. But for all of us it is also more. There is something in there, and we all, at some time or another, are aware that there's more than Dr. Freud's psychology, and there is more than depression and all of those things. There's more than emotion. There is a presence there. There are very few adults who will not say that at some time or another they've heard a voice. Or they have had a premonition. Or they engaged a dream consistently, night after night, until it began to take some resonance in their lives. They were engaging the spiritual world.

Spirituality doesn't have to involve religion. It can absolutely be freestanding. What has had the greatest impact on America's understanding of spirituality in recent times? It's Buddhism. And Buddhism is basically a nontheistic way of looking at the world. It calls itself a philosophy about as often as it calls itself a religion, because it is not organized in the sense that religion usually is. It is a way of seeing the world. But it is rife with spiritual practice.

Spirituality is traveling lightly but *awaredly* in the world of the interior. Spirituality is engaging living forces and agencies that do not have objective existence.

It does not have to mean that you're engaging God or that you're engaging divine agencies. It may be that you're engaging just the life force, just a sense of wonder, just a sense of pattern. One of the most deeply spiritual faiths is Taoism, which engages the pattern. And there is majesty in the pattern. Now, I would say that that pattern is proof of God or that it's a paradigm within which I see God. But you don't have to take that second leap. You can just say, "The pattern itself fills me with awe."

Spirituality is traveling freely enough and intimately enough so that you engage what's there. The minute you begin to see the things in the spiritual world as agents of God or as even God himself, you have begun to talk in terms of theology. You've become theistic. You are trying to define in terms of an ongoing metaphor what it is that happens to you in spirituality. The minute you have defined God, then you begin to want to know how to engage him—how to please him, how to move toward him, what the rules are. And that becomes religion. When a whole bunch of you begin to want those same things about that same theological conception, that same concept of God, you've got a major religion.

People talk about life being a gift. I think that's probably a crock. It's not that it's a gift to *you*—it's that your life was created to serve God. It is God's life. The fact that your awareness dwells *in* this life should not be confused with who owns it. You know, my awareness, perhaps, will die when I die. Who knows how much of it is neurological and how much of it is real? My obligation—my joy, my gift—is to see that this part of livingness that is me learns truly to celebrate its maker and to serve him.

Much of spirituality in bookstores is frightening to me, as a Christian, because it's a generic god, or it's just ooey-gooey. It's a feel-good, because it asks nothing. It makes no demands. And people who need that reassurance should be entitled to it. I'm not trying to be arrogant here or condemnatory. It's just that you can only live in that so long before its sheer sweetness will kill you. It's like eating too much icing.

Being in church does less for me now than it once did. When I was a younger Christian, a younger woman, I desperately needed that physical communion of the saints. I needed to hear the voices around me. I needed the discipline of the service more than I do now. Now, I rejoice in the illumination of the sermons. I enjoy the company of my fellow Christians, but I would not drop dead if I did not have that every Sunday in the same way.

Now, what I do have to have is the Eucharist. But when I take the Eucharist to my shut-ins,* and we sit in somebody's home, two or three or four of us, and we partake of the body of God, of the blood of God, and we do it with intimacy and with the candor that says, "Have my God, take him," and we know that we're going to face each other many, many times in life, having made that profession—that has become so much more meaningful for me. The institutional church has decreased in my sense of urgency, though I still believe in it. I love my parish church, you know. It's still the focus. But it's a different kind of communion.

---

* People, usually the elderly, who are frail and homebound.

31.

We're Spiritual and Religious

With one foot in religious tradition, many people are casting out and finding new spiritual venues such as retreat houses and meditation centers. One organization that helps churchgoers make these connections is the Shalem Institute for Spiritual Formation in Bethesda, Maryland, founded by Rev. Tilden Edwards, an Episcopal priest. Spiritual seekers, mostly from mainline Protestant churches, come to Shalem to engage in contemplative practices usually associated with Catholic monks. They also use icons, as do the Eastern Orthodox, and some practitioners like slow walking as well as other Buddhist mindfulness exercises. In 1999, Bob spoke with Edwards, and Gail Fendley interviewed Tina Brown of Wernersville, Pennsylvania, one of those churchgoers who have sought out the retreats and classes of Shalem. After a life-altering spiritual experience late one night in her living room, Brown became a seeker and, later, a spiritual director. Having at first assumed she would "opt out of the church because of the limitations," she now feels a pull toward service of some kind in the institutional church.

Tilden Edwards . . .

Something has been missing in mainstream churches. There had been a sense that what counted most was "right belief," a right intellectual assent to the doctrines of the church, to what scripture says, and that the way to find God is through thinking. What was missing was that there's also a whole other faculty of knowing in us—namely, what you could call a spiritual heart, which simply knows reality, knows life, knows God in a more immediate, albeit more obscure, way than the mind's categories know God. And there's been an imbalance between the head and the heart that's now being rectified, I think, in all traditions, at least in a desire for that.

I can define spirituality differently every day, because it is such a huge word. One way to speak about it, for me, in its broadest sense is to say it has to do with the way we probe and respond to that deepest yearning in us for the infinite, for that which is more than all the finite things that life gives us—our jobs, our families, our educations, whatever else there is that's definable. As St. Augustine said, we're restless until we rest in God. In that sense, it belongs to every human being, whether they use the word "God" or not, because it's, I think, part of our intrinsic human nature to have this longing for something more—the allness of reality, the fullness of truth, the greatness of love. There's something more that we yearn for.

Since every human being is made out of this larger spiritual stuff—as the great Jesuit Teilhard de Chardin said, we're not human beings on a spiritual journey, we're spiritual beings on a human journey—that means anything anyone is doing, any way that search is being manifest, has, in my book, God in it. God's desire for them is in their probing and their going to this workshop or what have you outside the church or inside.

But I think to really see it as a lifetime affair, a lifetime journey, you need to have a grounding somewhere that gives you a way of going deeper so that you can really have a chance to touch the deepest groundwater and not keep digging shallow holes everywhere. Otherwise you don't really find your own soul's depth, because you don't stay with anything long enough. One thing about a religious tradition is that it helps you stay with something until you touch the bottom of it.

People come to us with that more explicit hunger at a particular point. Our job is to help them notice what God's spirit is up to in their life, how they're being moved and guided into two things, because there are two basic callings, historically. One is a deeper, intrinsic communion with God, which is just an end-in-itself love affair out of which all other loves derive. The other is how that overflows into caring for the world—with your gifts and strengths and creativity and so forth.

Because everyone is unique, one thing we recommend for a lot of people is a spiritual director—namely, somebody they can meet with once a month, say, for an hour. They can talk about that hunger, how it's showing itself, how they're sensing that mysterious flow in their life, how they're sensing the way they're being called to do something or be present in the moment.

An enormous amount of spiritual practice is focused on how I can make myself better in a very kind of narrow, almost narcissistic, sense of that word. That's where it can be valuable for these things to be taught within a particular religious tradition, because one thing religious traditions bring is a sense that all of this is meant to overflow into the world and caring for the world. The spirit doesn't come to you in some private way—it comes to you to be circulated in the world.

I've always been so happy that it hasn't been the naval gazers, so to speak, who have come to us. It's been those people who most hunger for something that gives them a deeper personal ground for doing that caring and for doing the caring in a less frenetic way, doing it in a way that's coming from their own deep listening and letting God in on those activities, so they don't feel they're out there having to do everything on their own.

Tina Brown . . .

I had an experience late one night, on a Sunday before Christmas many years ago, when a kind of frightening thing happened with my husband's health that had never happened before. After everything was settled down at the end of that day, I was sitting in a chair in the living room. The whole house was quiet and the children were in bed and my husband was asleep. I was just thinking about what had happened that day, and I sensed a presence in me that I had never sensed before, and I just named that presence as God, or God named that presence as God in me.

That was all, but I felt the need to talk about it. I had never talked about God openly before, and I was a little bit embarrassed to. I was searching out in my mind who would I tell first, and I decided on two people. They were very receptive to me, thankfully. One of the people said, "I think you've been touched by God." And I was. I still believe that I was, and from that point on I started talking to more people about what was happening, and then someone, a friend of mine, thought maybe spiritual direction might be helpful for me. Would I like to talk with someone she knew about spiritual direction? I did, and I've been in spiritual direction for fifteen years since then.

I think that one of the big reasons I go on retreat is that it gives me some open-ended time to just be *attentional* to God in my life, God's presence in me, God's movement in me. Also, I can be *attentional* to my presence in God and my movement toward God or away from God and bring with me my daily circumstances as they are now to me, not last year or next year, but as they are right now to me. While I have some spiritual disciplines at home, they are part of my daily life. But on retreat I get to walk around for an hour here, two hours there and just have that more spacious time to put things into perspective, I guess I might say, because my greatest desire is to live out of God in me. I believe that God exists in me and I exist in God. I want to be faithful to that and I want to live out of that peace. For me, in order to do that, there are things that I need.

One of the things that I need, I've discovered, is the kind of time that I have on retreat and particularly the gatherings. I do need other people at times. So here I have a community of people, and while the community is a little different each time, it's still a community whose heart is centered in God. That's the common factor, that's what's really important for me. When I converse with others and when I listen with others, often times I get clarity and even a sense of expression from others that calls up in me maybe something that I can't quite express, and suddenly I can get a little more expression in that way.

Before making retreats I used to plan all the things that I was going to think about and pray about, and bring all kinds of books with me. That was maybe helpful to me at the beginning of some of my retreat journeys, but now I don't do that so much anymore. I get caught in that sometimes but generally not. I come here with how I am, and ahead of time I pray that I can be open to God. And being open means sometimes being vulnerable, too. It's a little bit scary. That's why it's nice to have people sometimes to talk with. But I find that I'm bringing fewer and fewer books and more and more paper to write with and blank pieces of paper because I like to journal. I do pray for that openness and vulnerability.

Thinking about God's presence in me is not something I can read out of a textbook. It's more of a sensing in me. It's a sensing of a love that leads me to be compassionate toward others and toward my prayers for the world. It's not a kind of love that says go out and fix everybody. It's not that at all.

I think that I listen to people more intently than prior to the years I had a conscious sense of God in me. I want to know about people's experiences with God. I just want to know and want to listen, and I want to be present to that. Maybe that is why I enjoy spiritual direction—and being a spiritual director.

I never thought I would become a spiritual director. It wasn't part of a plan. That's interesting because I've been raised in the American style, often times to plan out everything that I'm going to do. I think that somehow I was grown into that, and I think the relationship with God grew me into wanting to be present to other people in a way that my director was present to me.

I feel a call toward the corporate [institutional] church. It's been one of my struggles, actually, because I really didn't want that. I grew up in a church and had some pretty wonderful experiences. But I also find some limitations there, so I was thinking that I would just opt out of the church because of the limitations. The call, the inner nudging from God was—go and offer yourself, offer what you have to offer, in a church. I don't know where that's going. I have no idea. But that's where I am now.

32

Religion Makes Hospice Calls

Martin Marty—theologian, church historian, Lutheran sage—pondered the unbearable lightness of being spiritual without being communal, in this conversation with Bob in 2002.

———

Thirty and forty years ago most of the intelligentsia predicted that the future of America would be secular, godless. No reference to the transcendent, no magic, mystery, mysticism. A lot of the churches asked, how secular can we get and still be Christian?

All of a sudden we find that both the secular world and the already religious world are moving into a whole new understanding. They simply aren't satisfied by the meanings they get from daily practical life. They think there must be some bigger story. And they have to experience that bigger story that will endow their own joys and sorrows, their own successes and failures with meaning. They are going to find it somewhere. If their own church doesn't do it, they're going to find it at a megabookstore, at summer retreats or weekend retreats. Of course, the churches have adapted greatly and have gone into much more of an experiential and exuberant approach to worship.

I appreciate the spiritual search of the nonchurched, nonsynagogued people as being full of imagination, discovery, and satisfaction for the individual. But I once saw a bumper sticker that said, "Spirituality doesn't make hospice calls." Spirituality remains, normally, individualistic. You may gather for a retreat, and then you disperse. You may gather at the coffee shop or the bookstore, and then you disperse. The people who are handling the homeless and dealing with addiction and trying to improve senior care and who care about the training of the young—they have to bond together. If they don't do it in old-fashioned churches, they'll do it in new-fashioned churches. But I don't think it adds up to much unless there is some development of community, some bonding.

I once heard a paper by my counterpart at Emory University, Brooks Holifield, and I drew the conclusion that 40 percent of the American people are explicitly involved in visible religious quests and participation, year in, year out. I believe those who are actively involved probably have a larger vocabulary for dealing with religious issues. When bad things happen to good people, they can probably read the Book of Job, they can read the Psalms. When God is distant, they can read the medieval mystics. There's a vocabulary there, and they're not totally lost, and they kind of know each other along the way. And that probably is as good as ever.

So the drama is what goes on in the lives of people who say they aren't involved at all in religious quests and participation. Here I would say there are often astonishing acts of generosity. There are often evidences of deep philosophic thinking that has a religious touch to it. But I don't think it has led to the depths we'd like, because when one individual does it, it doesn't have a social power.

I'm interested in public religion. And if somebody tells me, "I'm on a spiritual search," and they describe what they're on and it has no consequence, I think, "Hmm, that's interesting." Some people read Goethe and some read Thomas Mann. Some read Toni Morrison, some read Alice Walker. That is, it's an aesthetic choice. And I love that they're doing it. I think it's a wonderful thing for the soul. But does it help the nation go deeper in its search for a way of addressing the profound issues of the day? I think it's bound to be superficial unless you have a community, the weight of a tradition, and the negative weight as well, and the grace that's mixed with it.

So I think across the board, from the most superficial to the most profound, people are sending out signals that they're reaching for things they haven't reached before. And my own view—the ones who are reaching deepest are those who are reaching into traditions that have been worked over for centuries.

I believe much of what is best is the same thing that people of long ago did. Somebody once said that in the case of Christians, it's a very material faith because you can't even get it going without a loaf of bread, a bottle of wine, and a river. Well, we still use bread and wine and water as the deepest material substances. There's something going on there.

33

The Good, without God

"The real risk we face now is that we may not survive the twenty-first century with the ethics of the twentieth century," says Rushworth Kidder, president of the Institute for Global Ethics in Camden, Maine, and author of such books as How Good People Make Tough Choices: Resolving the Dilemmas of Ethical Living. *Largely because of today's technologies, Kidder believes that ethics are perhaps more urgent than ever and that talking about ethics without necessarily talking about God is equally critical. Kidder himself is religious, a Christian Scientist and former senior columnist for the* Christian Science Monitor, *but he is alert to the growing number of people who seek the ethical life apart from religion and spirituality. During an October 2006 interview, Bill asked Kidder about those people who do not have religious reasons for wanting to reason morally.*

It's probably the oldest question in moral philosophy—why be moral? After all, the manifest advantages of the immoral life are lying all around us. If you want something, just steal it. Why bother to be truthful if you could lie?

Probably the oldest answer to that question is—because that's what God wants. That was, for a long time, the accepted and rather standard answer in the United States. You found an easy and natural discourse on the part of our Founding Fathers and of many people down through the nineteenth century around the topic of God's care for man and the understanding that we are fulfilling God's work in business, in government, in whatever we're doing. It was a much easier and commonplace conversation than it is today.

Here, in the early twenty-first century, it is still a very powerful answer for a lot of people: you lead a moral life because that's what God wants. But it is not and it cannot be allowed to be the only answer. In today's culture, we're no longer in a position to suggest that people understand their ethics through a spiritual framework. We're not willing to assume that people who don't have that framework not only aren't ethical, but can't be ethical or in some ways don't deserve to be ethical. There's too much of a polyglot and varying theology in this country today, and there are too many people who deliberately have no theology for us to rule them out and say, "Yes, we're assuming that when you don't have a god, you don't have ethics."

I happen to think that we are at a point where our ethics are no longer negotiable, situational, up for grabs. I think ethics at this point are a matter of survival. It's not an option. It's required. My reason for saying so is that our technology is now leveraging our ethics in ways we've never seen before. It is now possible for a single unethical action to have immediate, global, and catastrophic consequences. Granted, it's been possible in the past for tyrants with massive armies to do unethical things with devastating consequences over a broad swath of humanity, but this is different. We're not talking about tyrants with armies. We're talking about individuals armed with today's technology.

The great example for me is the meltdown of the Chernobyl nuclear power plant in 1986. I was, I think, the first Western journalist to visit Chernobyl three years after the disaster. The story of Chernobyl is not, alas, a story of innocent human error or a story of mechanical failure. It is a story of a profound and apparently deliberate set of morally unthinkable actions that led to the largest industrial accident in the history of the world. It was essentially caused by the decision making of a couple of people in charge of the plant that night.* There's nothing you could have put those two people in front of in the nineteenth century that could have produced damage at that level.

And where do you find in the nineteenth century the equivalent of the Love Bug computer virus that spread around the world in 2000? The virus was designed by a couple of kids in the Philippines—not terrorists, not kids out to line their pockets, just kids pushing the envelope the way kids have always pushed the envelope. What do you do if you're going to push the envelope in Manila and it's 1950? I don't know—you chase cats or you break

---

* Basically, the power-plant workers engaged in an unauthorized experiment that involved shutting down computer-driven alarm systems, according to accounts given to Kidder. Chernobyl is about eighty miles north of Kiev in Ukraine.

windows, you steal hubcaps. Now, you sit down in front of a keyboard, and just for fun, you create $5.5 billion in global damage. That is substantially and qualitatively different from what has happened in the past.

Given the way our technology leverages our ethics, the real risk we face now is that we may not survive the twenty-first century with the ethics of the twentieth century. Something profound has to change, because our technological progress is not going to stop. It is a steeply rising curve. I happen to think that our moral progress is also a rising curve. I'm not among the pessimists who think we are somehow going backward and losing whatever moral standards we had. But I think the moral progress curve isn't anywhere near as steep as the technological curve. The gap between them is growing. That's why we have to make sure people are tapping into their values.

As it turns out, there are a handful of moral values that we find in every culture that we visit, in every demographic slice that we work with, and we've done this work in about thirty countries.* It's not a surprising collection. It's rather obvious. Everywhere you go and ask people what constitutes the values that underlie the moral life, they'll talk to you about honesty, responsibility, respect, fairness, and compassion. That's a set of shared values all around the world.

Where do these values come from? Are they hardwired into people genetically? Are they part of a survival mechanism of some sort? Are they some part of our aesthetic concern for the beauty of the world? Or do they come from some divine source? We find that for the most part, we really don't have to get into the question of where values come from. People are comfortable just knowing that the values are there, because that cuts right through the moral relativism† that we've all grown up with in the last forty years.

Gathering the Philosophical Tools

There are three major ways in which individuals resolve ethical dilemmas, and at least two of these come straight out of the largely secular tradition of

---

* Referring to research performed by the Institute for Global Ethics.
† The idea that there are no objective standards by which to make moral decisions.

moral philosophy. When somebody says, "Look, I try to do what's best for everybody—the greatest good for the greatest number," that person is drawing on John Stuart Mill's utilitarian philosophy. Using a different principle, the teacher who says to a five-year-old kid, "Gosh, Johnny, if I let *you* do that, I'd have to let *everybody* do it," is actually speaking a fairly pure form of Immanuel Kant's categorical imperative—the idea that the only viable moral decision is one which universalizes what you're doing, so that if you can't say you'd want everybody in the world to do what you're about to do, then you're about to make an unethical decision. Third, there's the Golden Rule—do to others as you would have them do to you—which typically comes to us from a religious source but is as commonplace as the Native American adage, "Don't judge somebody until you've walked a mile in their moccasins."

Just observing the twenty-five thousand people who have gone through our seminars in the past fifteen years, we find them resorting to these three standards again and again. So whether they know it or not, there's a structure in place, and you'll notice that nearly everything we're talking about here has no reference to religion. And we've noticed there isn't any salient distinction between the moral reasoning capacities of people who are religious and those who are not religious.

In those seminars, we've been helping people expand their sense of ethics from simply thinking about it as right versus wrong, to an understanding that the toughest of our ethical decisions are right versus right. The question is: which of these two right courses am I going to choose?

I recently heard from a school counselor who was talking to a sixteen-year-old student. She came into his office one afternoon, shut the door, threw herself on a chair, and burst into tears. Her best friend had sworn her to secrecy and then confided in her that she had a serious eating disorder. And over the past month she had watched the friend grow thinner and thinner, weaker and weaker, and she told the counselor, "I think she's going to die." Here she was, absolutely torn up over that ethical conundrum. Now, if that counselor thought that ethics only had to do with right and wrong, he would have seen no place for moral reasoning here, because there's no wrong being done and no wrong being contemplated. It's not wrong to be sick. It's not wrong to be a teenager wanting to help your friend. That young girl is up against a profound right-versus-right tension, a truth-versus-loyalty situation. She longs to be loyal and to keep her word, but she deeply desires the truth to come out. Each of those sides is right.

Now, if the counselor thinks this through and helps her to unpack all that, it's quite possible to begin to apply the three ways of resolving ethical dilemmas, the resolution principles. On the one hand, if you want to do the greatest good for the greatest number, you might very well say, "There are a lot of kids out there who have made a lot of promises, and this question of loyalty is hugely important, and it may even be more important for me to remain loyal to the idea of keeping my word, even if one person dies." On the other hand, you could take this from the perspective of the categorical imperative, where Kant would ask, "Wouldn't you want everybody in situations like this to make a decision that would preserve life, rather than merely honor some concept of loyalty?" And the third way would be the Golden Rule. If you were that young women, the suffering student, even though you have said, "I want you to promise never to tell," isn't that a plea for help? If you were in such a position, wouldn't you want someone to help save your life? These three resolution principles might bring you to very different conclusions, and yet each one is a profoundly moral conclusion.

I'm not absolutely sure what happened to that sixteen-year-old girl, but I do know the counselor told her, in essence, "Look, I hope that in this case, you can understand that truth has to trump loyalty. Your friend may never talk to you again, but she'll be alive to make that decision. And you will have allowed her to be able to make that decision." In that sense you could say the counselor was actually using all three of the resolution principles. He was seeking the greatest good for the greatest number, sparing the whole community the trauma of losing one of its young. He was expressing the universal maxim that life should be preserved regardless of consequences, and he was illustrating the Golden Rule—if I were that girl's friend, wouldn't I want to be saved?

Ethical Seekers

There is a strong secular part of society which longs to be ethical but not religious. They're seeing what happens in schools, where the character element is missing. They're seeing this missing element in government, in the corporate world, in athletics, and the professions. The question is out there, and they understand that something needs to happen, but they're not saying, "In order for this to happen, I must somehow take up a religious understanding." They know the importance of cutting through the moral relativism, the idea that there really are no values and you could do whatever you want and it's just up to you to maximize your self-interests. I think there's an exhaustion and an annoyance with that language these days.

I think many people are putting ethics in what we would typically describe as a humanist structure. They're saying, "I want to live the very best life I can as a human. I understand the importance of humanity. I understand the importance of caring for other people, of living in a community where things seem to work well because we care for one another. I want to be able to look at myself in the mirror each morning and not be uncomfortable with what I see." I think these people will probably find [nourishment for the ethical life] in the creation of like-minded communities. They won't call them churches and they won't be there for worship, but there will be communities of individuals who share their sentiments about what constitutes the good life and what makes the world progress and how they can most contribute.

For me, the question is: is it possible to lead the ethical life apart from the religious or spiritual life, without simply continuing to drain down the reservoir? In other words, I wonder whether we are, in fact, living off the accumulated moral capital of our past. That capital was largely put into place in a theological context. Yes, I'm sure it's possible to lead the ethical life now and to help others lead that ethical life. But will we be effective at creating entire cultures of integrity, rather than little pockets of character throughout society, if we try to do it absent a set of theological constructs that posit a divine purpose underlying human ethics? I don't know the answer to that.

Will it prove possible for us to continue to replenish that reservoir of moral interest and concern if we don't know where our ethics come from? If our ethics arise not from a deific impulse, but simply as a matter of our DNA or out of a human love for community or from a dread of a dangerous future, are these powerful enough answers to compel us to continue replenishing our moral capital? Or will we just tap it down and keep going for as long as we can? That, for me, is one of the great questions before us in the twenty-first century.

CHAPTER 5

Being
Religious

Ask people what it's like to be religious, and some will tell of their experiences of the transcendent—no less meaningful within a traditional religious setting, they might say, than apart from it. They might speak of their celebration of the divine in congregational worship—stories, preaching, prayers, creeds, music, scripture, and often pageantry. Some will talk about theology, which helps them reflect upon their spiritual experiences, or about the history of their faith communities, as in the "salvation history" presented in the Hebrew scriptures and New Testament. Not least of all, many will speak of membership in a community of fellow believers who try to befriend each other and serve the world.

These and other basic elements of religious life are alive and not unwell, decades after commentators announced the "death of God," predicting the demise of religious belief and institutions.

True, the desire for a deeper sense of meaning and purpose has led growing numbers of people to explore their options in the open spiritual marketplace, beyond the bounds of church and synagogue. Yet "I'm spiritual but not religious" is only one sign of our spiritual times and not the sign that has, for many others, pointed back toward the accumulated wisdom of faith traditions.

For all the ways people are making their own meanings and for all the challenges mounted by science and secular systems of thought, traditional religion remains for diverse multitudes of believers the primary meaning maker. Surely, many Christians still find the essential meanings of their lives in the idea of being a disciple of Jesus or in the sacraments that reveal, to them, a divine presence. Many Jews find their ultimate meanings in their devotion to God, in the Torah, in the history of the Jewish people, and in the observant life. And five times a day, Muslims pause to affirm the one God and the Prophet who revealed him.

Theories of sweeping secularization that populated the sociological literature at one time have fared poorly in most parts of the world outside of western Europe. In the United States, a staggering majority of people say they are religious, and 80 percent of all Americans identify with one or another Christian tradition, according to polling sponsored by *Religion & Ethics NewsWeekly* in partnership with *U.S. News & World Report*. Similarly sound majorities say religion is important in their lives and that it helps them cope with personal and communal crises like the terrorist threat.

More than half of all Americans call themselves Protestants, with white evangelicals garnering about half that share. Nearly a quarter of the population is Roman Catholic. Jews add up to about 2 percent of the populace, as do Mormons. Muslims, Hindus, Buddhists, and all others who are religious but not Christian comprise about 3 percent.

We are religious, though not quite as religious as we think or say. Pollsters are aware that Americans are somewhat prone to exaggeration when they report how often they go to church and take part in other religious activities such as prayer meetings, though even allowing for embellishment, America is exceptionally religious by all conventional measures. The question is, how deeply are Americans seeking to draw on the deposits of wisdom in their religious traditions? By their own accounts, when making important decisions in their lives, Americans are far less likely to rely on the teachings of church or synagogue than on their own personal judgments or the opinions of friends and family.

Still, if 90 percent of life is just showing up, as Woody Allen put it, then each week extraordinary numbers of Americans are getting cued about life's purpose just by showing up at worship services. What is it like to be religious in contemporary society? What is the spiritual value of connecting to a faith community? What are the higher meanings that people draw from the symbols and imagery of religious tradition?

In these pages, religious believers and seekers throw light on what William James called "the varieties of religious experience," the spiritual, mystical, liturgical, and other forms of religious life. But most of all, they speak of their own religious communities and their personal, contemporary encounters with ancient faith traditions.

34.

All Is Gift

Eileen Durkin comes to her ultimate meanings as a cradle Catholic who grew up after the Second Vatican Council (1962–65), which instituted reforms such as wider roles for lay people. "My faith is what I breathe," says Durkin, who is rais-ing five children in the faith of her ancestors, although she does not echo the Catholics of yesteryear who were instructed to "pray, pay, and obey." In May 2002, Religion & Ethics NewsWeekly *special correspondent Judy Valente interviewed Durkin in the sanctuary of her neighborhood church, St. Mary of the Wood, on the northwest side of Chicago, while two of Durkin's daughters and her husband were performing an Irish step dance in the gym next door. Judy asked her, "What is it about Catholicism that gives you strength and solace in times of trouble?"*

It's the Catholic world view, which is that grace is everywhere. My view as a Catholic is that the world is sacramental with a small s. Everything has the potential for being holy because Jesus Christ came into our lives. All of life is gift, and we have to be aware of that in the rhythms of our lives, in the events of the world. Because I can look at life that way, I've got a great responsibility to be attentive to life and to feel that I'm at home in a church, in my family, in my job, and in other things.

I have five kids, so I've had five baptisms. The last one was Collum's. He's the youngest of five. And as we approached the baptism, his older sib-lings were getting to understand more of what was actually going on. We gave them little jobs to do at the baptism, because we wanted them to feel involved. So one of them got to pour the water into the pitcher before it was blessed. Another got to hold the candle. Another got to hold the oil. This was a way of welcoming Collum as a child of God, as one of the community. We had already welcomed him in the sense of our family, but this was the public welcoming, the public celebration, the public reminder. I see sacraments as great reminders. If all of life is little sacraments, if all of life has potential for being graced and holy, then the big sacraments are the times we really stop publicly and remind each other of this.

I remember with my oldest daughter, holding her in my arms one night when I was nursing and saying, "I just want you to always know that you're loved," because I knew life was going to throw a bunch of curve balls her way. Baptism for me is an initial reminder that this child is loved and that this child is a member of a family larger than our own.

I asked my daughter the other day what it meant to her to be Catholic, and she said, "Celebration." So they're very attuned. When we do the sacraments, when we do the baptism, we always have a celebration. When we do first communion, we always celebrate. And one of our most successful family ways is during Advent, when we light the Advent calendar and say a short prayer every night, and the baby sings "O Come, O Come, Emmanuel" very loudly, and there's this sense that this is the family, this is the prayer, this is joyous.

We say grace every day at meals. And since September 11th, actually we've been adding a little tag line that we always say, "For peace in our world and love in our hearts," because we're really trying to communicate to them that there are events happening in the world, but we have a duty to do our small steps along the way, and we've got to begin at home. We have to begin that peace at home, both with prayer and with trying to not fight, but particularly with prayer.

My husband and I met at a church. Certainly part of our courtship was an understanding that faith was important to us. We were both involved in a lot of volunteer programs, so we saw that as something important, and we had a sense that you took your faith and you brought it outside and tried to help those less fortunate, tried to transform the world in your own little way. So that was our attraction to each other. And then we got married in the church, and we attend Mass together, so that's something that grows with us. And at different times in our lives we've done prayer together. Frankly, those are the times when we're both the best in our marriage. During the seasons of the year, during Lent and Advent, we're able to take time from our busy lives and kind of really focus on growing spiritually together.

It's sacramental to us. We're very aware that our marriage is to reflect the love of God, it's an ongoing process, and if we're not growing in our marriage, in our love, in our faith, if we're keeping it inside, if we're just keeping that love between us or in our family or in our home, then that's not working either. So our marriage should reflect—and hopefully it does, in some ways, in our family life—God's great love for the world.

I see Catholics as able to embrace all of life—the good and the bad—and to kind of bring it all together, bring it to the liturgy, to the Mass, and offer it up, and live with the good and live with the bad and say we believe that the good ultimately triumphs, but we acknowledge the bad. And still it's worth celebrating the good. It's still worth embracing art, embracing culture, embracing all of life. I'm not saying that because this is of the earth this is bad, or because this is of humanity this is bad, but that God made this, it's good, and it's up to us to see how it can be celebrated.

I think there's also a great obligation to serve the poor and those less fortunate. And I see this in other religions as well, but as a Catholic, I feel very strongly that that's part of the story. You have been blessed, you have gifts, and your job is to share those gifts with other people.

I relate all this to the story of Jesus Christ, who was divine but became human. For me, personally, this means my life has the potential to experience that divinity, so therefore I have a responsibility to see my whole life as potentially holy. Sometimes when I vote, I'm doing that as a Catholic. I mean, I'm doing it as a person, I'm doing it as a citizen, but I don't see that as separate from my identity as a Catholic. And when I recycle—it's part of my identity as a Catholic to care for the earth.

My faith is what I breathe. I mean, I'm not thinking about my faith every minute, but it intrudes a lot into my life. I get up every morning, and I give the day over to God. I usually make the sign of the cross and try and make some commitment to spend that day in the name of the Father, and of the Son, and of the Holy Spirit. As broken as I am, I try to do that. And then, taking care of my children and doing any other work I do, trying to treat people with respect, trying to do my work well—all these things are from my faith identity—trying to be a person for other people, and understanding when I fail, when other people fail, and trying to be compassionate, trying to be forgiving, all that.

And at the end of the day, I'll review where I've gone and try to come to some understanding. But I suppose it's because of my faith that I get up the next morning and try again. And I have to be humble and understand that I'm not doing it right all the time, but I think I'm able to try again because I think about it in a faithful way all the time.

I have issues with the structure of the institutional church. But I was really lucky. My uncle is a priest, and my mom's a theologian. I was always exposed to the church, so I have great respect for church leaders, but no reverence. I mean, I save the reverence for God. And so, if I don't agree with particular leaders or particular structures of the church, that doesn't affect my faith in God, in the Holy Spirit at work in the people of the church. That's how I'm able to live with those differences, although I work for change.

For me, probably the biggest issue with the institutional church is the issue of women's ordination. At the start of the new millennium, I told my daughters that I was going to pray every day for women's ordination, and I do. I have wonderful daughters, and I cannot personally see how they could not reflect the wonders of Christ if they chose to be leaders in prayer and service. And although women's voices are heard in the church, they're not heard every week. We're losing the wisdom of half the human race.

Catholicism is more to me than just pronouncements. It's life. It's lived. It's the people I'm with. It's the experience of Jesus Christ in my life. I think there are good people out there trying to live their lives in the world, respectfully, in committed relationships. The church has to listen to people who are in homosexual relationships, in premarital relationships, people who may be using birth control.

Parsing the Mass

I bring whatever is in my life to Mass. So if things are going well, I'm bringing it all to Mass. If things are going poorly, I'm bringing it all to Mass. So when I approach the Mass, I'm ready to have some distillation of my daily life in this hour or so on a Sunday.

The beginning of Mass is some kind of introductory rite with the penitential rite, so I'm ready right in the beginning to ask for forgiveness, because, especially when there's turmoil in my life, I like to settle in. And so the opening—Lord have mercy, Christ have mercy, Lord have mercy—is a wonderful reminder to me to reprioritize my life and to ask for forgiveness and to be given a chance to try again. I love that that's at the beginning of each Mass. I need to be at peace with people here, and at prayer, and with my world.

I love to listen to the stories of the scripture. We have usually an Old Testament and a New Testament reading. There is great drama in the scripture stories and, again, reminders—I've heard the stories before because they're repeated every couple of years, but I'm a different person every time, and so each time the story hits me in a new way, and I think of something else.

I should mention the music, because that's probably my favorite part of the whole Mass when it's done well. There's the opening song that brings the whole community together and kind of proclaims, "Here we are!" And then between the readings there's usually a psalm sung. That's always a real reflective time for me and a meditative time, at that psalm between the readings. It is very prayerful to me.

Then there's the homily. I've been blessed, through my life, with attending churches where I've had great, great homilies. They are always very good at making me think and challenging me. And I'm usually sitting there, as I'm listening to the homily, thinking about how I am going to apply this to my life, or what—if the priest tells a story—what his story reminded me of or who it reminded me of. That's a very active thought time for me, and a challenge time, and a time of renewal. What am I going to take from this homily and bring out to the world?

Then after the homily we do the prayers, the general intercessions, the prayers for the whole world. And I love those prayers, because those are the times we pray publicly as a community for peace, for those who are sick, for those who are suffering, for those who have died. It's opening us up to the whole world. That's one of the things I like about being a Catholic—that we have a responsibility to pray for the whole world and to be blessed by the whole world.

And then the liturgy of the Eucharist is the meal. It's when we gather around the table. It's when everybody comes, and we actually do this in remembrance of Jesus. We bring the gifts of bread and wine to the altar, and then they are broken. And I always like the part where we talk about Jesus blessing the bread and breaking it, because that reminds me of life. Life breaks and my life breaks. And I like the sense that the brokenness of life is up there as well. I mean, it's the meal, it's the party, it's the thanksgiving, but it's broken, and yet it's that broken bread that nourishes us at Communion time when we go forward and receive the body and the blood of Christ.

I love the sign of peace.* This takes place after we end what's known as the Eucharistic Prayer and after the congregation recites the Lord's Prayer, the Our Father. All of a sudden we open up again to the community. And the sign of peace is just a reconciling, a concrete way of reconciling, first with my family, if we argued on the way to church or something. I can give one of my kids a kiss and say, "The peace of Christ be with you." And then we reach around to the people around us, who we may or may not have met, and wish them Christ's peace.

Then we have Communion, and that's the actual walking. I mean, physically, we walk. We walk forward to receive the body and blood of Christ. And it's a minipilgrimage. You're in your pew, and then you step out, and you have to walk. You have to take a journey, and you have to go forward. There's just this movement in the church, all the people coming forward. And then someone shares a meal with you. It's another human being who shares the meal and says, "Body of Christ," and then you say just "Amen." That's food, and so you got fed, and then you proceed back to your pew.

And what I always think when I see all the people coming forward is that nobody's shallow. I don't know if I can really explain this, but each of these people, whether I know them or not, has this entire depth that I may not see and other people may not see, but they have a life, and they may have somebody who is sick in their lives, they may have somebody who was just

---

* An exchange of greeting among Mass goers that comes before Communion.

born in their families. And I don't know what it is, but I know that I've got a lot going on in my life, and they do, too, and we're in this together. And as they're walking up and committing to being nourished and being a faithful person, so am I. And I'm there for them, and they're there for me. And it's a great unifying thing.

Usually we have a meditation song after Communion, and again I find the music really brings it all together. Then comes the blessing and then the dismissal, the sending off. It's the commissioning. Go out into the world and be more joyous. Be more forgiving. Be more loving. Be more compassionate. Do the work of God in your daily lives, in your work, in your families, in our world. And usually the last song is always very uplifting, and it has the sense of an anthem and going out there.

I always love going out after Mass, because that's when I get to talk with people and check in with people, see how their lives are going, pick up the parish bulletin and anticipate bringing it home and reading everything that's going on, all the activities, and trying to decide what to get involved in. On the way home, the kids are thinking about whether we're going to get donuts or not. But I'm thinking about how I'm feeling better, even if I've had a bad day, or a bad week, or a bad month. The liturgy always reprioritizes my life. I'm grounded. I feel refreshed. I feel renewed. I feel empowered. And because of this experience I feel like I can tackle the day. At least I can tackle the next six or seven days, and then I'll have to come back and do it again.

Being Catholic is such a fulfilling part of my life that I can't imagine not being Catholic. It's part of my identity. I'm of Irish ancestry, and it was passed down through grandparents, and great-grandparents, and great-great-grandparents who really suffered for their faith. And so I really feel that it's a heritage that was passed down to me, and I feel an obligation to pass it down. It's a joy and a privilege to pass it on to my children.

In Touch with the Cosmic Matriarch

My prayer life is constant—and constantly in need of improvement. So I feel very humble in that I have a vision of an ideal prayer life which would involve a regularity and a depth which is not present in my life at this time, with my little kids. And yet it's an ideal, something I aspire to.

I give the day over to God, and I talk to God at various parts of the day. I will either thank God or I will beseech God. So there's this sense that God is with me throughout the day, and I consider that part of my prayer life. And we pray with our children, individually, before they eat, before we put each one down to bed. If I have friends who are sick and who are suffering, or if I know somebody who is dying, I keep that with me all day. I don't really know how to describe it. But those people are in my mind, and I call them to mind, and I tell them I'm going to call them to mind.

At the end of the day, I like to call them to mind again and offer prayers for them up to God. And I find prayers to the mother of Jesus to be so wonderful for that, because I find her a wonderful model of somebody who suffered, who knew suffering, who knew loss, and who knew great joy, and who persevered, and who was faithful. The traditional Marian prayers weren't necessarily part of my childhood, but I'm coming to them more as an adult, seeing them as great sources of solace and challenge as I experience more suffering and loss.

The Memorare is one Marian prayer. "Remember, O most gracious Virgin Mary, that never was it known that anyone who fled to thy protection, implored thy help, or sought thy intercession was left unaided. Inspired by this confidence, I fly unto thee, O virgin of virgins, my mother, to thee I come, before thee I stand, sinful and sorrowful. O mother of the Word incarnate, despise not my petitions, but in your mercy hear and answer me." I hope that was right.

That prayer is particularly moving in my life, because it was one of the last prayers that my dad said when he was dying, and it was his childhood prayer. It was just a wonderful thing for me to see that he had something from his childhood, that he had a faith from his childhood that he brought with him and that was comforting to him and inspiring to him at the time of his death. The span of everything that had taken place in between was something I wanted, something I wanted for myself, something I wanted for my children.

I had learned the prayer as a child, and I can stand some improvement still, but I say it every night now when I call to mind people who are sick, because it is a prayer of humility, I think. I don't focus on each word and what each word means, but I focus on the tradition and that it was passed on to me from my parents and from perhaps people who are wiser than I am. The heritage of the past—I want to go back and see what they had that was of value, and I want to respect it.

My daughter Nora made her first reconciliation* in fourth grade last weekend, and it was a very moving experience. She had been baptized and then made her first Communion, and now she was going to experience the sacrament of reconciliation. We gathered for prayers and readings in the church, and then each of the children went up with their parents individually to the altar, and we kind of sent her off.

She sat in a chair opposite a priest and really talked to him about what she considered to be a sinful part of her life. And we, my husband and I, were standing there, and we weren't a party to what she was saying, but we just both had tears in our eyes as we looked at her because she was sitting—first of all, she was right under Our Lady of Knock, which is one of the Marian images, and I have family right near Knock in Ireland. So it connected. I said, "Butch, she's under Our Lady of Knock, so she's in good hands."

I could see at one point that she looked like she was going to cry, and my heart just went out to her. I thought she's so brave to kind of look at her life and see where it needs improvement. And then she seemed to get over that moment, and she was talking with the priest and smiling, and obviously being reminded of God's forgiving love and celebration.

And then she came back to us, and we dipped our hand in the holy water and put the sign of the cross on her forehead and just thought of her baptism. And she's the child I have such an image of holding in my arms when she was a baby and saying, "I want you to always know you're loved." I think she was reminded she was loved, so I was very happy.

---

* Also known as confession.

35.

Eileen's Uncle and His Catholic Imagination

In the preceding reflection, Eileen Durkin mentions in passing that her "uncle is a priest." That man is none other than Andrew Greeley, the prolific, insightful, and frequently contentious commentator, novelist, and sociologist. Judy Valente asked him in 2002, "What's the essence of Catholicism?"

I think it's the stories. If we get you in the early years of your life and we fill your head with all of the Catholic stories, then it's very hard for you to stop being Catholic. Catholics are Catholics because they like being Catholic. They like the stories—Christmas, Easter, May crowning, the souls in purgatory, the saints, the angels, the mother of Jesus. These are enormously powerful religious images. Some people might think they've become clichés through the centuries, and maybe for some they have. But for most Catholic lay folks, the images and the stories are what hold us in the church despite, sometimes, our leadership.

The kernel is the belief that God is love, and in Catholicism, God's love is present in the world. It is in the sacraments, in the Eucharist, in our families, in our friends, in our neighborhood, in a rediscovered love. And when there is forgiveness in the touch of a friendly hand, God is there. God lurks everywhere. That's the fundamental Catholic instinct on the imaginative and poetic level. Right down the street, right around the corner—there's God.

People have decided they're going to be Catholics on their own terms. They are Catholic, they're strongly Catholic, they like being Catholic, but they're not going to let church leadership dictate the terms of belonging. Immediately after the Second Vatican Council, there was the euphoria and the effervescence of the council, and in a remarkably short period of time, the people and the lower clergy changed the church. By 1975, all this had happened: birth control wasn't wrong, premarital sex wasn't wrong, priests leaving the priesthood wasn't wrong, nuns leaving the religious life wasn't wrong. You didn't really have to go to Mass every Sunday. You didn't have to go to confession before receiving communion every time. All of these things, which they never really understood and they didn't like, were just swept away. Now, a whole generation later, church leaders have not been able to restore the acceptance of those teachings. And I don't see how they ever will.

The Catholic imagination is metaphorical and sacramental. It sees God as present in the world. The Protestant imagination, the dialectical imagination, [is wary of] identifying God with his creatures. Catholicism has no problem with that. It sees God present in his creatures, in all of the creatures, and especially in those creatures that love us and that we love.

We don't believe that we have a monopoly on truth. We believe what we have is true, but it's not the whole truth. And we can learn a lot from the other religions if we listen to them respectfully. We don't give up our heritage—we expand it. There's a great story about Saint Augustine of Canterbury. He went to England when the Anglo-Saxons had taken over, and he liked them; they seemed to be good people. He wondered whether it was all right to adapt their customs to Christianity. And Gregory the Great, who was pope then, in 600, wrote him a letter saying, "Well, of course. As long as these are good and true and beautiful, and there's nothing unnatural about them, then of course they can be adapted for Christianity." That's been our policy ever since. Sometimes we've violated it, but that's the official policy. We can learn from everybody. Catholicism means, "Here comes everyone."

I don't think Jesus was an exclusivist. He said, and we believe, that he is the unique representation of God in the world. But that doesn't mean this is the only way God can work: "Now, God, you've got to work here and no place else." Nobody puts constraints on God. She doesn't like it.

The Most Serious Problem . . .

The church just has not been able to cope with the demands for fairness and equality from women, so they're very angry. For a long time, the bishops could console themselves—and I think some still do—that these are just radical feminists. But the radical feminists include their sisters and their nieces and their mothers and all the women in their lives. They just don't like the way the church treats them. And this includes lots of parish priests who are just awfully sloppy in their respect and sensitivity toward women.

There has always been a certain proportion of people who leave the church on issues of authority and sex. That hasn't changed since we started doing research on it back in the early 1960s. The increase comes from people who've had marriage problems. Dean Hoge and his colleagues* have done work on young Catholics, and they find that very few young Catholics don't think of themselves as Catholic anymore. Young Catholics want to stay, even if they don't go to church much.

Once a Catholic, always a Catholic. If you're a Catholic and are filled with Catholic images and stories in childhood, you don't want to give them up. You like being a Catholic. And how fundamental are these teachings? What's more important? Life after death or birth control? What is more important? God's forgiving love or premarital sex? The sexual ethic is important, but it's not the only thing in Catholicism. I'm afraid sometimes our leaders—and the media, too—have made it sound as if the only unique thing about Catholicism is sexual teaching. The lay people know better.

I think one of the conclusions that many Catholics drew from the Second Vatican Council is there're just a lot fewer mortal sins than there used to be. So we don't really have to confess them, and we can make a good act of contrition, as we used to say, and receive Communion, and it's fine. Part of it is just the decision that confession before Communion isn't necessary. This is a conclusion that the laity have reached. And the lower clergy have not disabused them of that notion, because they think the same thing. People still go to confession and the penitential services at Easter and Christmas. They're very, very popular. But we realize now that we really don't have to run to confession every Saturday afternoon if we want to receive Communion on Sunday.

I'd say that Catholicism in the United States has the distinct advantage of being in a pluralistic society, where your religion contributes something

---

* At the Catholic University of America in Washington, DC.

to your identity. So you tend to define yourself as a Catholic. I'm Irish, Catholic, a Democrat from the West Side of Chicago, and that's pretty much my identity. For most Americans, that relation is part of their identity, so you come to them and say, "Where are you from?" or "What are you?" when they move into a neighborhood, and they'll say Protestant or Catholic or Jew. It's the preprogrammed response. I don't know how I would explain it to people who live in a country where everybody's one religion, but I would try to say that religion is a part of who we are and what we are. It gives us something to belong to and something to believe in, in our lives.

I think Hispanics are a great grace for the Catholic Church in this country, because their religion has so much festivity and celebration in it. We European Catholics tend to be somewhat grim and dour and straitlaced. We shouldn't be, but we are. We can learn from the Latinos that Catholicism is a religion of festivity and celebration.

They have a very strong sense of family and local community. Of course, so do the Italians and the Irish. But I think it's stronger among Hispanics. One Hispanic woman was telling me about her religion, and all she was talking about were the parties, the festivals. And I asked, "But what does all this mean?" She would tell me about another party or festival. I finally said, "No, no. What's the theology?" "Oh," she said. "Well, I think we believe that God is part of our family. And when we have celebrations, God comes and celebrates with us." I like that. I think we should have more of it.

36.

Stuff Counts

George Weigel, the author of Witness to Hope: The Biography of Pope John Paul II, *spoke with Bob on several occasions marking the life as well as the death of the Polish pope. Weigel is also a senior fellow of the Ethics and Public Policy Center in Washington, DC, and here, he examines the core of Catholicism, remembering the Catholic whom he believes embodied "the Christian proposal."*[*]

I would say the essence of Catholicism is Jesus Christ—the sure conviction that in Jesus of Nazareth God entered human history in the person of his son for the salvation of the world, and the further conviction that that saving mission continues in the church, which is an extension of Christ, which is, indeed, the body of Christ. To meet Jesus Christ is to meet his church and become incorporated into that church, and to live that Christian life through the church—through its sacraments, through its moral teaching, through its community of fellowship, through its service to the world. But at the heart of it all is the person of Christ. Christ is the essence of all Christianity. Christ is the essence of Catholicism.

Catholicism understands itself to be the fullest embodiment of the Church of Christ in history. Namely, Christ intended not only a fellowship, a community of disciples, but a structure for that community. Key parts of that structure are the episcopate, the office of bishop as the pastoral leadership of the church. The chief bishop, the bishop of Rome, the successor of Peter, is a crucial part of that structure. So is a sacramental priesthood in which the priest is understood not as an ecclesiastical functionary who's licensed to do certain kinds of church business, but as an icon of the eternal

---

* These remarks are culled from Bob's conversations with Weigel aired in 2002 and at the time of John Paul's death in 2005.

priesthood of Christ, whose priesthood continues in the church. Those notions—and particularly the centrality of the Petrine ministry as the continuation of Christ's mandate to Peter, embodied now in the bishop of Rome and, thus, a connection to the apostolic origins of the church—are very much at the heart of Catholic Christianity.

One of the distinctive things about Catholicism is its intensely sacramental understanding of the world. In a Catholic vision of reality, everything discloses something else. Water and salt in baptism disclose the salvation of God at work in an individual life. Bread and wine in the Eucharist become the body and blood of Christ. Marital love within the bond of fidelity discloses the truth of God's self-giving love to the world. Stuff counts in Catholicism, and that sacramental imagination about all of reality is intensely expressed in what Catholics call the seven sacraments of the church.

John Paul's Catholicism

In his encyclical on Christian mission, *Redemptoris Missio*,* Pope John Paul II said very explicitly, the church proposes, the church imposes nothing. The church has a proposal to make to people about the nature of the human condition which it believes has been redeemed in Jesus Christ. The pope also says in that encyclical that there are many who are saved who are not formally part of the church, but all who are saved are saved in some sense because of Jesus Christ. And they have therefore in some sense a mysterious relationship to the church. As he once said to Muslim teenagers in Casablanca, "I'm sure God will explain all of this to us someday." For the moment, the thing we need to focus on is what we agree on, particularly about the moral life and how to live decent, free civic lives, so that all of our truths can be in conversation with each other.

I think this man embodied the Christian proposal to the world in a singularly compelling way at the end of a terrible century and thereby prepared the church for its third millennium. More than any human being in the twentieth century, he embodied the Christian vision of the greatness of the

---

* Latin for "Mission of the Redeemer," issued in 1990.

human possibility. And he did that in the face of all of the awfulness of this century, much of which he experienced personally: the Nazi occupation of his city, thirty years of communist occupation of his country. He came out of that convinced that the Christian vision of the dignity of the human person and the greatness of the destiny of humanity was the most compelling answer to the question that tortured the twentieth century: What are we doing here? What is this about? Who are we? What's this for, where is it going? He gave an extraordinarily compelling answer to that question.

His answer was that human beings were made for communion with God. Had been intended for that communion with God from the beginning. Had lost the capacity to be that. Were redeemed from that incapacity through Jesus Christ and now ought to live as if they were people capable of being the friends of God. That's a remarkable statement and a remarkable act of faith, but he believed that with every breath he took.

John Paul II planted a time bomb in the Roman Catholic Church between 1979 and 1984 in a series of 140 audience addresses that taken together comprise what is called his "theology of the body." This was the most comprehensive intelligent Christian response—not just Catholic response, Christian response—to the sexual revolution that had been laid out since the 1950s. I say this is a time bomb because in the first instance, most people don't even know it happened. And in the second instance, even those who have read those audience addresses have not even begun to come to grips with what it means, for example, when the pope says, as he did, that marital intimacy is an icon of the interior life of God. This is an astonishing statement. This repeals fifteen hundred years of Christian nervousness about the *embodiedness* of human beings. Marital intimacy is an icon of the interior life of the Trinity. Now, fifty years from now, a hundred years from now, when that time bomb goes off, we're going to have to rethink virtually every doctrinal category in the church to take account of this new concern for the fact that we're not simply souls temporarily trapped in bodies. We are, in fact, embodied spirits, whose *embodiedness* has something to say about our relationship to God. This was entirely missed by clergy. I have yet to hear a sermon laying this out.

I think the effects of that will be to set aside the notion of sexuality as something embarrassing, vaguely distasteful. No, this is a great good, this is a great gift. It is also a great power to be used with care. The second thing it will do is provide a much more compelling account of who we are as sexual human beings than the sexual revolution has done, which simply reduces us to a set of urges, reduces sexuality to another contact sport, football without pads, if you will. This is not terribly interesting after a while, and it does enormous damage to human beings. It doesn't add to the sum total of human happiness.

I think it's a mistake to divide his pontificate into precollapse of communism and postcollapse of communism, which is rather the conventional way to do it. The themes were consistent throughout: the dignity of the human person, freedom, not as some free floating, "I can do what I want because I want to do it," but freedom as the capacity to do the good, what we ought to do. And in that respect, what he was saying to communist rulers pre-1989—let my people go—was exactly what he was saying to new democracies and old democracies in the 1990s. Think about freedom seriously. Get freedom reconnected to moral truth and to the pursuit of goodness, not simply the pursuit of pleasure and the pursuit of wealth.

The pope, I believe, came a long way in his understanding of the way modern societies operate. He really had not had a lot of experience of the West prior to his election. And I think if you trace his addresses in the United States from 1979 to 1987 to 1995, you see an evolving understanding and indeed appreciation for this kind of messy, glorious, confused, decent-spirited business we call democracy. The Holy Father came to understand that the United States was not Western Europe times ten. Western Europe really was de-Christianized in the post–World War II period. The United States was not de-Christianized in the post–World War II period. And I think he came to appreciate that difference, came to appreciate the vitality of Christianity in the United States and wanted America to live that religious vitality in a more politically serious way, which is hard to say we've done since the Cold War.

The Roman Catholic Mess

The clergy sexual abuse crisis is fundamentally a crisis of fidelity. If a man truly believes that he is what the Catholic Church teaches he is as a priest—namely, an icon, a living representation of the eternal priesthood of Jesus

Christ—he does not behave as a sexual predator. So at the bottom of the bottom line here, we have a crisis of fidelity. We have a crisis of failed discipleship. The normal reaction to that among people is a deep sense of betrayal, a deep sense of hurt and anger that the pastoral authorities in the church have not dealt with sufficiently. It's important to remember two things here. One is that the overwhelming majority of Catholic priests in the United States are leading faithful lives of heroic virtue. The second is that betrayal has been part of the story of the church from the beginning. It's interesting that in constructing the New Testament, the church did not eliminate the story of Judas. Judas is in the New Testament, but Judas is not the story line. The story line as it plays out in the Gospels and in the Acts of the Apostles is fidelity. And that is what I believe, at the end of the day, will come out of this current crisis—a renewal of fidelity to integral Catholic faith.

This is a real problem, and it needs real solutions. The real solution is for the church to become more Catholic, not less Catholic. I mean people living integrally Catholic lives. I mean the recognition that "cafeteria" Catholicism is simply unserious. The Catholic faith is not a smorgasbord down which you can walk, saying, "That looks good, that doesn't look so good." It's a complete package. And when we try to convince ourselves that it is a smorgasbord, a cafeteria, a certain corruption comes into the whole enterprise. That's what we're seeing played out.

I think this is actually a great opportunity. "Crisis" in the language of the Bible means a mess—our conventional meaning of the term. It also means an opportunity. This is an opportunity to really complete the reform of the priesthood, of the episcopate—and, indeed, of all of Catholic life—mandated by the Second Vatican Council.

I have in mind a Catholic Church in which sixty-five million people live the fullness of Catholic faith, live the truth of Catholic faith, participate vigorously in the liturgical life of the church, are actively in service to society, and are bringing the wisdom of Catholic social doctrine to our public life. That's what I mean by a renewed and reinvigorated church.

The way out of this is not Catholic lite. It's real Catholicism, full Catholicism. And I think that's exactly what's going to come out of this—a reinvigoration of classic Catholic faith.

37.

Is God Still the Center?

For many years, historian of religion Mark Noll taught at the evangelical Wheaton College near Chicago. He has been a leader in encouraging evangelical scholarship and criticism, especially in his 1994 book The Scandal of the Evangelical Mind. *In 2006, Noll joined the faculty of the University of Notre Dame. Judy Valente interviewed Noll in 2004.*

———

Evangelicals usually stress conversion to Jesus Christ. Evangelicals stress the authority of the Bible as their chief religious authority. Evangelicals are activists in some areas of life, principally in trying to share the good news about Jesus. And evangelicals usually stress the death of Christ and his resurrection as the key, central Christian teaching.

To evangelicals themselves, they're wonderful people that make everything nice when people listen to them. Often, to those who don't appreciate evangelicals, they're seen as rednecks, as cryptofundamentalists, as people without education, as people without a brain.

The truth is that evangelicals are an American brand of Protestant Christianity, strongly influenced by revival traditions but moving in many different directions.

Evangelicals tend to be not as political as they have often been portrayed. There is a very strong pietist* tradition in evangelical Christianity, which

---

* A strain of Protestantism emphasizing Bible study, prayer, and personal religious experience.

means that evangelicals often focus upon their spiritual lives and on the good they can do in a community, rather than in mobilization for political life.

The diversity of evangelical Christianity is extreme. Evangelicals would include people with no time for higher education and a full roster of PhDs, MDs, LLDs.

Usually the terms "evangelical" and "fundamentalist" are used with distinctive meanings. Fundamentalism would be one variety of evangelical Christianity. Fundamentalists historically have been defined as those who are especially influenced by the revival traditions of the nineteenth century and sometimes by their attitudes of separation and militancy toward the rest of the religious world and the rest of the world. Evangelical Christianity as a whole includes some fundamentalist tendencies, some fundamentalist groups, but probably most evangelicals would not want to be called fundamentalists themselves.

I think it's possible to suggest that evangelical Christians have become more prominent in public space over the last thirty or forty years because of signal events, turning points, as it were. Certainly, the presidency of Jimmy Carter was important. Here was a Southern Baptist who said that he was born again and tried to live by his faith. This was nothing new in the South and in many parts of the rest of the country, but it was new for a public speaker to talk like this. Certainly, the debates that have taken place over moral issues—the debate over abortion on demand, for example—led to a certain kind of militancy in public life by a certain kind of Protestant that seemed new, although it actually went far back in American history with many traditions. And other issues that have been part of what are sometimes called "the culture wars" have drawn more attention to groups of Protestant Christians that were there all along but have now surfaced in the public. It is also true that since World War II, the proportions of churchgoing Americans have shifted. In very rough terms, one used to be able to speak of about the same number of Roman Catholics, mainline Protestants, and evangelical Protestants taking part in church activities and being active religiously. Since the end of the Second World War, Catholics have grown somewhat, mainline Protestants have declined, and the number of evangelicals, however defined, has increased quite dramatically.

Evangelical Christianity is a tradition of religion that is adaptable. Evangelical Christianity began in the eighteenth century with people who were willing to preach outdoors at a time when that was a very radical step. In America, evangelical Christianity was promoted most dramatically in the early nineteenth century by Methodist circuit riders and by Baptist lay preachers. Both were innovative techniques for church organization. In the twentieth century, evangelicals were pioneers in the use of radio for religious purposes. Since World War II, evangelical churches have adapted to current culture in ways that other groups have been slower to do.

Evangelicals have been pioneers in the outreach of Christianity in suburban areas. Some of the new megachurches around the country, most of which are evangelical in one way or another, look a little bit like shopping malls. They are able to put people at ease who are used to going into shopping malls and are not perhaps used to going into traditional churches. At the same time, some of the newer evangelical churches realize that people need identification with a small group—auto mechanics, or Alcoholics Anonymous, or youth clubs. Evangelicals have innovated in all of these matters and in many more in trying to provide a religious interface with people where they actually are living and hurting and feeling and taking their day-to-day existence.

Evangelical Protestants have been leaders in the use of modern musical forms in church. This is actually quite offensive to some traditional evangelicals and some traditional Protestants of other sorts, but it has been an adaptive strategy. It's been a way of using the musical language of television and of the modern mass media to bring it into church, to sanctify it, to baptize it, and it has been attractive.

Music has always been important to evangelical Protestants, right from the days of Charles Wesley, the great hymn-writing brother of John Wesley. "O, for a Thousand Tongues to Sing" has been the Marseillaise hymn of Methodism since the 1740s. Hymns for evangelicals, I think, fill several functions. They fulfill a teaching function. They express what is important at any one time and era for evangelical Christians. Evangelicals do not, generally speaking, emphasize the sacraments of baptism and the Lord's supper. And so singing—something bodily—becomes quasi-sacramental in evangelical churches.

One of the constant features of evangelical history has been new music for new times. So at the end of the nineteenth century, there was a great quantity of what we now call Gospel music that was written. Fanny Crosby's hymnody was a very important addition to American and to worldwide Christian music. Her hymn "Rescue the Perishing, Care for the Dying" was an appeal to reach out to the new urban masses in America who were not as well churched as had been the case in earlier Protestant America. And now, in the last forty or fifty years, we've had a great boom of song—praise song, worship song, scripture songs.

I think some of them are fine. I think some of them are terrible. As a historian and a lover of hymnody, I worry that some of the older, very good hymns are simply being turned aside because they're not now fashionable, don't have a strong enough beat. But as a historian, it's obvious that at different times the music expresses new things. And evangelicals are among the first to jump on the bandwagon and use the new kinds of music.

Throughout evangelical history, the strength of evangelicals in adapting to cultural change has always been marked with a weakness in being able to adapt to cultural change. When a religious tradition adjusts to new conditions, there is always the chance of having a great appeal for that religious tradition, but there is also a chance that what had defined that religious tradition can be given away. An example would be that traditional evangelical preaching customarily accentuated the notion of human sinfulness. People were alienated from God. God was holy. Humans were sinful. God judged sin. Because God judged sin and provided redemption through Jesus, it was possible for people to be reconciled with God. In the modern world, we are more diffident about sin. We are more reluctant to point the finger and say, "You are a sinner who needs to turn to God." Some evangelical churches, traditions, denominations have adjusted an awful lot. Some critics say they have adjusted too much and have, in fact, lost the message of salvation, because they have lost the sense of human sinfulness.

It does seem to me that some evangelical groups do water down the content of the Christian Gospel in order to make an appeal. But I am reluctant to stand in judgment.

The Christian faith is always a faith that calls people away from themselves, *toward* God, but always attracts people because it offers something *from* God. It is the maintaining of that balance, of what God gives to Christian believers and then what God expects from Christian believers, that is the critical matter for all varieties of Christian faith.

One of the interesting aspects of evangelical history today is the awareness that what takes place in the United States is really now only a small part of what could be considered a broader evangelical history for the world. Tens of millions of Africans, tens of millions of Chinese, tens of millions of Latin Americans, both Catholic and Protestant, practice forms of the Christian faith that look pretty similar in many ways to what we define as evangelicalism for the United States. The way in which evangelicals in the United States interact with these evangelical-type groups around the world will, I think, be a very important factor in the future of world Christianity as well as just the future of evangelical Christianity.

I think evangelicals may still feel marginalized and as minority members in a hostile culture, in large part because of the national media and because of the national systems of higher education, which do tend to reflect less of the ordinary religious perspective of the country than actually exists on the ground. Television is not a particularly religious medium in the United States, even by comparison with some of the European countries, where there are far fewer religious practitioners. The movies are not a particularly strong domain for religious expression. The movies and television, and much of what is present in the popular national press have a local effect as these media come into localities. So it's entirely reasonable that a region where there is a strong evangelical presence may still feel put upon if the national media that they participate in, that they read, or have some awareness of do not reflect what they experience, day by day and week by week, on the ground.

The emphasis on personal experience has been a main feature of evangelical history since the mid-eighteenth century. Even though some of the early leaders of evangelicalism, like Jonathan Edwards and John Wesley, were first-rate intellectuals, they communicated a message that said that personal experience of God was a key matter. Always, however, when you stress personal experience, the risk is run that you, rather than God, will become the center of religion. Does this risk exist now? Yes. Has it existed before? Yes. Has God brought people through this risk before? Yes. Can he do it again? Yes. Will he? We don't know.

38.

The Inerrant, Infallible Word of God

The largest evangelical Protestant denomination by far—the largest of all Protestant denominations—is the Southern Baptist Convention, with more than sixteen million members. Its primary spokesman is Rev. Richard Land, president of its Ethics and Religious Liberty Commission. He spoke with Bob in 2002 about core Southern Baptist beliefs and about the successful campaign by church conservatives, in the 1970s and 1980s, to remove from leadership positions those who taught anything other than a literal understanding of the Bible.

The whole controversy was about one issue—one doctrine and one doctrine alone—and that was the infallibility and the authority of the word of God. There were a lot of attempts by people on the moderate and liberal side to confuse the issue, and the reason is quite simple. When polls were taken, they found that over 90 percent of Southern Baptists, when they were asked, "Do you believe the Bible is completely true?" said "Yes." And so there were attempts by those who didn't believe the Bible was completely true, who were teaching in our institutions and agencies, to confuse the issue and say it was a question of interpretation. It was not a question of interpretation. We have considerable latitude for different interpretations about what the Bible says, but we don't have any latitude for understandings about what the Bible is. It is the inerrant, infallible word of God. The issue was always about whether or not the word of God was completely true, or were we going to put question marks at the end of God's sentences, and were we going to practice dalmatian theology, which says the Bible is inspired in spots, and we're inspired to spot the spots.

Southern Baptists believe that Jesus Christ is the son of God. That he

235

came and died on the cross for our sins. That he was resurrected on the third day. That he is coming back to judge the quick and the dead. And that every human being needs to have a personal relationship with Jesus Christ. And we believe that the biblical forum for people who are converts to Christ is to worship in local churches that require baptism by immersion after a profession of faith. We believe that the Bible is absolutely true from cover to cover, and that as New Covenant or New Testament churches, our manual for faith and practice is to be the entire New Testament, from Matthew 1 through the end of the Book of Revelation.

The central focus of our churches, the central focus of our worship, the central focus of our lives is to come to the place where we personally understand that we are sinners, that we need to be saved from our sins, and that Jesus Christ died on the cross to pay that penalty, and that if we ask him to forgive us and we ask him to come into our hearts, that he will do so and he will forgive us, and he will live in our hearts forever. That's the born-again experience. We are born again from above. And it is absolutely critical and essential as the foundation of every Christian's life. Baptists have always believed that. We will always believe that. It is the central core of the Christian faith to personally profess Jesus Christ as Lord and Savior, and to trust him and him only for salvation.

In my own case, I had an overwhelming conviction as a six-year-old boy that I did things I shouldn't do and I said things I shouldn't say, and that as a result of that, it was necessary for Jesus to die on the cross, and that he loved me so much that he was willing to come and die on the cross for me and every other sinner as well. And so I asked him to forgive me. He says that he stands at the door of our heart and knocks, and if we'll open the door, he'll come in and fellowship with us, and he's promised that he will never leave us. And that happened to me.

And it happens to all of those who ask him to come into their hearts, because he is a keeper of his promises. And if we ask him to come into our hearts and we trust him and him only for salvation, he will come into our hearts and he will live there forever. He has promised that he will do that— not because of anything that is inherently good in us or anything that is inherently better in us than in anyone else. The only thing that a Christian can bring to his salvation is the sin from which he needs to be saved. And I can only tell you that it has been forty-nine years now since I made that decision, and there have been far too many times when I have not been all that he would have me be, but there has never been a single moment when he has not been everything that he promised he would be to me and more.

We as Baptists, of course, have had a longstanding tradition of soul liberty. We believe that no one—no government, no one—has the right to interfere with a person's personal relationship with God. It's too sacred to allow any mere person to interfere with it in a way that is compulsory or in a way that is forced or coercive. From Roger Williams and the Anabaptists right on down to the present day, we believe in soul liberty. That means we respect everyone's right to believe whatever they want to believe. But we also ask that they respect our right to believe what we believe. And to say to us that we shouldn't witness our faith when we believe that everyone needs to come to a personal relationship with Jesus Christ as their Lord and Savior means they don't respect our faith. Witnessing, evangelizing, sharing our faith is an act of love, and it is a command from our Lord and Savior, Jesus Christ. So to ask us, out of some misguided concept of respect, not to share our faith in a noncoercive, voluntary way with others, and saying if we do so is to disrespect their faith, means that they disrespect our faith, because part and parcel of our faith, part of its essence is sharing our faith with everyone we meet.

I think Southern Baptists increasingly understand that they are living in a culture that discriminates against evangelical Christians. It doesn't persecute them yet, but it does discriminate against them. It caricatures them. If you said the kinds of things about any other group that you say about evangelical Christians, you would be accused of rank prejudice. And I think that this has been a shock for many Southern Baptists who grew up in the culture friendly South, but the South has become far more like the rest of the country. You know, we now have a pretty homogenized culture so that the South, increasingly, and the Southwest are as hostile toward overt expressions of the Christian faith as any other part of the country.

Southern Baptists and Israel

It is the overwhelming belief of most Southern Baptists that God made promises to the Jewish people and that God does not make conditional covenants. And one promise was that the land of Israel was given to the Jews forever. So for most evangelicals, and certainly for Southern Baptist evangelicals, we believe that we, as a matter of faith, must support Israel's right to exist. In a very real sense the Bible Belt is Israel's safety belt.

We believe that God is a keeper of his promises, and if God promised that land to the Jews forever, he promised that land to the Jews forever. I get rousing amens every time I say from a Southern Baptist pulpit that the main reason God has blessed the United States of America to the extent that he has is because we have been in the West the least anti-Semitic nation, and that we recognized Israel in 1948, and that we have consistently supported Israel. God blesses those who bless the Jews.

39

The Genius of Evangelicalism

Randall Balmer is an evangelical, a historian, and a professor of American religion at Barnard College at Columbia University. Kim Lawton interviewed him in 2004.

———

One of the characteristics of being an evangelical is that you want to share your faith, or at least you feel you should share your faith or proselytize, bring others into the kingdom of heaven. And certainly that's warranted in the New Testament. My sense, however, over the last thirty, forty, even fifty years is that most evangelicals talk about doing that a great deal more than they actually do it. They tend to hire professionals to do it, so you have these large, particularly suburban churches, megachurches, or even churches that are not quite that large, that have a visitation pastor or an evangelicalism pastor on their staff as a way of fulfilling that part of what it means to be an evangelical.

There's not a whole lot of difference between proselytizing and evangelizing. I think that generally proselytizing has more of a pejorative connotation, and evangelicals talk about what they do as evangelism. They use the term "evangelism" more than "proselytization." Besides, it's easier to say.

Evangelism's always changing, and I think the genius of evangelicalism throughout American history is the way in which evangelicals have adapted to the cultural idiom, whatever that may be at any given time. In the eighteenth century you had George Whitfield coming with the Great Awakening, doing open-air preaching, very persuasive rhetoric; he was somebody who had been trained in the London theater, and so he understood the importance of dramatic pauses and contemporary settings. He could bring tears to your eyes simply by saying "Mesopotamia"—he was that riveting a preacher. In the nineteenth century you had the circuit riders;

later in the nineteenth century you had colporteurs who rode on the trading lines bringing Gospel tracts and Bibles to the western territories. In the twentieth century you had the great urban revivalists, beginning with Billy Sunday and later with Billy Graham and so forth. So evangelicals are always crafting their message and using the media with extraordinary success in order to bring their message to the masses. The suburban megachurch, of course, is the great paradigm, now, for evangelical adaptability to the larger culture.

In the case of Willow Creek,* they recognized that they were locating this new church in a suburban context. So they speak the language of the corporate culture all around them. In the mid 1970s, when Bill Hybels began the church, he did a door-to-door market research survey to find out why suburbanites were staying away from the church. He found they didn't like religious symbols—crosses and icons—anywhere in the church. The building itself looks like a corporate office park or even a suburban shopping mall with a food court.

Evangelicals understand that the message is what is important. The vehicle for communicating that message is quite pragmatic, and they're willing to try a lot of things. One of the reasons for the success of evangelicalism, if you compare it, say, for example, with mainline Protestantism, is that evangelicalism is always looking for novelty. It's looking for innovation, always looking for the latest edge in communicating to the larger public. In more tradition-bound religious movements, whether it's Presbyterianism or the Episcopal Church or something like that, you have liturgical rubrics, you have centuries or at least decades of tradition, and people are reluctant to countermand that tradition. Evangelicals have no problem with that.

The day for the popularity of hellfire and brimstone preaching probably is past. It was popular in the nineteenth century and the earlier part of the twentieth century when people really did have an innate sense that the world was a dangerous place, that there was eternal punishment. These days I don't think Americans feel that so acutely, so it's a message that doesn't resonate quite so clearly. Evangelicals have quite rightly emphasized the

---

* Located near Chicago, Willow Creek is considered one of the first megachurches.

grace of God rather than the anger and judgment of God, and I think that's what the Gospel is all about.

I think that fits in with the therapeutic culture that is all around us. We don't talk much about sin any longer in the culture, and you don't hear it much from evangelical pulpits. When I was growing up as an evangelical thirty, forty, almost fifty years ago, I heard a lot of hellfire and damnation sermons.

Pluralism is a huge challenge for evangelicals. Changes to the immigration laws beginning in 1965 suddenly changed the complexion, quite literally, of religion in America. Evangelicals were unprepared to compete in that marketplace in the way they had in the past. The response generated by that was, politically, the rise of the religious right, which effectively tried to turn back the clock, tried to reintroduce evangelical Christianity as a kind of hegemonic expression of faith for the entire culture rather than compete in that marketplace. I think that's a mistake. I think evangelicals need to understand how to compete within a religiously pluralistic environment.

The real danger for evangelicalism is in trying to impose its religious values on the larger society, whether it's posting the Ten Commandments in the Alabama judicial building or trying to prescribe some form of prayer in public schools. I think that is a mistake, because religion has flourished in this country precisely because the government has, for the most part, stayed out of the religion business. Once you begin to specify or to codify religious beliefs or behavior, I think you kill it.

The biggest challenge facing evangelicals is how to communicate their faith. What are the ground rules in a multicultural context? What is appropriate for me as an evangelical making faith claims for myself or for my tradition, listening to others, trying to find a balance in that dialogue that would do no violence to the other and allow the other to be heard, but at the same time representing my faith with integrity, as Jesus would? We're still struggling with that.

40

Who Is Winning—Evangelicals or American Culture?

Alan Wolfe is a sociologist who directs the Boisi Center for Religion and American Public Life at Boston College. He told correspondent Jeff Sheler in 2002 that he thinks evangelicals are neither as discriminated against as they think, nor as evangelistic as they claim.

We used to talk about evangelicals as if they were kind of a countercultural force, as if they were marginalized from society. But if the culture we're talking about is the popular culture, the culture of NASCAR racing and Grand Ole Opry and all the things that I see when I turn on cable television, then the influence of evangelicals is everywhere. There is a kind of emotionality to our culture that I think owes a great deal to evangelical forms of worship. There is a kind of populism to our culture that grows out of the way evangelicals structure their entire approach to religion.

Evangelicals, unlike fundamentalists—with whom they're often confused—are charged with a mission to go out and make converts. The Great Commission in the Bible speaks of this: make disciples of all nations. So evangelicals can't ignore the culture. Their whole religious sensibility is based upon meeting the culture halfway. At the same time, American culture—just like American religion—is an enormously powerful force. It will change religion, just as religion will change culture. One of my arguments really is that evangelicals often lose this battle. They're far more shaped by the culture than they are capable of shaping the culture to their own needs.

The whole megachurch phenomenon is premised upon the idea that we can't do anything with people unless we get them to church first, so the priority is to get them in there. But to get them in there, you downplay the

Christian symbolism, you take the crosses off the church, you make the pews as comfortable as you possibly can, you put McDonald's franchises in the lobby. Sometimes you don't even know you're in church when you go to church, because the church doesn't look like a church.

It's clear that that's what people want. If you're in the business of getting the people there, you've got to give them what they want. But it comes at a huge cost. They call themselves evangelical, but they're not strict, not demanding. Willow Creek, the most famous of our megachurches, doesn't even have a cross outside the building. It won't identify itself with any specific tradition. It wants to grow. And the way you grow is by trying to be all things to all people.

The job of an evangelical church is not to reach out to a guy like me. I'm the kind of person that loves Johann Sebastian Bach. When I think of church, I think of organs and Bach chorales. These are the first things that evangelicals throw out of their churches. Sometimes I'm asked, what's a megachurch? My one-sentence answer is, a megachurch is a church without an organ.

Whatever you want to call the old-time religion, it doesn't seem to be that much a presence in American life anymore. If you think that religion is what you saw if you watched the famous movie *Inherit the Wind*, with the born-again Christians out there demonstrating against the modern world, that's not what religion is anymore. Even among people who would call themselves conservative Christians, it's a very different way of understanding what faith is and what the Lord requires, and I think it influences all of America's religious traditions.

The individual just plays a much bigger role. It's not that God plays a smaller role, necessarily. That can vary from one tradition to another. But the idea that religion is going to be a set of commandments that are written in stone, for which obedience is sacrosanct, and there's going to be no questioning of what those commandments are—that's just not a realistic picture of where Americans are these days with respect to religion.

And Persecuted Evangelicals?

I think most Americans think that they're looked down upon by most Americans.

If you're a religious believer, you think that the whole world is organized by secular humanists and atheists who hate you. But if you're an atheist, you believe that the United States is dominated by Christian fundamentalists who hate you. We're such a complex country that anybody can find something that will make them feel marginalized and victimized. Religious believers, in that sense, are like everybody else. There's a kind of culture of complaint, as one writer called it. And being an evangelical doesn't excuse you from the culture of complaint.

Evangelicals really aren't that marginalized. Like everybody else, they worry about where they stand with respect to the markers of identity. So they look at the media, and they have a problem. That's such a classically American thing. All ethnic groups—for example, Italian Americans, Jewish Americans, Irish Americans—would say, "We haven't been accepted by the media yet." And they'd complain, and they register letters. Then, before you know it, they've got television programs. Then they feel that they belong. I think we're witnessing much of that same kind of phenomenon here.

Because of a sympathy effect—in other words, because people want other people to believe that they're going to church—there is a tendency for people to exaggerate how often they go to church. The same kind of effect can be seen in other poll questions. I think evangelicals think they play fewer video games and watch less violent television than they actually do. On some statistics, like out-of-wedlock births or rates of divorce, evangelicals really aren't all that different from nonevangelicals. This is a finding of pollster George Barna, who works for the evangelical community. He finds this over and over and over again.

I don't see that explicitly proselytizing, witnessing, heavy-duty evangelization has much of an impact. This is America. You've got to let people find their own way. And the way evangelicals generally do this is to say, "I'm going to do sort of a lifestyle form of evangelicalism. I'm going to lead a good life. Then I'll shine and I'll have this glow and people will see it and they'll ask me about it. Then I can tell them about Jesus." But the notion that you go up and ring doorbells, which Jehovah's Witnesses do and Mormons do—that's not what most evangelicals do in America. It just doesn't work.

41.

God Is Not Going to Whomp You

Through most of U.S. history, the Protestant mainline was the country's religious establishment. It included among its members the leaders of American business and government, and its ideas influenced all of American life. But beginning in the late 1960s, for more than twenty years, the mainline lost millions of members. In some denominations the number of people fell by a third before the hemorrhaging stopped. In 2006 Bob spoke with historian of religion Martin Marty about the mainline and its problems, and about what American Protestants believe.

The easiest way to [say what Protestants believe] is with a little chart: God on top. God comes through Christ, revealed through the scriptures. All Protestants believe in God. All of them believe God reaches us through Christ. All of them somehow relate to the scriptures. And they believe that God's basic action to us is undeserved grace.

The central idea of Protestantism is a gracious God. And that means that God is not going to whomp you, not going to devastate you. There is a strong sense that you can be forgiven and can start over. I think all the religions know they can't get anywhere just with hellfire and damnation and a punishing God. Grace, grace, grace.

Mainliners may be very serious about works, as their ancestors the Puritans were. But they wallow in the concept that, essentially, God is a gracious God.

The second common feature is that the main authority is always the Bible. But whereas the people to their right, who have come to be called fundamentalists or pentecostals or evangelicals, tend to draw boundaries, have very clear definitions, like to speak in absolutes, and have everything solved, the mainline has always encouraged people to come with a sense of questioning, with a sense of seeking authority but not thinking they've finally found it. They want to come to a place where the serious questions get asked, but you don't get pushed into a certain conformity. I guess I would use the adjective "open." They are very insulted if you suggest they're less Christian than other Christians. They're very insulted if you think they all think "anything goes."

Mainliners are porous, with gaps in their boundaries. Most people who are in the mainline would say, "Yes, we believe these things, maybe somewhat differently. But we don't think that we're compromising. We think that's the nature of reality. The Bible is full of inner contradictions. Read the Book of Job, read the Psalms."

The delight of being a Calvinist or a Lutheran or an Anglican today is that you are responsive to tradition, but when you go back to the foreparents, you find that however emphatic they were about what they believed, they also were setting you up for a form of Christianity which has a great level of personal responsibility. The confessions of the church—the thirty-nine articles in Anglicanism, the Augsburg Confession, the Lutheran Catechisms, and so on—are not so much saying, "This is what you have to believe to belong to us in the mainline." Rather, they are saying, "These are the things we believe and we're exuberant about. We're running up a flag and seeing who salutes. And if that's not where you are and you move on, we wish you'd stick around, but we're not going to condemn you to hell for having moved on."

In the sixteenth century most of the antecedents to the mainline churches began proclaiming the priesthood of all believers. What they meant by that was that all believers have equal standing before God. There is no pope or hierarchy closer to God than all members. In the Catholic church of their day you couldn't have anything important happening if a priest weren't there. In that concept the priest is supposed to be a channel between a human and God, but he could also be a barrier or a block. So we like to say all humans are priests, but I prefer words like "the ministry of all the baptized."

Individual responsibility does not mean you make everything up as you go along. Mainline Protestants are very conscious of the fact that they are supposed to be a community, that they are, somehow, the body of Christ.* They have more difficulty getting that across in a day when we all choose our church as opposed to inheriting our church. But still it comes out pretty strongly.

Freedom in the eighteenth century in the United States was not what people think it is today. What you needed freedom for in the eighteenth century was to be a responsible citizen. If you didn't have freedom, you couldn't do that. So the concept of individual freedom in Protestantism is not that you can do anything you want, make up anything you want. Basically, you need freedom in order to come to the kind of decision that makes you a responsible member of the body of Christ.

The division in the nineteenth century that became drastic in the early twentieth was [between social and personal ethics]. One set of Christians said that the gospel of Christ and the mandate to care affect all society, and this means all of the powers: economic power, education power, entertainment power, political power. All these powers can organize themselves in such a way that they make victims of people, and therefore they have to be confronted. The itch the mainliners have had was to say, "If we want to bring freedom to South Africans, we've got to kill off the structures which are holding them down. Let's deal with church investments that do business there."

On the other hand, the main interest of the antecedents of today's evangelicals was in personal ethics, those things you could change if you as an individual were converted. In the nineteenth century, this meant opposition to dueling, to shopping on Sundays, to drinking. The assumption was if you could get a woman out of prostitution, then that problem would be solved by at least one. The evangelicals used to say if you didn't have an abortion, if you didn't practice birth control, if you didn't shop on Sunday, that's [enough]. It wasn't your business to move out further.

There is great suspicion of ideology in the modern world. That is, we have known fascism, communism, all the other isms. And people are sus-

---

* "The body of Christ" refers to all baptized Christians.

picious of dogma, doctrine, stipulated rules. It does not mean they disagree with them. It's just that they aren't so moved by them. They are moved by story. All over the world Protestants are moved by the stories of Jesus. The good Samaritan. The prodigal son. But they don't only want to hear that two thousand years ago interesting things happened. They want to experience it now. And I think they share with almost all people in the world today that impulse to have experience. The evangelical sector has surged in impact because they minister so much to the theme of experience and then you have to tell somebody else about it.

I think another reason for the relative decline in the mainline would be recruitment. Mainline churches for 150 years have been a little embarrassed at the notion of knocking on somebody's door or handing out tracts at the airport. This isn't done.

I think what happened was that almost all the churches I've mentioned as part of the mainline just assumed that their children would follow them in the faith, and they didn't. Right up until the 1920s, 1930s, and 1940s, if you were Methodist, your kids were Methodist unless they married somebody who wasn't and changed. Then all of a sudden radical choice came in, and the mainline wasn't equipped to whip into action and learn this style. Whereas the evangelicals and pentecostals had the understanding that if they didn't convert their own children, they wouldn't have a church tomorrow. And if you didn't convert your neighbors, there wouldn't be a church tomorrow. I think the mainline never really learned that. They thought they were well set, and they kind of settled back and didn't hit personal experience nearly as much as others. So when membership in a church became a matter of choice, when it became a market, when you picked and chose, these groups sort of said, "We're the traditional, we're the aristocrats, you come to us and we'll put you to work. You come to us and we'll give you a good message and good music. You come to us and we'll give you good fellowship. But we're not going out to the highways and byways to get you."

Most mainline churches have not bought into pop culture. They don't come in and say, "Hiya, folks. I've got my Hawaiian shirt on. Jesus is our buddy." In other words, the chummy relationship. At its best, the mainline will have a choir march in, sedately, then a big organ blast. This is a time when I am prostrate, not because I have no inner dignity, but because in order to express my inner dignity I have to know that I have faced the [divine] Other. If you look at the grand hymns of the tradition, and the mainline preserves them, all is grounded in some sense of keeping you in your dignity but saying God has to confront you and restore you and move you into something else.

I think the mainline also suffers from the fact that, as one sociologist said to us one time, "You won." That is, so much of what mainline Protestantism stood for became a part of the larger culture.

When you go back to the founders of the nation, they were reasonable sons of the Enlightenment. But they were all Episcopalian, Presbyterian, Congregational, and so on. And that got so stamped in our culture. And with all that as a head start, they could bond with the environment, they could shape it. They helped pass its laws, they helped found it in the constitutional era, they helped give impulse to its business. When modern industry came along, Protestants were running the show. And it got so fused with the environment that you don't have to be Protestant to seem Protestant. No matter who comes to America they take on that style.

The slaves, what did they do? They became Protestant with their own stamp on churches called Methodist and Baptist. When some Asians come they remain Buddhists, but they call it Buddhist Church. If I go to Honolulu, I go to a Buddhist church. That's an oxymoron in Japan, but it has pews, it has an organ, it has envelopes for offerings, it has charity drives. It looks just like the Presbyterians down the block.

To my knowledge, no one called the mainline the "mainline" until the second half of the twentieth century, even though their ancestors have been on this continent since 1607 at Jamestown. Now and then some individual would use a term like "Standard Brand Denominations," and for a while people talked about "Mainstream." But the word "mainline" really got invented when it became apparent that they and their old kin, who they called evangelicals, were coming somewhat further apart. I think the name was born at the same time that the word "WASP" was invented—"White Anglo Saxon Protestant." To a lot of people that was used negatively and pejoratively, as was the word "fundamentalism."

Protestantism with a capital *P* has no constituency anymore at all. There are almost no organizations in the phone book that are called Protestant. There are very few ways you can offend someone by calling them Protestant. There's no banner that people are going to come up and fight for. How do you insult Protestantism as such? That would be a very hard thing to do. It doesn't have a single national profile any longer. For one thing, it used to get its profile because it was anti-Catholic. And it isn't that anymore. So it is in the individual local churches—that's where the pulse is. That's where the vitality is. The mainline is healthy in many tens of thousands of local bases.

People in the mainline would like to have a sense that people in the year 400 were thinking about the same things we are, and not all the illustrations have to come from cable TV, or MTV, or anything like that. We won't mind if now and then you quote Calvin, or Pascal, or St. Teresa, or Augustine.

Augustine nailed it when he said, "Thou hast made us for Thyself, and our hearts are restless until they find their rest in Thee."

If you go to church and hear two lines like that, you're off and running.

In a 1998 interview for Religion & Ethics Newsweekly *and* The Newshour with Jim Lehrer, *Associated Press religion writer Richard Ostling, then of* Time *magazine, asked Marty about the unique characteristics of being Lutheran. Marty is an ordained minister in the Evangelical Lutheran Church in America, which is, despite its name, part of the traditional Protestant mainline.*

Martin Luther is believed to have said that God carves the rotten wood, God rides the lame horse. That is, the Lutheran vision is very nonutopian. There is not what Paul Tillich called a "metaphysic of progress." We don't believe that behind the scenes of the human drama every day and every way the human race is getting better.

The Lutheran vision also says you have to be content with the buttocks of God, the hind parts of God. That is, you don't believe that by your studies you can climb up into some transcendent realm. You are always caught in the drama of normal human history. That's somewhat different from the standard American vision in which there had long been a belief that we would progress and bring in the kingdom.

In our tradition, Luther is quoted as having said, "If the world were to end tomorrow and they would tell me that, I would still plant my apple tree today." That is, each day has an intrinsic value that you invest. There's no guilt left from yesterday, there's not supposed to be worry about tomorrow, and you plant the apple tree today.

42.

Vital Signs

Diana Butler Bass, a scholar and author, spent three years studying fifty healthy mainline congregations to find out what they are doing right. Her findings are in her book Christianity for the Rest of Us. *Bass spoke with Bob in 2006 about the vitality of the individual churches she attended and about how moving it was for her to worship in those congregations.*

One reason for the mainline decline was mobility, and people leaving the towns and cities in which they grew up, mostly in the north and east, and moving south and west, and when folks move their religion typically changes. So if you move to Georgia and are looking for a good church, you're as likely to end up being a Southern Baptist as you are to stay in the mainline.

Some people blame the decline on liberalism, saying that by the time you get into the mid-1960s the leaders of most of these denominations had become so theologically liberal and so politically liberal that they lost touch with their constituencies.

I actually think that it's related to the fact that these churches had really hitched their wagon to middle-class, mostly white, postwar culture—the privileged culture. And that was a culture that was being questioned and criticized by the civil rights movement, by the feminist movement, and by confusion over the Vietnam War. And when that culture dissolved, mainliners had no idea how to voice their theologies and how to do their work. There was a whole generation of spiritual seekers coming of age and wanting spiritual experiences, and the mainline had nothing to offer them. I think it surprised the heck out of church leaders that their once-dominant message didn't resonate with the longings of the new group. It caused a lot of self-doubt.

And then, when birth control was more widely available, mainline women were more likely to have fewer children, and when the birth rates started dropping off mainliners could not replace themselves.

Also part of that culture in the postwar period was privatized religion. People were taught that it was impolite to talk about their faith in public. So there wasn't a lot of talk in the 1950s and the early 1960s about personal religious experience or transformative religious experience. There wasn't an emphasis on teaching people how to pray or an emphasis on personal Bible study, and they really did lose a kind of spiritual energy and spiritual vision.

The mainline today is troubled, certainly. Most people are over sixty, and the typical mainline congregation would have around 100 or 150 people in it. They tend to use more old-fashioned music, they tend to be fairly cerebral. They're not very experiential, and what's really sad, of course, is that that kind of stuff feeds on itself. If a new person walks in the door and experiences a church like that, they're going to think, "Well why should I join a community like that? It seems they're disheartened, there's not a lot of energy here, there's certainly not a lot of vision. What's in it for me spiritually?"

My job for the last three years has been to go out and look for examples of vital and growing mainline churches. I studied fifty congregations across all of the mainline denominations in all different regions of the country. And every congregation was a growing congregation. They were not churches where you find a sort of spiritual boredom. They were churches where you walk in the door, and you could sort of sense that something dynamic was going on. People were alive and offering hospitality and had a sense of mission, real spiritual passion. They were congregations where there was a purposeful embrace of Christianity and spiritual practices. So they paid attention to things like prayer, theological reflection, offering hospitality, Christian formation, the practices of worship, and they put a lot of thought and energy not only into doing those things in community, but also into teaching one another.

And so they had created communities where people were on a journey of learning about the Christian life together. They really understood Christianity not as a set of abstract doctrines or creedal statements that you have to sign your name to in order to get into heaven, but they understood Christianity as a way of life that offers people meaning in the world.

Sometimes when I am sitting around in a room somewhere with leaders who are saying, "What are we going to do with our church?" I think to myself, "It's not really rocket science. What does it mean to be the church? It means to be the people of God on a journey to God, and enacting God's justice, and learning and teaching one another along that way." How does that happen in a contemporary setting and in this cultural setting? These churches that I studied, these vital congregations, had all figured out a way to do that.

Almost to a person, people would testify that being in a mainline church was a different kind of spiritual experience for them. It was the place where they could go where they didn't have to park their brains at the door. They talked about a connection between their minds and their hearts and their hands, where they could think about God, they could ask questions, they could experience God, and where they could actually enact what they think is God's dream for the world in serving the poor or taking care of homeless people or whatever the mission of the church was.

And I heard in their stories an amazing cultural need for communities that are open Christian communities, not closed ones. There are Americans who are not looking for certainty, but rather they are looking for an open spiritual community in which they can ask their questions. We heard that over and over again: "This is a Christian community where I can ask questions, where I can still have doubts, where I can explore a variety of answers, and yet God is still present here, and I feel it."

I think as a researcher I was a little surprised at the strong reaction I had to all of the congregations I visited. I felt connected in a way that I don't in any other part of my life. People feel very fragmented, and even folks who are very faithful churchgoers and good Christians all their lives can say there is a kind of meaninglessness in the larger world, and they are not quite sure where they belong or how they fit, and their lives feel splintered.

I feel this, too. I feel this constant pressure in my life, a sense of chaos that I feel I'm always hovering close to. And when I go into a congregation and I experience the worship life as these churches do it, I begin to move away from that chaos into a deep sense of connectedness. I begin to see and feel and experience connections that I don't give myself room to experience in the rest of my life internally, and I feel more connected to the people around me.

I can't even begin to say how many times I have been in church, and I'll be sitting there with my family and my heart will sort of melt, and I'll realize that I have not been as intimately connected with my family and as gracious as I should be. So I begin to experience my family and my neighbors in a new way.

And then from that I begin to think about God. And that worship service is the one place where I have an hour and a half during the week that I am focused on what it means to be a Christian, and who God is, and how my relationship with God has an impact on the rest of my life. And so I move to this place that I do not have in the regular bits of my life, and I move there not by myself.

I really do not think it is possible to be a Christian without that larger community because as I get connected with God and myself internally, I am sitting there in a room where a hundred or two hundred or five hundred other people are doing the same thing. And in that movement of the community toward God there is something that happens that is very transcendent, and it becomes not just about me and my fragmented life, but it begins to be something about us, about being a community of people who are in this together. I understand that God has not just created us as individuals so we can go to church to feel better. God is creating a community of people who are on a journey together so that they can really move out into the world and enact their callings, their vocations, their jobs, their careers in ways that are transformative and that enlarge God's dream of peace and justice for all humanity.

So for me that's what happens in worship. Those connections begin to get stitched again for me, they are deepened and reinforced, and to experience that as a community calls me out of the spiritual navel gazing and self-centeredness that can happen if you are there just to feel better about yourself.

In this culture, where you have a lot of people talking about spirituality and their spiritual journeys, it's very easy for that to become a kind of self-centered quest. You know, you go and get your spiritual high, and then everything is sort of fixed for you.

But it takes it to the next level to be part of a community that is experiencing God, because it's not just about me, it's really about the world. And these churches I studied were able to move from deep practices, like centering prayer and personal Bible study, through corporate worship out to doing and enacting mercy and compassion and justice in the larger public square. Mainline congregations have cared for a long time about justice. And now what they seem to be doing is taking that vision of doing social activism and justice and really knitting it to some of the deepest, most intimate parts of a person's spiritual life, and saying this is all of a piece.

I think the future of the mainline could be pretty good. I have friends who are rabbis who are interested in synagogue renewal, and one of them said to me once that they wanted to create communities where people could have an authentically Jewish experience. And I thought that was one of the clearest ways of expressing hope for congregations in the future. I think that needs to be the vision of these mainline churches as well—a sacred community where people can have an authentically Christian experience.

43.

Safe Harbors and Defiant Spirituality

Robert Franklin is President of Morehouse College in Atlanta, and he wrote about challenges facing the African-American church in his 2007 book, Crisis in the Village. *An ordained minister of the African Methodist Episcopal Church, he spoke with Bob in 2006.*

I like to refer to the African-American church as the safest place on earth, and I say that because black churches have always served as houses of refuge, of safety. They were safe harbors over history for people who faced uncertain social environments where there was a constant threat of being apprehended or brutalized. Certainly during slavery and then afterward, when African-Americans often faced harassment, when Sunday came, they could finally make it to the church, a safe harbor. So there's that sense of basic personal security, a place where one can finally exhale from the rigors and the traffic of a busy week.

Another phrase that comes to mind as I think about walking in and being seated, and looking around and listening to the music begin, and having this sense of a collective experience with the holy, is the phrase "together again."

Each week, there's that sense of our effort in the worship service to transcend our individualism and transcend the fragmentation that we experience, and that I think is really the norm in contemporary American culture. So the church becomes a kind of community for bonding people, reconnecting people. And then another important dimension of this for me is not just the sort of contemporary sense of being together with others, but the historical glimpses I experience whenever I'm seated in a black church, whether it's with fifty people or five thousand, a sense of the church itself as something of a miracle when we look at American history. It is a kind of defiant response to institutional racism in the society because it says that despite the way society tried to define blacks, we are a people of dignity, of unity, of culture, and we are able to celebrate that and celebrate the God that has enabled our journey. So there's that sense of the historical memories that creep in and haunt every black church service for me.

In a way the black church has a sense of a left-hand and right-hand strategy. On one hand, there is this need for a safe harbor, a core where we maintain and preserve tradition, and I think that this gives rise to a rather conservative cast to much of black culture, certainly with respect to family values, personal morality, and outlook on the world. Again, in a world of tremendous uncertainty and dynamic change, there's this quest to preserve some place that is relatively stable. The theologian Lovett Weems uses a wonderful definition of leadership in our time as "stability in motion," and I think that captures part of what's happening in black churches as they maintain stability on one hand, but on the other hand there is a sense of a need to bring the power of a liberating Gospel into an immoral society, and hence there is a need to change. You can't simply accept or accommodate the status quo when it is unjust. And so there has always been alongside this fairly conservative liturgical, congregational, ethical culture, an openness to innovation and social change, a defiant spirituality.

I think we can't find a better example of this than in Montgomery, Alabama, in the life of Martin Luther King Jr. at the Dexter Avenue Baptist Church in the mid-1950s. I mean, think about this. Here is this young pastor in a congregation that is relatively middle class, kind of a black bourgeois congregation. Many of the members of the church were professors at the local Alabama State University, and he was preaching sermons and nurturing the congregation when Rosa Parks and the movement sort of invaded his life, and what's remarkable to me is how Dr. King found another voice. I don't think it changed. He continued to preach those fairly dry intellectual sermons on Sundays. But when he addressed those mass movements, he realized that he was a poet of the people. He had to speak to the sorrow and the aspirations of the people, and another voice emerged. And so there is that tension, and I think we see it in King's own life: the pastor of a conservative, traditional, black Baptist congregation, at the same time leading a movement to transform American democracy and dismantle legalized segregation.

What I like to call the "rich cultural ecology" of black churches is one of America's great international exports to the world. I mean, everyone loves black gospel music. And then there are the musical genres that emerged from black gospel, and even before black gospel, the black spirituals, the work songs, the famous glee clubs of Fisk University and Morehouse, places like that. So there's this rich musical tradition, and here again the point is valid, I think, that there is an effort both to preserve the best of the song tradition of the past, but also to engage in a bit of experimentation, and so gospel emerges as a break with the spiritual tradition of the past and the hymnals, and we see today in gospel rap and gospel hip-hop continued innovation. Of course jazz and Motown and other musical traditions emerged from black church culture. But other parts of that rich ecology, of course, include something I've described as the full sensory-engaging worship service, where there's a lot of foot tapping and clapping and backslapping and hugging and the visual stimulation of colorful choir robes and movement. So worship should engage all of the senses. Another dimension is that of the cathartic prayer, the altar prayer that happens in most black congregations. A single voice articulates the woes and aspirations of the people to God, but everyone sort of gathers, and the moves, the moans that are a part of that prayer are important.

And then, of course, last but not least, one has to talk about the power of the prophetic pulpit and the role of preaching in black culture, interpreting events of the world but doing that in light of the biblical story. I think of a sermon that I once heard as a younger person about The Exodus and how God sort of stepped into history to accompany the people out of bondage, out of slavery and move them toward freedom. And for some reason, as a teenager hearing that sermon, being together with all those people, it was just a powerful kind of shift for me. I had a greater sense of participating in the Christian story, in the black American historical experience. And I think it had to happen in a communal, worshipful context. I'd read the story hundreds of times, but it all sort of came together with my own emotional response of feeling the awe of God acting in history, feeling the pain of the people who had been enslaved for so long suddenly beginning to see the promised land ahead, moving forward. I was just overcome with tears and a new sense of commitment to that struggle. And that was a dramatic worship moment for me. It really deepened my Christian commitment and faith.

I think there's a reaction to the derailment of that prophetic preaching tradition by the prosperity gospel movement.* People are trying to preserve the prophetic, preached word that transforms people's lives, but also transforms social institutions and policies. So it becomes a kind of public preaching, a public theology. At the same time, you're doing this work of social analysis within the context of the sermon, naming social evils, naming the demons, and there's this effort to employ language that is poetic and evocative, that reaches deep into people's imaginations. I think that's the artistry that we see in many of the great black pulpits today. I think the great preaching tradition of Martin Luther King and Howard Thurman and Adam Clayton Powell and Benjamin Mays and so many others of the past may have planted seeds that have been dormant for a while but are now flourishing.

It's always a challenge generalizing, but what I see is real hope with respect to the pipeline of leadership. I think in contrast to the white mainline churches, where there's a real challenge in recruiting, preparing, and placing younger and intellectually astute religious leaders, black churches are doing pretty well there. I mean, in some of the larger churches there are a dozen younger ministers in apprenticeships learning from the senior pastor, anxious to go on to college, to seminary, and to serve their own congregations. A lot of energy, a lot of imagination. I worry a bit about some of those young clergy who are influenced by ministers who focus on the gospel of individual piety and prosperity, and that's a tension in black church culture today. In fact, I think the greatest single threat now is this prosperity movement that is inviting the assimilation of so many younger black clergy.

---

* The controversial, but often popular, claim that being a faithful Christian will bring worldly success.

Another issue confronting black churches: some of the large megachurches are paying more attention to mentoring young males. Black churches are largely populated by black women, and many of them are single mothers or primary caregivers with children, and a lot of them have sons. And you can see almost on a monthly basis the frustrations of black church women over the relative absence of men in their children's lives. We all know about the phenomenon of "father absence" throughout the culture and certainly in African-American communities. And these women come to church hoping that they will encounter positive role models for their sons, and that happens. What used to be fairly accidental has become very intentional, so we are now asking men in the church, deacons and others, to become mentors, to gather these young men up, take them away for weekend retreats. That's very exciting work, because our society, secular nonprofits, and government are all struggling with what we do with young men who don't feel that they've been integrated into the society. There are higher rates of incarceration for these young men. They make bad choices, but black churches are stepping up in a really exciting way.

The other side of that is the reentry into the community of the young men who've been in prison. Everywhere I go and I talk about this issue, the room is packed with people saying, "We don't know how to do prisoner reentry. Help us think about this." And so there are some good and encouraging things on the scene there.

I think the one big issue that continues to be a fault line in black church culture is the issue of gender and how the church provides equal opportunities for women in ministry and in decision making. I think we're making important strides, but there's still a lot of work to be done.

44.

The Miracle of Existence

Blu Greenberg is an author who has published widely on subjects ranging from feminism and the Jewish family to Orthodox Judaism and interfaith dialogue. In the late summer of 2006, Bill interviewed her in her warm and welcoming home in the Riverdale section of Bronx, New York, where she and her husband, Rabbi Irving Greenberg, raised five children in a purposefully observant house- hold. Her living room was decorated with family photos, including those of her nineteen grandchildren, and stacked on coffee tables were oversized books with titles such as The Jews of Cracow *(a variant spelling of "Krakow") and* Mapping the Human Journey. *Bill asked her about the Jewish map of the human journey and about her personal journey as a Jew—which has very much to do with how she spends her Friday nights.*

I would say the Jewish map of the human journey begins with the covenant, with the Torah, which is the story, the history of what brought the Jewish people to this day, to this place, and many places. I see myself connected all the way back.

Beyond my great-grandparents, I don't know where my ancestors came from, other than that they descended from those Jews who stood at Sinai. And the Jews standing at Sinai descended from Abraham. Since there weren't many conversions into Judaism all along the way of Jewish history, the likelihood that I'm a direct descendant of Abraham and Sarah is quite high. But even if that's not literally so, it's close enough to the mark for me to consider my ancestral roots going back well over four thousand years to Abraham and Sarah.

That is the sense of Jewish *peoplehood*, which is a very powerful force in my life. Because of our history as a minority, as such a small people who made it this far, I have a sense that miracles are possible. And I've observed a few in my lifetime.

Just yesterday, I was telling a friend of one miracle I witnessed. I was talking about the Scud missiles that Iraq fired into Israel in the early 1990s. A Scud is a huge, heavy multithousand-pound bomb. These Scuds landed in the heart of Tel Aviv and didn't kill anyone. I interpret that as nothing short of a miracle.

Then there's the ingathering of the exiles, the whole historical movement of Jews back to Israel, even the return of the Ethiopian Jews to Israel. You can walk on a street in Jerusalem or Tel Aviv and see people from every part of the world.

And to see the renaissance of Jewish life in the former Soviet Union is part of what we call *techiyat hametim*, the revival or restoration of life. It's one of the blessings we say every day, when we pray to "the God who restores life, resurrects the dead."

But, as I said, the Jewish journey begins with the Torah, which is the sum total of religious behavior and ethical behavior. That includes the interpretations by the rabbis, who carry the "chain of authority." Without undue modesty, I think I would be an ethical person even if I weren't an Orthodox Jew, but a good part of my behavior is guided by my tradition, the whole notion that you're put here on earth to do some good, to improve the world, to repair the world, to make a difference. That is one of the most powerful teachings of Judaism.

It's something we're taught at a very young age, so it becomes a natural part of your life. You don't have to keep asking, "What's my mission in life?" You simply go through life with that understanding. Life is not just for your pleasure, although it is also for your pleasure. Life is a responsibility.

What is my perception of God? I'm not sure. But when I make comments about that to Yitz,* he says I have a primitive sense of God. On the one hand, I see God as a source of miracles, of all good things on earth. But I also see

---

* Rabbi Irving "Yitz" Greenberg, Blu's husband, whose reflections on evil and suffering in light of the *Shoah*, the Holocaust, appear in chapter 2.

God as the God of the *Shoah*, and I'm not satisfied with any of the explanations of the Holocaust given by theologians—including my husband. So I'm left with that struggle. If you play that out on a larger canvas, it is the old question of good and evil in the universe. I haven't resolved the "evil" part.

I believe there is a God in the universe, and I have my quarrels and my gratitude. That's where I am. I'm probably less pious than I once was. I'd like to be more certain in a number of ways, but that certainty wasn't given to me. I still have to say that for me God does very much operate in this world, which is why I have my questions. There are many times when I feel like the man in the Yiddish joke who complains, "God is running this world, but not like a *mensch*."*

On the other hand, I have to say that the promise to Abraham that the Jewish people would last forever is the most powerful proof of God's existence, because by all logic, by all historical reasoning and happenstance, the Jewish people should have disappeared a long time ago. Ninety-nine percent of the nations, the peoples and races and religions of ancient times disappeared from the face of the earth a long time ago. Not only have the Jews made it, but they've also made an incredible contribution to the world.

So for me, it's been a long journey—which has also taken me deeply into a feminist critique of the tradition. But I've remained as I always was, a faithful and loving Orthodox Jew.

Thank God It's Shabbat

Jewish ritual is wonderful, and I think the most important part of that is Shabbat,† which is the most important part of my life as a Jew, aside from the ethical content of Judaism. Shabbat has an impact not only on my identity as a Jew, not only on the way that I received the tradition from my parents and the way my husband and I have transmitted these values to our children, but also on the very way my family's life has been organized. Shabbat has truly been an orienting force in my life.

---

* A Yiddish word usually taken to mean "a great guy."
† Hebrew for Sabbath. The Shabbat observance begins at dusk on Friday and ends at nightfall on Saturday.

I should say that being an observant Jew means, first, that you observe the ethical laws of the Torah. I should say this because unfortunately there are some who feel that only the ritual defines you as a religious person. It's like the saying—"I see ye pray in church on Sunday and *prey* on people all week long." I know some Jews who are more ritually observant than others, but I would not consider them ethical people.

So the ethical teaching is primary, but certainly in the ritual area, Shabbat is far and away the most significant aspect of my life as a Jew. And there are so many different aspects of Shabbat. First of all, there's the Shabbat ambience, the preparation of meals, the household, the dress. It's all about creating family time, home time, community time.

You simply carve it out. I am not a workaholic, but I love my work. I'd be very comfortable working right through Friday and Saturday. It wouldn't bother me in the least. I think I wouldn't feel deprived at all if I didn't have a specific, formal day of rest. But having it as a gift to me from my tradition, I realize how much I need it and benefit from it.

The Shabbat family meal is the equivalent of having a Thanksgiving dinner every week. It's like having a dinner party every week, really two dinner parties—Friday night and lunch on Saturday. Typically, we have company and extended family. You sit for two or three hours at a table, just being together, talking and learning about life from each other. At one point I decided if we could sit through Friday night and nobody feels a need to go off and do something else or talk on the phone or watch television, why can't we do this during the weekdays, too?

So I told the kids no answering of telephones at mealtimes during the week. At first, I remember J.J. came up with every imaginable emergency at the other end of the ringing line. But actually he, too, got used to it, and the children all grew to like it. Soon, they didn't like anyone interrupting dinner with a telephone call.

That was one way of taking a bit of Shabbat into the weekday. Plus, we always had company, and the kids learned to meet all different kinds of people, including people who were not Orthodox or Jewish, sitting with them and talking to them in an intimate way. That wasn't their universe. We lived in an Orthodox community. Our children went to an Orthodox school and had Orthodox friends and neighbors and so forth. So in a sense, that most intimate Jewish experience—Shabbat—provided our kids with an opportunity to experience a broader spectrum of Jewish and non-Jewish life.

The rituals of the Shabbat are strong and binding for creating family life, extending your friendship group, bringing you into contact with community—things you don't do if you just inhabit the workaday world. Doing this week in and week out does shape your life.

It anchors you in a particular way as a human being connected to other human beings. You don't have a sense of isolation or anomie. And since you have to be present, you can't be in a bad mood, which doesn't mean you have to be cheerful every single Shabbat of your life. I've been grouchy plenty of times during Shabbat. I've felt that I'm working too hard and nobody is helping me or that I had to ask too many times for help. You don't have to be cheerful and smiley, but on balance, you do have to be a sociable human being.

We bless our children every Friday night, and now we bless our grandchildren. On some Friday nights when my kids were teenagers, the last thing in the world I felt like doing was giving them a blessing. But they came to expect the ritual, even when they didn't want to hear your voice or see your face.

We sing Sabbath table songs—*zemirot* is the Hebrew word. Some of these *zemirot* are 400, 500, 600 years old. They're part of the Sabbath tradition. When our kids were teenagers, they used to bring their friends home for Shabbat dinner, and sometimes they would talk while we were singing, make jokes, or do things they knew would get my goat. And I would glare or say, "Come on, guys." But I had a secret, which I would say to myself—"Oh, am I lucky! Blessed is the mother whose teenagers think that their adolescent rebellion is expressed in not singing *zemirot* instead of smoking pot on the corner."

You knew you had to come to the table dressed. You had to be ready for the Sabbath in your nice clothes. You had to get to the synagogue on time—well, that one we didn't do so well. And because we observe all the kosher laws, you had to be mindful when you were out, mindful of what you were eating, because you are part of this larger entity or unit, this Jewish family and the Jewish people.

All of our children have recreated these rituals in their own homes, which is something I always wanted to see. This doesn't mean they wouldn't have been wonderful human beings choosing something else, but I'm sure happy they chose this path.

On Shabbat, you celebrate what you have, and you take for granted life and health. The High Holidays—Rosh Hashanah and Yom Kippur—are very different. They're about turning yourself around, reexamining your life. They're about the deeper questions of life.

J.J. died two days before Yom Kippur.* Because we couldn't travel on Shabbat,† we couldn't get to Israel immediately. We were here for Yom Kippur, and I went to the synagogue that day, still in a state of shock.

I had never realized before then how many times the word "life" appears in the liturgy. So even though I didn't understand by then what had happened to J.J., I understood on some level that this was about life and death. In the past, it hadn't been the most powerful theme for me because I simply took life for granted. Of course, I knew that everyone was eventually going to die, like my father who died at ninety-one. I grieved over that. I was very close to my father. But it was natural. Everyone in my family enjoyed good health and relative longevity. I realized that the Yom Kippur liturgy is so much about life and who will be given life, and if you have any kind of vulnerability at all, you have to think about it. You get life as a gift every day, and you make it worthwhile while you have it.

Those are the themes of the High Holidays, and you don't think about those deeper questions on Shabbat, which is quite a different mode of looking at life. On Rosh Hashanah and Yom Kippur, you look life and death right in the eye.

All the Jewish holidays have such different meanings. Succoth is a harvest festival. It is about not taking bounty for granted, not taking your food and the way nature works, the whole earth and ecosystem for granted. Passover is really focused on redemption from slavery and on how you treat others, remembering what it was like to be a slave. And Shavuot is about receiving the Torah, which you know you receive every single day, but you relive that particular covenant experience intensely once a year.

---

* Jonathan Joseph "J.J." Greenberg was thirty-six years old when the bicycle he was riding was hit by a car in Israel on September 13, 2002. He was, as the *New York Jewish Week* reported, "an ascendant star in Jewish communal service."
† Travel by any mechanical means is prohibited on Shabbat, in the Orthodox observance of Jewish law.

And Chanukah is about historical miracles. Both Chanukah and Purim are about historical saving, which goes back to the miracle of Jewish existence. Even though you're reminded of all of these things in your daily prayer, it's lifted out in a very intense, purified form on the holidays.

There is always a feeling of living on the edge as a Jew. I don't live every day thinking about my vulnerability as a Jew. My daily realities are much the same as everyone else's, but sometimes I say to myself, I wonder what it's like not to be Jewish and not to have these existential anxieties. On the surface, I don't feel them at every given moment, and yet there's this undercurrent, something different about being a Jew, an added dimension, an added responsibility—added anxieties.

But more than anxiety, I feel very privileged. I feel blessed that I was chosen at birth to be a Jew and was raised in a very Jewish family. In a sense, I never really chose Judaism. It chose me. It was a matter of divine election.

It's so special to be Jewish. It's not a matter of being the chosen people. Jews are the chosen people, but so are other peoples. Lots of people have been chosen, but the Jews were chosen for a special role, and the sheer longevity of the Jewish people is very special.

I think about what it took for my ancestors to maintain their commitment to Judaism, to be Jewish in a world that was sometimes hostile. My grandparents left Europe because it was not a good place for Jews. They were fortunate that they got out.

Miracles Unceasing

My father was very deeply religious, a very modest man, a very sweet, good, kind person, and I'll tell you a story about him, because it reflects how prayer can affect your attitude about life and can give you a new orientation. In 1973, my brother-in-law suffered a massive heart attack in New Orleans, where he and my sister were visiting. Fortunately, they happened to be near a modern heart hospital, which basically revived him. Still, there was damage to his heart, and he was forced to retire as a young man.

Then, a year later my sister's daughter was mugged on their nice street. Several months after that, my sister's house burned down in an electrical fire. They rented another place while their house was being rebuilt. But six months later, early Thanksgiving morning, a week before they were supposed to move back in, another fire broke out, caused by a careless contractor's cigarette, and it was another several months before they could move back in.

That Thanksgiving morning, I was talking to my sister—she is Orthodox, as I am—and she said, "You know, somebody up there doesn't like us." I said, "I know, Judy, I was thinking the same thing myself."

Then I called my mother, who told me that my father was crying while he was reciting his morning prayers. My father wasn't a crier. I saw him cry very rarely in his lifetime. I was sort of dreading talking to him because I understood that he was so heartbroken over this.

When I called him a half hour later, I said, "Dad, I'm so sorry. What were you thinking of when you were *davening*?" That means "praying" in the Yiddish. He said to me, "All morning long, I couldn't help but think, *Hasdei Hashem ki lo tamnu.*" That is a biblical phrase meaning, "God's acts of loving kindness never cease."* My father said, "Once again, they were saved."

There it is, once again, the miracle of existence—of God's saving grace.

---

* From the Hebrew scriptures, Lamentation 3:22.

RABBI ALAN LEW

CANTOR ABRAHAM LUBIN

RABBI JOEL TESLER

45

Reading the Book of Our Life

Tradition is cherished in Judaism and most profoundly during the High Holidays that formally begin in the autumn with Rosh Hashanah, the Jewish New Year. Here we explore the holidays with three spiritual authorities, each reflecting on this solemn season of contemplation. According to Alan Lew, formerly the rabbi of Congregation Beth Shalom in San Francisco, the spiritual mood of the holidays is actually set a month earlier on Tisha B'Av, often called the saddest day in Jewish history, when the destruction of the Jewish temples in ancient Jerusalem is mourned. Before he became a rabbi, Lew practiced Zen Buddhism for ten years and now blends Jewish and Buddhist traditions in his spiritual practice and teaching. His reflections are followed by those of a cantor, Abraham Lubin of Bethesda, Maryland, descanting on Yom Kippur, the holiday that ends the holidays, the day of atonement when observant Jews spend all day in synagogue fasting and repenting. In Jewish worship, it is the cantor, also known as hazzan, who leads the congregation in ancient, sung prayer, pleading for God's forgiveness on that day. And there is a necessary turn toward human forgiveness, as told by Rabbi Joel Tessler of Beth Shalom congregation in Potomac, Maryland. Correspondent Kate Olson spoke with Lew in 2006, Susan Grandis Goldstein spoke with Lubin in 2001, and Bob spoke with Tessler in 1997.

Rabbi Alan Lew . . .

The point of the High Holidays is atonement, reconciliation. It's a restitution to wholeness. So it makes sense that a journey that ends that way should begin with an acknowledgment of alienation and estrangement, and that is the theme of Tisha B'Av. Tisha B'Av is the time when the temple was destroyed,* and the temple was the place where one felt the palpable presence of God.

After acknowledging that we are, in fact, estranged from ourselves, from others, from God, for the next thirty days there's a very rigorous period of introspection. The essential gesture of this entire period is to become more mindful, to become more aware both of our own situations psychologically and spiritually, and those things that we've been doing that aren't so productive.

So the closer we are to being in the present moment, the more mindful we are, the closer we are to God. God is here; if we are elsewhere, we are estranged from God. The blowing of the *shofar*† is connected to this mindfulness, this process of becoming mindful; it calls us to it. It wakes us up literally. It's an alarm clock.

When we are really immersed in the act of prayer, we are not so much asking for things, and we are not so much trying to bend God's will to our own, which I think is what we ordinarily think of as prayer, but we are really engaging in an act of self-judgment.

Part of the reason that we are able to effect a reconciliation with God during this season is because we realize how desperately we need God, we realize we can't do all these really difficult things without a sense of a transcendent consciousness beyond our own.

Rosh Hashanah is the day when the gates to heaven open, and it's a very rich symbol, suggesting access to the presence of God during this time, extraordinary access, and suggesting a time of transformation—that if we read the book of our life, we can see ourselves and we can stop jumping into fires and stop doing unconscious hurt to others.

Yom Kippur, the very end of this process, is a time when we literally rehearse our own death, and we intone this endless liturgy of who will live and who will die, and we abstain from all activities that living people engage in, like eating and sexual activity.

---

* The fasting on Tisha B'Av marks the destruction of both the First Temple in 586 BCE and the Second Temple in 70 CE, as well as other tragedies throughout Jewish history.

† A ritual trumpet usually made from the horn of a ram, used in worship mainly on the High Holidays of Rosh Hashanah and Yom Kippur.

We can evoke the power of our death to show us our lives. The most intense times are those last several hours of *neilah*[*] when the gates are closing. I can almost hear and feel those gates clanging shut.[†] And then the *shofar* blows, and there is a tremendous feeling of lightness.

We spend the rest of the year in a greater state of awareness.

Cantor Abraham Lubin . . .

We are instructed to have what is known as *heshbon hanefesh*, to have an inventory of our soul. We count those things that matter for our hearts, for our souls, for our conscience, and for our very life. Those are the themes for the High Holidays.

One of the centerpieces of my work, and that of every *hazzan*, is to lead the congregation in prayer, to hopefully inspire them in wanting to pray, to create a mood through the music, through liturgy, through the intensity of your own input into the service, to create that kind of environment. To lead them and to worship with them. The congregants put themselves into the prayer and sing along and read along and find meaning in the sentiments expressed by the prayers.

Prayer comforts the afflicted and prayer should also afflict the comfortable, those who are smug, blasé, "everything is great." The *hineini* prayer is a classic prayer. It was written by a humble cantor in medieval times. And the sentiments in that prayer really speak to my heart as they do to all *hazzanim*, all the cantors who lead the service on the High Holidays. What it asks is: am I worthy of leading the congregation in the act of worship? We ask that God allow us and give us the strength to lead the congregation in prayer.

Our lives are sometimes hanging on a thread. Our lives are so vulnerable. We don't know from day to day what life may bring, and so once again, the High Holidays are a time to reflect on these issues and should lead us to a better kind of life as we reach the end of the year.

---

[*] The last of the five Yom Kippur services.
[†] Referring to the symbolic closing of the gates of prayer as Yom Kippur ends.

One of the salient prayers speaks of the book of life, and on Rosh Hashanah, the New Year, the decree of God is written. On the day of the fast of Yom Kippur, our fate is sealed for the year, and so we ask: Who shall live and who shall die as we usher in the New Year? Who shall be hungry, who shall be poor, who shall be rich? Who shall die of this illness and who shall die of that? These are serious questions, and we don't know the answers. But the prayer ends on such a wonderful, hopeful note. It says that with repentance, with prayer, and with good deeds, with righteousness, we can avert, God forbid, any decree that is not of a positive nature. And we are very positive and hopeful that the year will be a peaceful one, a year of harmony, of good health, a year of life. That is what we wish everyone for the High Holidays.

Of course, we do think of Israel, the lack of peace, the absence of peace. And we pray for absolute *shalom*. The High Holidays will focus on that theme and on harmony among people and harmony among nations and peace in Israel, throughout the Middle East, and in fact the whole world.

There's a certain magical symbolism here of a prayer that speaks to our hearts. It talks about vows, it talks about words, and words are very precious. We have to be very careful in what we say, because we can never take it back. Saying the wrong word can be as violent as doing something physically wrong.

What are the hopes of the people when they come for the High Holiday services? To have a better year than the previous year, to have a year of greater harmony and less dissonance, to have a year of good health and less illness, to have a year of greater compassion on our part toward people, greater understanding, greater sensitivity to the needs of others, to listen a little more and talk a little less, because by listening we recognize better what is in the hearts of people. And we need to listen to our own hearts, to our own conscience—to have a sense of integrity and honesty in our lives and have a conscience in whatever we do and whatever we say.

Ultimately, those are the feelings of all human beings. What do we want? We want harmony, we want peace, we want good health, and most of us are willing to do our part to bring that about, to be better people.

The Hebrew word to pray is *l'hitpallail* in a reflexive form of the verb, so that we reflect upon ourselves when we pray. Rather than to try to change God, so to speak, prayer should change us, should make us better human beings. That is the ultimate purpose of prayer. If you bring a sense of honesty and integrity into the act of worship, then you can have a better chance of leaving the service feeling better, motivating you to be better.

We are human beings, we've got failings and that's expected and so forth. We should be understanding of people and we should be forgiving, and yes, we should recognize that we have the capacity and the potential for being better, for doing more good.

We think of the sovereignty of God because there are things greater than ourselves. We can't control life, but we can make an attempt to make life better about us. These are simple things and simple themes, but they are the ultimate and most important things in our lives, if we would only think about them.

Rabbi Joel Tessler . . .

As a rabbi, I must tell you that people assume that if they go to the synagogue and spend the entire day in fasting and prayer on Yom Kippur, all their sins are sort of wiped clean. But in truth it's crucial to be able to seek out those who we think we've wronged in the course of the year and ask them for forgiveness.

The actual process is recorded by the rabbis in the Talmud as, first, really acknowledging what I've done as incorrect and then making a *vidui*, or a confession. Finally, we make a resolution for the future: I will try not to do the same thing.

Let me tell you a quick story. My daughter is seven years old, and a little girl threw a stick at her and actually hurt her on the playground. Just yesterday she got a little note from the little girl in big handwriting saying, "Dear Safira, it's before Rosh Hashanah, and I just want to say I'm sorry." There it is, at seven years old they learn.

46.

The Soul Is Hovering

In February 2004, Religion & Ethics NewsWeekly *aired a memorable segment on the Jewish tradition of tahara, the washing and purifying of a dead body, which is considered one of the greatest of all good deeds—mitzvot. Those who perform taharas are volunteer members of the burial society, Chevra Kadish, which brings together women who attend to deceased women, men who attend to men. In Jewish practice, a body is buried within twenty-four hours if possible, and there is no embalming. Our producer Susan Grandis Goldstein found three women in Westchester County, New York—Rochel Berman, Nancy Klein, and Mina Crasson—who have been doing taharas for more than twenty years and agreed to describe their work. In keeping with the tradition of respecting the dead, they did not invite press coverage of an actual tahara; they used a mannequin, instead, to demonstrate the ritual. Berman's commentary is interlaced with prayers and readings by her and her tahara team.*

No matter what is going on in my life, before I walk into the *tahara* room, no matter how troubled or obsessed I might be about something, it totally disappears during the time of the *tahara*. It is the most profound connection with my Judaism. Both task oriented and spiritual at the same time, it's so intensive that it's almost a lesson for how to do other commandments.

I think it's considered the greatest *mitzvah** because the person that you are serving, the deceased, can't say, "Thank you."

The purpose of the *tahara* is to provide comfort for the soul and care for the body. We talk very little, except about the tasks at hand. When we are working on the deceased, we never pass anything over the body. We always walk around as a sign of respect for the dead. I have a distinct sense that the

---

* A good deed.

soul is hovering and is in transition as we do this, and that makes us that much more careful with the body.

> *May it be your will, Lord our God and God of our Fathers, to bring a circle of angels of mercy before the deceased, for she is your servant daughter.*

It's definitely changed me. For one thing, it's put my own mortality in a much sharper focus. I don't think I have a fear of death, and I could kind of imagine what that would be like. I have thought about my own *tahara*. And I also find it so enormously uplifting and rewarding that if I get a call to do it, why wouldn't I do it? It makes me feel so good about myself; it gives a lift to the rest of the day.

Tahara is analogous to a three-act play. There are three distinct parts: there is cleansing, there's purification, and there's dressing. In the cleansing phase of the *tahara*, we remove all the bandages and anything extraneous on the body.

> *And I will pour upon you pure water.*

The purification is a cascade of twenty-four quarts of water that are poured by the entire team in a continuous flow. And it is analogous to a *mikvah*, which is a purification that women go through following their menstrual cycle. It's as if we were washing away all the suffering of the last periods of their lives. It is like a veil that you leave behind.

> *Tahara he, tahara he, tahara he. She is pure. She is pure. She is pure.*

And then the body is dried, and the final stage is dressing it in the shrouds. The shrouds are fashioned after the garments that the high priest wore in the temple on Yom Kippur, and they're white, usually made of linen, hand sewn with no knots, so that they will disintegrate easily. They also have no hems to signify their impermanence and no pockets, so that you take no worldly goods with you. And everybody, rich or poor, young or old, religious or nonreligious, are all buried in the same garments.

And then the body finally is placed in the casket and wrapped in a large sheet, which creates almost a cocoonlike image. And there is a sense of protectiveness as the person enters the world to come.

We sprinkle earth from Israel at the bottom of the casket before we place the body in there, and after the deceased is completely shrouded, we place earth on the eyes and on the heart, and that is our connection with our homeland.

At the end of the *tahara*, before we close the lid, the team gathers around the casket to ask forgiveness of the soul for any errors of omission or commission, and assure the soul that we have done everything within our power to do this correctly, in accordance with our customs.

> *Dina, daughter of Jacob, we ask forgiveness from you if we did not treat you respectfully, but we did as is our custom. May you be a messenger for all of Israel. Go in peace, rest in peace, and arise in your turn at the end of days.*

We address the deceased by name, and that makes it very specific and personalized. And I usually wish her well.

47.

Bearing Witness
to the One God

Seyyed Hossein Nasr is a Muslim and a native of Iran, where he taught at Tehran University and was also the school's chancellor. He became an American citizen twenty years ago and is now a professor of Islamic studies at George Washington University and the author of many books, among them The Heart of Islam: Enduring Values for Humanity. *In a February 2003 interview, Bob asked Nasr to explain the essential ideas of Islam, usually referred to as shahadahs—"to bear witness to."*

To be a Muslim, one bears witness to two truths. The first is the phrase, "There is no god but God." There is no divinity but the Supreme Divinity, God with a capital *G*—bearing witness to the oneness of God. And the second is, *Muhammadun rasul Allah.* That is, "Mohammed is the messenger of God." These two truths define for Muslims the Islamic tradition—to bear witness to the oneness of God and to accept the *messengership* of the prophet of Islam. Perhaps of all the religions of the world, Islam is the simplest one to embrace from the point of ritual, because all you need is to bear witness before two other Muslims and repeat these two sentences.

Islam considers itself to be the religion of unity, what in Arabic is called *tawhid.* That is really the pivotal reality, the axial reality of Islam. But *tawhid* has two different meanings. First, it means emphasis upon the oneness of God. Islam, like Judaism, is totally uncompromising in its emphasis upon the oneness of God: "Say the Lord is one," the Old Testament says. Secondly, it means to integrate, because oneness does not imply only one divinity sitting up there on his throne in heaven. *Tawhid* means also unity in creation, interrelatedness, integration. Islam tries to emphasize the integration of society; the integration of our soul within ourselves; the interrelation with the community, with other human beings, even with other creatures of God, the nonhuman world. It has a very wide application to many different domains.

There is no domain, according to Islam, where God's will and God's laws do not apply. There is no extraterritoriality to God's creation, in the same way that theologically we say God created the whole world, not only part of the world. He created the whole universe. Islam sees that as meaning one's religion should also encompass the whole of life. Of course, this is not religion in the narrow, usual sense of rituals one performs in a mosque, or a church, or a synagogue. The principles of religion should apply to ethics, to morality, to politics, to economics, and even to domains of knowledge and art—to everything.

The Koran, for Muslims, is the verbatim word of God. If we ask ourselves, "What is the word of God in Christianity?" it is Christ. So, in a sense, the Koran corresponds in the religious and spiritual life of Islam to both the Bible and to Christ.

The word *ummah* means community or a collectivity united. In the Koran, Abraham himself is also called an *ummah*, because he symbolizes the whole of the monotheistic family. Christians are called the *ummah* of Christ. Jews are called the *ummah* of Moses, and Muslims are called the *ummah* of the prophet of Islam.

Turning more specifically to the Islamic case, *ummah* means the totality of the Islamic community, which is bound together by the links and the attraction toward one single religion, one single revelation. It refers to the bonds of brotherhood and sisterhood, bonded by following a single, divine law; by ethics; and by many, many other issues. It's a very profound and strong bond that unites the members of the *ummah*, or the Islamic community, together, regardless of where they live.

After the first century of the history of Islam, Islam was never politically united in one single unit. But the idea that the *ummah* is united, that all the members of the Islamic community are united, has remained very strong throughout Islamic history, no matter where you live, no matter what kind of ethnic background you have. Whether you're Arab or Malaysian or Chinese or Persian, no matter what language you speak—that is secondary to the idea of this primal and very essential bond.

You can have in religion a very strong ideal, but not everyone follows it. Charity is central to Christianity. There are many charitable Christians, but there are also many who aren't charitable, because human ambitions, greed, ethnic and tribal bonding, and other things have not died out completely. Islam tried to replace all of those with a bond of the *ummah*. And it succeeded to a large extent, but not completely. For example, the Prophet was against tribal bonds. Arabia was a tribal society. And to a large extent, the tribal allegiances were transformed to allegiance for the *ummah*—but not 100 percent. You still have tribes in Afghanistan. Other places in the Islamic world present very, very strong links between particular groups of people. We have had wars, as has the Christian West.

The Inner Jihad

Jihad is a crucial term that needs to be redefined and discussed extensively, because now it has become a popular word in the English language, and practically every author is trying to push the word into the title of his book to sell more copies. There is so much misinterpretation.

For a long, long time, many centuries, jihad was translated as "holy war." This is false. The word "jihad" in Arabic comes from the root "to use effort." It means to use one's effort in the path of God. Over the centuries, jihad took on two meanings, in the same way that in English the word "crusade" has two meanings. One is the historical act of the pope ordering the Crusades in Europe in the Middle Ages. And one is the popular, everyday word, like the crusade of President Lyndon Johnson against poverty, or something like that, which we use in the English language regularly.

Jihad also has two meanings. One is general—whatever you exert yourself for in a good way. For example, in some countries you have jihad for helping the poor, jihad for reconstructing slums—this kind of thing. It would be exactly like the word "crusade" that in the Western mind originally was a holy war, but it now means any kind of effort. But the original meaning, the more profound meaning, is the one that is now being misconstrued and mistranslated and discussed all the time as "holy war," almost like going to fight against others. This is not true at all.

One type of jihad is to defend—not to bring offense, but to defend—one's religion and home and property when one is attacked. That's called the external jihad, the little jihad. The greater jihad is a jihad within oneself against all the negative tendencies that are really the source of all the external frictions in society—greed, evil, envy, all of the unnecessary rivalries, the kind of fighting that we have to carry out within our soul to create peace within ourselves. And that is called the greater jihad.

When the Islamic community had just established itself in the city of Medina north of present-day Mecca, the Meccans were still not Muslims. They tried to attack the Medinans and destroy the early Islamic community. The Battle of Badr was fought in which the Muslims, although a much smaller number, were victorious. So everyone was very happy. When they were coming back to the city, the Prophet said to those around him, "You have now come back from the smaller jihad." And they were all surprised. What could be greater than having gained this victory which would protect the early Islamic community? They asked, "What is the greater jihad?" He said, "To fight against one's inner passions, against the evil tendencies within oneself." So human beings should always be in an inner jihad to better themselves, to overcome the infirmities and imperfections of our inner soul.

Throughout the history of Islam, governments have attacked other governments, armies have attacked other armies, even within the Islamic world. In the name of jihad that occurred, because this was a very important symbol within Islamic society, like, let's say, the Catholics' and Protestants' fight against each other for a hundred years in Europe. Each was using religious legitimacy on its side. That has occurred. But legally, from the point of view of Islamic law, jihad should only be for defense.

In Shiite Islam, religious scholars have said that jihad should always be for defense, and they've never supported any jihad that has been offensive. In Sunni Islam, which was much more powerful militarily during most of Islamic history, occasionally the attack by a particular state against another state or against another army was condoned as being a legitimate jihad on the basis of "the best defense is a good offense." Sometimes that has occurred. But technically, that would be against the teaching of the Prophet.

In every religion, you have people with a sense of blind self-righteousness. When Oliver Cromwell was beheading Charles I, he thought he was acting as a very good Christian. The terrorists of 9/11 are people who are blinded by their own narrow, exclusivist interpretation of religion. And these people think that, in fact, they are the true interpreters of Islam.

But if you look at the whole of the Islamic world, the background from which these people come, even theologically, is a kind of heresy. I don't like to use the word "heresy" any longer, but they're at the very margin of the spectrum of Islamic thought, both Sunni and Shiite. They're not really traditional, orthodox, mainstream Muslims by any means. The fact that you have small groups taking recourse to violence, of course, is not unique to Islam. You right now have it in India in Gujarat among Hindus, who've done pogroms of the worst kind, and you've had it historically in Christianity.

I think if you take the whole of the Islamic world, the people who are called traditional Muslims—who are neither fundamentalists nor Islamists nor extremists on one end, nor rabid modernists and secularists on the other end—these people still constitute about 90 percent of the Islamic world.

The beliefs and practices of a traditional Muslim are rooted in the Koran and the sayings and actions of the Prophet—the *hadith* as it has been interpreted over the centuries in various schools of law, theology, and ethics, in mysticism and philosophy, and as it has flowered over the last fourteen hundred years. That's traditional Islam.

The most eminent representatives of Islam, the various muftis of the great, important countries—Syria, Morocco, Pakistan, Shiite Iran, Indonesia, and others—all of them came out with very, very clear and categorical opposition to terrorism after 9/11. It is the killing of innocent people. The surprising thing is that there was so little reported here by the American media. There was a lot more opposition by these people against the terrorists, the exclusivists, than there has been in the United States by mainstream Christians against those extreme voices who call Islam a religion of evil and try to demonize Islam.

Waiting for Mr. Jefferson

Democracy is a means to an end. It is not one single institution. Democracy simply is the Greek word for "the rule of the people." The voice of the people must be heard. There's no innate contradiction with Islam.

If somebody says, "Well, why wasn't Thomas Jefferson born in Cairo?" the answer is, of course, that in the West itself, it was a long historical process from the Magna Carta and so on until George Washington and Jefferson and the American constitution and modern democracies.

For most of its history, the Christian world was like the Islamic world. It had an emperor, or a king, or some kind of absolutist monarchy. The fact that this development took place in a particular area of the world called the West doesn't mean this was part and parcel of Christianity. Christianity accommodated itself to it.

There's no reason why Islam cannot accommodate itself to democracy— unless if by democracy we mean cutting off the voice of God. That's something else.

The Muslim people do not like freedom any less than anybody else. It is in the nature of human beings to like freedom. You don't think somebody sitting in a shop in, say, Damascus doesn't want to be free to travel to Cairo without ten stops at the border? No, he wants the same thing we have here going to Canada and back. It isn't that Muslims are against democracy or freedom. The problem is that sometimes these terms are defined exclusively upon the basis of the Western experience, which is culturally bound, which has taken many historical transformations to become what it is. And yet we expect to transplant that right into Iraq. You cannot even transplant it into Bolivia or Mexico, which is just south of the border. Mexican democracy is very, very different from American democracy. So it needs time. And if the West is friendly and its interest in the Islamic world is not only its own interest, but it also wants to have a friend with whom to trade, to negotiate, to exchange institutions that we call in the West democratic, democracy in the Islamic world would grow up much more rapidly.

Unfortunately, since the colonial period, the experience of the Islamic world has been that usually the West has not supported democratic movements in the Islamic world, but has supported any regime that would protect its interests, whether that regime was democratic or not. That has been the experience of the people. So they are, of course, very skeptical.

48

The Hajj

"Imagine a crowd a quarter the size of New York City, only more diverse, all trying to do the same thing at the same time in the same place. The common language is Arabic, though not everybody speaks it well. The common goal—the worship of God." This is correspondent Anisa Mehdi's description of the annual Hajj, or pilgrimage to Mecca, one of the five pillars of Islam. Each year during the last month of the Islamic calendar, millions of Muslims converge on Mecca, near the west coast of Saudi Arabia. One of their first ritual acts is to circle the Ka'aba, a cubical shrine Muslims say was built by the patriarch Abraham as the first sanctuary dedicated to the worship of the one God. (Both Muslims and Jews trace their spiritual ancestry to Abraham: Jews through his son Isaac, Muslims through his son Ishmael.) Every adult Muslim who is physically and financially able to do so is expected to make the five-day hajj at least once during his or her lifetime.

In the spring of 1998, one such pilgrim was Abdul Alim Mubarak, a CNN videotape editor who lives in New Jersey and whose pre-Muslim-conversion name was Ronald Carl Rowe; his wife, Audrey Rowe, has kept his former surname as well as her devout Christian faith. Religion & Ethics NewsWeekly *correspondents followed Mubarak on his often-grueling desert journey, which all too many pilgrims have not survived, and Mehdi (part of whose narration is presented here) caught up with him again four months later in Maplewood, New Jersey. At the time, this African-American Muslim was still mining the spiritual meanings and cultural implications of the sacred path Muslim pilgrims beyond number have walked for fourteen hundred years.*

—

Hajj is a sacrifice. It is a very personal sacrifice, and it's not something to be taken lightly. Hajj is a duty that all of mankind owes to Allah. It recognizes the sacrifice and the contribution of the first of our primary prophets, Abraham, and the dedication with which he built the first house for Allah in

Mecca. It shows that it is a religion for all of humanity, a religion that all of the prophets from Abraham to Mohammed accepted. And "accepted" means that we resign our will to the will of God.

The Hajj brings humanity together as one, recognizing the oneness of the one God, the oneness of all of his prophets, the oneness of his creation, the oneness of his revelation. Muslims accept all of the prophets that God sent to mankind. And we commemorate that oneness here on Hajj, when we visit the Ka'aba here in Mecca, when we circle around the Ka'aba as Allah has commanded all of mankind to do.

The Ka'aba is in the center of the Haddam Al-Sharif, the noble sanctuary. Opening to the sky, three stories high, the sanctuary is big enough to hold 750,000 worshippers at once.

It's huge, and it's so imposing, you're dwarfed by it. The huge marble columns, the huge marble minarets just dwarf you. And you feel like this tiny ant, walking in this vast expanse. It empties out into this vast courtyard, and right before you, you see the Ka'aba. And this is what I've been praying toward. This is it.

The Ka'aba itself is a very simple, yet imposing structure. It is nothing more than a focus, a place of worship. The Muslims don't worship the Ka'aba, they worship the Lord of the Ka'aba. Coming here is also an answer to Abraham's prayer, because Abraham was commanded by God to call the people to come to this house. We respond to the command of God by coming here to sanctify this house, this structure.

You see, the universe itself is built on structure. A human being is built on structure. If we didn't have structure in our whole physical body, we would fall apart. So everything in creation is built on structure. Allah, who is pure and perfect, establishes structure and rules to discipline the human being, to evolve the human being in a structured, orderly fashion.

I'm standing on the roof. I see the believers swirling around the Ka'aba, sanctifying the house of God. It's like a galaxy in motion. A galaxy of humanity evolving around God. Worshiping him. Evolving. It ebbs and it flows as human beings do.

Before circling it, we have to enter into a spiritual state of purity—this is what's called *ihram*. Men dress as you see in a simple piece of white, unstitched cloth. The reason for that is to put all of us on one level, plain. You can't tell a pauper from a rich man. You can't tell a beggar from a thief. You can't tell a king from a janitor. It is the great equalizer because in Allah we are all equal.

On the other hand, women must be completely covered down to their wrists and their ankles.

Many of the Muslim countries operate under a sort of patriarchal mindset. But the Prophet was egalitarian in his dispensation of Islam to women. He put women on an equal footing. In the pre-Islamic era, women had no rights. Women were treated as nothing more than cattle or cannon fodder to be used at the pleasure and whim of men. Men buried their daughters alive. But in that darkest period of history Allah shined a great light, illuminating the whole world and sending a prophet to his people.

Women were given equality in the Koran,* and an example is the way the Prophet treated his wives and the way he regarded other women. If you look at the Prophet's wives—Hadijah, she was a businesswoman, she had her own business. Aisha, she was a scholar in Islam. People came from all over the world to sit at her feet and be taught. There were many more women scholars who came after her; scholars from all over the world, men and women, came to sit at their feet and be taught. So we have to go back to the authentic sources, because that's the spirit of the Koran, and the spirit is with us here on Hajj.

The ultimate goal of the Hajj is the valley called Arafat, a few miles to the west— where the prophet Mohammed gave his final sermon and where it is said that God answers all prayers. En route, pilgrims spend the night in a city of tents called Mina.

Arafat is Hajj. If one does not make Arafat, your Hajj is not going to be acceptable to God. So you camp here overnight. And you prepare yourself spiritually. You rest. You contemplate. You remember. You work to remem-

---

* The holy book of Islam, also rendered in English as Qur'an.

ber your Lord. Contemplate what you're going to say. Contemplate what your existence is. The purpose of existence. Then tomorrow, we go to Arafat, and we engage in a one-on-one conversation with the Lord.

You beg him for his mercy. Beg him for his forgiveness again. Begging that he will even accept your Hajj.

When we go to Arafat—where it has been reported that Adam and Eve went*—we go back to our origins. We go back to our spiritual origins, and we go back to our human origins. As Muslims who come here to Mecca to make our Hajj, we are commemorating the whole of the religion—the whole of God's religion—here in Mecca.

I will offer sincere repentance to Allah for my sins and my shortcomings. I will pray for my mother, father. I will pray for the souls of my grandparents. I will pray for my children. I'll pray for my wife. I'll pray for my friends.

I will pray to Allah for guidance, for health, for wealth. I'll pray to Allah for spiritual enrichment, to increase my faith, to increase my repentance. I will pray to Allah for peace for all the Muslims, for prosperity for all the Muslims. And I will pray to Allah to unite all the Muslims in the world.

It's quite a journey. "Patience, patience, and more patience," someone told me. You get through it by recognizing that these people aren't there to hurt you. It's not like you're trying to find a seat on the subway in New York. On the subway, they will crush you. They will stab you. Believe me. But at Hajj, their passion, their zeal is to worship God. But God wants us to— excuse me, Allah, pardon me. *Allah* wants us to worship him, not just with passion or zeal, but with rationality and reason.

[After Arafat] Those were six grueling hours at Arafat, and I was out in the blazing sun. I had no cover on my head. I was dripping, soaking wet with sweat. You think to yourself: only for Allah I'm doing this. You wouldn't do this for any man. You do it only for Allah. You go through this process, because you know that you're doing it for Allah and Allah will reward you for it.

---

* After being expelled from Eden, according to legend.

At times, I've really had to control myself. I wanted sometimes to scream and lash out, because of the pushing and shoving. I felt like grabbing somebody on a few occasions, because of how impolite and how rude and how un-Islamic they were behaving, even in the holy house, the holiest of holy houses.

But you have to restrain yourself because if you don't, you blow your whole Hajj. Allah says be patient and persevere. You know, Allah knows best.

Months Later: Remembering the Stones, Living the Lessons

We moved to Muzdalifah* after Arafat, and then we threw the stones, which are really just small pebbles. Those are what you use to throw at the stone pillars—which represent Satan. Abraham took seven stones and threw them at Satan, so we commemorate that experience. But we are also stoning the devils in our own lives, because we're always tempted by the devil, every single moment of our lives, inwardly, outwardly. The big Satans that operate in the larger society, the Satans that operate within our own particular consciousness and souls, the Satan who is an open enemy to Allah—those Satans are always tempting us. We have to always fight them. And we stone them.

The zeal with which people behave sometimes really astounds me, and with the crowds and all, it becomes dangerous. I almost lost it myself. The stoning was an ordeal, because you had to protect yourself. There was the real possibility that you could be stampeded and lose your life. So many a time the old couldn't make it because of the risk. And the young adults who were able bodied did it on behalf of the old. It was very unsafe for women on many occasions because of the crowd and everything. There was one sister who asked me to stone for her. And I did it, but you would get in there, you stone, and you get out.

If you slip out of your sandals, you keep on going. People just left them there, because if they bent down, they would get trampled. So it was precarious. There were those who did not make it, and they lost their lives.

---

* Where the pilgrims take part in ritual stoning, recalling when Abraham was tempted by the devil to ignore God's command to sacrifice his son, Ishmael, according to the Koran. Abraham threw stones to drive away Satan.

But those who lose their lives—Allah grants them instant paradise. So I wasn't worried about my life, even when I almost fell back and I almost lost my glasses. I almost stumbled and fell into the crowd. For a brief moment, I thought, okay, this may be it. But Allah knows best. I gathered myself together, I got into a football stance, and I just went through the crowd. I had to do that just to get there for my own safety.

When I got back to work, a lot of people were asking me, with sincerity—"Oh, did you get caught up in that stampede? Wow, that must have been really something." And I explain to them what had happened. But I use that as a wedge to explain what the whole Hajj was about.

I say the Hajj broadens your humanity. It broadens your human scope. You're not as narrow-minded and not as closed-minded. You're not as subjective in your human understanding as you were before.

I was saying to my wife that I now have a very low tolerance for ignorance of other cultures because I've begun to realize how much knowledge there is out there in the world that we as Americans don't have a clue about. We are truly a global community, and when we get on the Internet, we get plugged into the whole world, everyday. But most of us don't know what's going on in the world. We're so ensconced in our own little comfort zone.

I was telling my wife something else the other day, and she was amazed to hear me say this, because she always had this opinion of how I'm trying to change her. For seventeen years she let me know that you can't change a person. We were talking about another incident, regarding one of our family members, and I said, "You can't change a person." And she says, "Well, honey, you can—one person can change somebody." I say, "No. You can't change anybody. You taught me that."

But what you can do is share knowledge with the person. And that person will, in time, if Allah so pleases, change whatever's within their own soul until Allah will change them. So only Allah makes Muslims. Once I deliver that message, then I'm done.

One of the beautiful things over there is that I met Muslims from every corner of the globe. So I now have friends in London. I have friends in South Africa. I have friends in Sudan. I have friends in Mecca, Medina, Jeddah.

I take from those people lessons about life. We share information on the state of Muslims in the world. Islamic life in our respective countries—how can we improve it? What lessons can we draw from it? What ideas can we draw from each other?

So you come back from Hajj intellectually strengthened. You come back spiritually strengthened. You come back morally strengthened. It has a psychological impact on you. It has an emotional impact on you. Hajj is all of that, plus. You can add whatever plus you want to that.

49.

A Message from the Dalai Lama

In June 1999, Religion & Ethics NewsWeekly was invited to interview the living symbol of Buddhism at his home in Dharamsala, India. Correspondent Lucky Severson traveled into the foothills of the Himalayas, where—as he reported—most of the faces you see are Tibetan, because that is where their spiritual and political leader, the fourteenth Dalai Lama, lives in exile. Some call him a god-king, though he told Lucky, "I'm just a human being, a Buddhist monk. I think a happy human being, perhaps." Forced out of Tibet by the Chinese in 1959, the Dalai Lama remains one of the world's foremost symbols of hope and peace. How does he keep from despising those who have brutalized his Tibetan homeland and oppressed his people? The answer lies at least partly in Buddhist meditation, which he practices for five hours every morning.

As a human being, whether you're a believer or nonbeliever, you have the seed or potential to develop a sense of caring, a sense of sharing with each other. So I think we are all social animals, we human beings.

These are basic human values, but there are also Buddhist values and the Buddhist method. All sentient beings—not only human beings, but all sentient beings—have limitless potential. And this belief is called the Buddhist nature or Buddha seed. Everyone has the potential to become enlightened, like a Buddha, to strengthen my compassion, my sense of caring for the other, the sharing of one another's sorrow or suffering.

How to do this? Channel the mind. First, make clear your different thoughts. Analyze what thought or emotion is beneficial. What is harmful? Analyze clearly. Then find out the contradictions among these different emotions or thoughts. Once we realize an emotion such as hatred or resentment is very bad, very harmful to your health, very harmful to mental peace and to society, then think about opposite thoughts: love, kindness, compassion. These thoughts, these emotions are the antidote. Eventually you will develop some kind of conviction: "Now, this I need," or "This is my real enemy." That kind of attitude itself makes change. This is what Buddhists call analytical meditation.

Analyze, then familiarize. Think about compassion. Look at examples, and you'll see that hatred, through history, brings about a Hitler, a Holocaust; it brings about racial prejudice. On the other hand, we have a Martin Luther King, a Mahatma Gandhi. We have examples of nonviolence and equal rights. So that is the proper way: to analyze and familiarize. That's the training of the mind.

My fundamental belief is that all religious traditions have the same potential to make better human beings, good human beings, sensible human beings, compassionate human beings. I have experience of this. As a result of my meetings with some genuine spiritual practitioners, such as Thomas Merton,* I have developed a genuine appreciation of Christianity. I look at Mother Teresa. How did she become like that? It is because of Christian tradition, Christian belief.

I have a full conviction that among the 5.7 or 5.8 billion human beings, we need a variety of different religious traditions, many different religious dispositions. I have found that some of my Christian brothers and sisters—very good Christians, very faithful to the concept of a creator—are at the same time using some Buddhist methods or Buddhist techniques to increase spiritual forgiveness or tolerance and compassion. Similarly, Buddhists can learn. There are actually many useful traditions among Christian monks and nuns and some Christian practitioners, which are useful to learn.

However, there are big differences among the traditions. And this is partly due to the Buddhist concept of the law of causality, that everything comes and happens due to cause and effect, cause and effect, cause and

---

* The late American Trappist monk and writer.

effect. This indicates there's no central cause or creator, a belief that is very powerful in Christianity, Islam, Judaism, and many other important world traditions. We're talking about very different philosophies.

My view is that whether you believe or don't believe, that's an individual right. But once you take a religious faith, then you should be very serious and sincere, and implement what your faith teaches. The religious belief should be part of daily life. Your life should show: I am a believer. I'm Buddhist. I'm Christian. I'm Muslim. I'm faithful to God in my actions, in my karma. I have to face the consequences.

I have a firm belief that people like westerners, like Americans—you people should keep your own traditions. You should not change your faith. But then there will be some individuals who really find their tradition no longer has any effect. They don't believe in it at all. Meantime they want some spiritual practice or spirituality and find Eastern traditions more effective, such as Buddhism. In that case, think carefully. You have to be fully convinced that this possibility, this new tradition, is more effective and that you really feel this can change your life.

After that, there's one important thing we should keep in mind. In order to justify your position, you may have a critical view toward your previous religion. That you must avoid. That the tradition no longer has any effect on you does not mean it no longer has any effect on humanity. No. Millions of people get their inspiration from that tradition. So you must respect it.

A final point: there are some unqualified sorts of people who carry spiritual teachings, including Eastern religious traditions that have become a fashion. Of this we should be very careful. I think the real teacher, at least in the Buddhist tradition, is not one who claims to be enlightened. Buddha was a real teacher, and when Buddha was fully enlightened, he did not go around shouting, "Oh, I'm enlightened! Come and listen to me!" He never said that. He remained quiet, in the forest. Then some people asked, insisted, "Please, give us some teaching." And then he started.

50.

Being Mindful and Engaged

In the United States and Europe, the other best-known Buddhist leader, besides the Dalai Lama, is the renowned Vietnamese monk Thich Nhat Hanh. When he was sixteen he became a Zen Buddhist monk, and like other Vietnamese monks, was given the title "Thich," which means that he is symbolically a member of the Buddha's extended family. During the Vietnam War, Nhat Hanh actively opposed the fighting, offending all sides. He developed what he called "engaged Buddhism," going beyond meditation to campaign for peace, care for refugees, and rebuild bombed villages. ("If you hear the bombs falling, you know that you have to go out and help," he explains here.) Because of his antiwar activities, Nhat Hanh had to leave Vietnam; in the 1980s, he founded a Buddhist community in France and has spent most of the years since teaching, leading retreats, and writing more than seventy-five books. Many people find Nhat Hanh's teachings utopian, though he is convinced they are practical and proven. And one great peacemaker who agreed with him was Rev. Martin Luther King Jr. who nominated Nhat Hanh for a Nobel Peace Prize in the 1960s.

In September 2003, Bob caught up with Hanh during the late afternoon rush on Capitol Hill, where Hanh had given a talk at the Library of Congress about peace in a time of terror; he recommended that members of the bitterly divided Congress practice what he calls deep listening (to each other) and gentle speech. The next day he led a retreat for members of Congress, teaching the simple practices he says can ease the suffering of any soul.

Buddhism teaches us not to try to run away from suffering. You have to confront suffering. You have to look deeply into the nature of suffering in order to recognize its cause, the making of the suffering. Suffering is the First Noble Truth, and the making of the suffering—namely, the roots of suffering—is the Second Noble Truth. Once you understand the roots of suffering, the path leading to the transformation of suffering is revealed. And if you go on that path—namely, the path of right thinking, right speech, and right action—then you can transform your suffering.

The Buddha spoke about suffering in terms of food. Nothing can survive without food, even your love. If you don't feed your love properly, your love will die. Your suffering is there because you have been feeding it. If violence, hate, despair, and fear are there, it is because you have been feeding them by your unmindful consumption. Therefore, if you know how to recognize the source of the nutrients of your suffering, and if you know how to cut off that source of nutrition, then the suffering will have to vanish.

This is a very important teaching for our time, because the amount of violence and craving in us and in our children comes from our practice of unmindful consumption—watching television, reading magazines, having poisonous conversation. We bring a lot of poisons and toxins into our body and into our consciousness. If you don't stop producing these toxic items, and if we don't know how to protect ourselves by mindful consumption of these items, there's no way out.

We need not less, but right consumption. There are very wonderful television programs that can water the seed of understanding, compassion, joy, and happiness in us. We don't have to consume them less, but we have to refrain from consuming the kind of television programs that can mean to our body and mind a lot of craving, a lot of violence and despair. It's not a problem of less or more, but right or wrong—right consumption, mindful consumption.

Engaged Buddhism is just globalism. When you have enough understanding and compassion in you, then that amount of understanding and compassion will try to express itself in action. And your practice should help you to cultivate more understanding and compassion. If not, it's not true practice. When you have these two kinds of energies, they always seek to express themselves in social action. And that is called "engaged Buddhism"—Buddhism applied in your family life, in the life of your society.

Suppose you sit in meditation, and you hear bombs falling, because meditation is to be aware of what is going on in yourself and around you. If you hear the bombs falling, you know that you have to go out and help. But you try to help in such a way that you can be keen, be calm, and at peace, with the concentration in you, and not lose yourself in the act of service. That is engaged Buddhism—active, but still maintaining the spiritual element within yourself.

The level of violence in society is very high—violence in families, violence in schools, violence on the streets. We do not seem to focus our efforts in order to transform that violence; we are trying to invest all our time and energies and money in order to fight violence outside. But we don't know that violence is there within ourselves, within our society.

If you see someone who is trying to shoot, to destroy, you have to do your best in order to prevent him or her from doing so. You must. But you must do it out of your compassion, your willingness to protect and not out of anger.

If you look deeply, you see that you* have not been able to remove terrorism, especially in the mind of the people. You might have created more violence, hate, and fear in the minds of people. That is why you have to reflect deeply on the situation and see whether there are different ways of doing it more effectively. We have been inviting Israelis and Palestinians to come to our practice centers, and we always succeed in helping them in becoming brothers and sisters, removing wrong perceptions, cultivating brotherhood and mutual understanding. If that can be done on the international level, we can succeed. But our political leaders are not trained to do these kinds of things. They are trained in political science. They are not trained in mindfulness, deep listening, compassionate listening, and loving speech.

Our practice as monks is not only to improve the quality of a person, but also to improve the quality of the life of a community. Community building, *sangha* building is our true practice. And without a community, your practice cannot be strong enough. That is why it's not true that Buddhism only offers a practice for individuals. Everything you can achieve as an individual can profit our community and our nation.

Meditating with Cops and Congress Members

During our retreats in Madison, Wisconsin, police officers learned to go home to themselves and release the tension in their body, release the fear,

---

* Referring to Americans.

the despair in the mind, learn how to get in touch with the positive elements of life that are in them and around them for their nourishment and healing, so that they can better relate to their families, their colleagues, and better serve the people. They are called peace officers, and they should be—they should have enough peace in themselves in order to do so.

During the retreat, we all practiced the basic Buddhist practices, like mindful breathing. You're breathing always, but you are not aware of it. In these exercises, while you breathe in, you become aware that you are breathing in. And you may enjoy breathing in, because breathing in shows that you are still alive. That is called mindful breathing in. When you breathe out, you focus your attention entirely on your out-breath. That is called mindful breathing out, and that practice alone can bring you home to the present moment and help you to be fully present, fully alive. It can be very healing and nourishing. It's a pity if you don't know how to do it. Everyone can practice mindfulness without becoming Buddhist.

We also practiced mindful walking.* We embraced our pain, our sorrow— the negative things—in order to transform. And transformation is healing, is possible. I think in that retreat, the police officers had the first chance to really listen, and they had the first chance to release, to make known the suffering and difficulties. They learned many things in order to protect themselves and their families, and to have more peace in order to serve in a better way.

One message was: you carry a gun, but it's perfectly possible to carry a gun with a lot of compassion inside. You carry a gun to say, "You should not do that. If you do that, you may get into trouble." But that is a message that can go together with compassion.

During the retreats for members of Congress, I did not tell them anything, except to offer them concrete tools in order to have more time for themselves, more time for their families, so that they can release the tension in their daily life, bringing some joy and happiness into their daily life, so that they can serve better their nation and the world. I am not a politician. I am not going to prescribe a political solution for them. I am only a monk, and the best thing I can do is help them be more of themselves—more peaceful, more compassionate.

---

* Slow walking, concentrating on every movement.

We know that violence cannot replace violence. The work of the police officer, as it is now, is only to deal with the symptoms. That is why we have to look deeply to find the practice that can deal with the roots of violence. If you rely on police officers to keep the peace, well, you are truly too naïve. They can do only the things on the surface, but the violence is always there, trying to explode. That is why you have to use other means to look deeply and to eradicate, to remove violence from a street.

I realize that many elements of Buddhist teaching can be found in Christianity, Judaism, Islam. I think if Buddhism can help, it is through concrete methods of practice. We have the same kind of teaching, but in Buddhism there are more concrete tools to help you realize what you want to realize, namely, more understanding, more compassion, and absence of discrimination.

There are many Christians who practice Buddhism, and they become better and better Christians all the time. In my retreats over in Europe and in America, there have been Catholic priests and Protestant ministers receiving the teaching and practice formally. They even receive the Three Refuges and the Five Precepts.* They don't see any conflict between the teaching of the Buddha and the teaching of Jesus.

Regardless of tradition, it is the individual who can effectuate change. When I change, I can help produce change in you. As a journalist, you can help change many people. That's the way things go. There's no other way. You have the seed of understanding, compassion, and insight in you. What I say can water that seed, and the understanding and compassion are yours and not mine. You see? My compassion, my understanding can help your compassion and understanding to manifest. It's not something that you can transfer.

If you want Mr. Bush to have that, you have to touch the seed of compassion and understanding in him. You cannot transfer yours to him. It is like a father—the wisdom of a father you cannot just deliver to the son. It is very frustrating. You have to help him develop his own wisdom. It is always like that.

---

* The Three Refuges are the Buddha, the Dharma (or teachings), and the *Sangha* (or monastic community), which offer refuge from an unsettling world. The Five Precepts are against killing, stealing, sexual misconduct, hurtful speech, and intoxication.

51.

The Smaller Sufferings

Helen Tworkov is the author of Zen in America *and founder of* Tricycle *magazine, which serves a broadly diverse community of Buddhist converts. While Thich Nhat Hanh speaks of spiritual suffering in terms of dark forces such as violence and mindless materialism, Tworkov seems just as interested in the little sufferings, the everyday stresses and frustrations that she believes exact an excruciating, if usually unexamined, toll on the human mind. In 1997, she spoke with Maureen Bunyan about what she sees as a plague of "dissatisfactoriness" in modern society and about the Buddhist remedy—which has to do with forgiving the burned toast.*

—

We talk a lot about how we're stressed out. Everybody's stressed out. Every magazine has articles on stress. Every countertop at every drugstore and health food store has medications for stress. What is stress? I mean, stress is some fundamental distortion of mind. It's some fundamental way in which something is out of reality. If you're stressed out, you're not seeing reality clearly.

So you get up in the morning and you're going to work, and you get to the bus stop and the bus pulls out, and you say, "Oh, damn it." About a hundred times a day, this is what stress means. "Oh, the train just left, the milk spilled, the garbage didn't get picked up, the faucet is leaking, the toilet broke, you just burned the blouse," and it just goes on and on and on.

People tend to think about suffering in some big huge way, like in the Holocaust, or race battles, or cancer, AIDS—huge, monumental, seemingly insurmountable problems. But another way of translating *dukka*—it's the Sanskrit word for suffering—is dissatisfaction, *dissatisfactoriness*, living with a tremendous amount of *dissatisfactoriness*.

I think that's the sense of *dukka* when we talk about our lives. And in fact we're not growing up in a concentration camp. When we talk about urban

315

America, we're talking about the problems that basically the mind is creating for itself all day long. And this is one of the great teachings that Buddhism has to offer this country that I don't believe is available through other forms. There's this emphasis on the capacity of the mind to create and to dissolve suffering, dissolve *dukka*, dissatisfaction. And, so, how can Buddhism help this sense of feeling annoyed all day long? Annoyed, grouchy, grumpy. That's what we call stress.

There's some way in which you're taking this personally. We talk about stress as a state of being fundamentally out of reality, because how could you take spilled milk personally? How could you take the bus pulling out personally? But if you look at your body, your body motion, that's what you're doing. Oooh, the bus left me.

So one of the most primary teachings in Buddhism is this sense that you're functioning from the place of your egocentric small mind. This is the mind that is taking it personally. This is the mind that is creating *dukka*. It's creating dissatisfaction that lives in a state of *dissatisfactoriness* all the time. And that mind is a very small mind. It's gotten very locked on you. Your response to that bus, your response to the burned shirt, your response to the burned toast—it's not a very spacious mind. It's just not seeing that the toast did not burn itself to hurt you. The shirt did not get burned to have some big negative effect on your mind.

So there are many ways in which Buddhism can address this. But let's say you sit on the cushion. Let's say you're talking about meditation, because even though there are many forms of Buddhist spiritual practice, for the new Buddhist in the United States and in the West, meditation is by far the most common practice, and for many of us or for most of us it's the core practice. So if you sit down on the cushion with relatively little instruction, if you just sit quietly and start to look at your mind, it's just astonishing what's going on, how tyrannized you are by your thoughts. And when you're sitting so quietly you begin to get a sense of why you're getting angry at the bus, because even when you're sitting there and thinking, you can feel what happens in your body when you think a negative thought, what happens in your body when you think a positive thought. You can see how much that thought, as it comes in like a cloud, how much it can affect how you feel.

You might not be able to begin to tame your mind, you might not be able to control your mind, you might remain quite tyrannized by your mind, but you can begin to get a taste of what, for me, are the essential Buddhist teachings, which is the nature of mind. And you begin to get a taste of what this mind can do, how destructive it can be—and if you work with it, how constructive it can be. It goes both ways.

But for the most part we're living without any sense of the functioning of the mind. It's not just that you live tyrannized by it—we don't even understand what it is that's tyrannizing us. We don't even know that the mind has that capacity. Until we deal with it and look at it closely and personally, we don't really know that the mind is muttering, muttering, muttering, affecting how we see the world all day long, affecting how we see the bus, affecting our response to other people on the street, affecting the way we communicate with everybody around us. We keep thinking it has something to do with the outside.

I often ask: what does Buddhism offer this country that we're not getting anywhere else? As a Buddhist I want to study the Buddhist precepts, but I also think it's a mistake to think that they are vastly different from the Christian precepts. This is a Christian country. Buddhism has a way of studying morality, but I don't think that ideas about morality are what are missing in America.

We see a lot of people getting involved in social action work. It's wonderful work. It's wonderful when Buddhists do it, and it's wonderful when Christians do it. I'm not sure I understand what makes it Buddhist. It doesn't have to be Buddhist. So I keep asking: what does Buddhism offer that we don't already have? And that's what I would like to see offered in this society, so that we're not just doubling up on what we have, so that there is a sense of pluralism. Do we have something to offer that's not here? Because if we don't, why bother? To me it comes down to some very specific things. It has to do with the nature of mind. And that's an aspect of Buddhism that I think is not in the culture and that I think we desperately need in the culture. Our culture desperately needs a sense of how to work with our minds, and the sense of personal responsibility that comes with understanding the nature of mind.

The Buddhist Phenomenon

There are so many different forms Buddhism can take. I think at this point it would do us well to encourage a kind of tolerance for all kinds of forms rather than making very exclusive statements about "this is what it means to be a Buddhist, and if you don't believe this and you don't believe that, and you don't do this and you don't that, then you're not a Buddhist." But you have a lot of people who are calling themselves Buddhist and are doing some kind of meditation. And with the proliferation of Buddhism and the enormous interest in Buddhism in this country, of course we're seeing all kinds of different manifestations of Buddhism.

Most of us, and that means Christians and Jews, were told maybe to believe something and to perform some rituals, but we weren't told that it was our responsibility to transform our lives and here's how to do it. There are many aspects of Buddhism that are steeped in belief systems the same way that certain aspects of Christianity and certain aspects of Judaism are also based on belief systems. But the kind of Buddhism that the new Buddhists in this country were attracted to has to do with the fact that the teachers were telling us to do something. They were telling us sit down, watch your mind, do something, learn something about yourself by doing something on your own. Don't read this book that somebody else wrote. Don't read what the Buddha wrote. Do something. Learn something for yourself. Experience something for yourself. Get a taste of your own mind. You have to do that on your own. Suddenly there was an engagement, an engagement with a tradition. It wasn't just out here. We weren't watching it on TV. There wasn't a book that we were pulling off the shelf. It wasn't just a teaching sitting up on a podium or a ceremonial altar.

There's an American sense of self-reliance that appealed to us, because in some ways the Buddhist teachers were saying: Test it out. Try it. Do one hundred thousand prostrations. Okay, I'll try that. I'll go like that and get on the floor. I'll see what it feels like. What does it feel like with my whole body, not just to sit in a pew in a church or temple? What does it feel like to have your whole body on the floor? What does it feel like to bow? What does it feel like to actually use your body as an instrument for this practice, to engage your body with it? One of the things the Buddha taught was to try it. And that was so radical for us who had grown up in Christian or Jewish households. No one had ever said to us, try it. No one had ever said that there's something to do. There was a belief or a ritual, but there was no way to engage your actual mind and body.

In America today I think we're taking stock. And we don't like what we see—the environmental destruction that I think the younger generation is extremely aware of, the tremendous violence in this society. And I think that there's a tremendous need all across the country for people to create some spiritual dimension in their lives. You might say that Buddhism is in the right place at the right time, because it's not as if Buddhism has teachings that are superior or more effective spiritually than Christianity or Judaism. But for many of us our experience with those traditions is that they lost their capacity to function as moral witnesses for our time. Through their own institutionalization and bureaucracy and corruption, they lost the ability to communicate in a clear way.

What happened with Buddhism in this country is that it came to us— and this is like a honeymoon—it came to us not completely, but mostly unpackaged from the same kind of bureaucratic and institutionalization problems in Asia as Christianity and Judaism have in the West. If you go to Asia today, even historically, the Zen establishment was in cahoots with the Imperial Army. The people destroying Burma are "Buddhists." You see tremendous Buddhist political corruption all through Thailand, through Sri Lanka. So what are we talking about here? We're talking about a fabulous honeymoon in which we could hear these teachings. These teachings came to us like pure music from the oracles, so unfiltered, so raw and fresh. And the language was so clear.

There is a great deal of Buddhist activity in America. But I think it's far too soon to talk about an American Buddhism. There is no American Buddhism right now. It's all over the map. There's tremendous diversity. There are different forms. There are all kinds of experiments going on. I don't think at this point there is any coherent way to talk about American Buddhism. And I don't think we have any clear-cut direction ahead of us.

Now what we're seeing in this country is the resurgence of the mystical traditions in both Judaism and Christianity, and that clearly has been kicked up by Buddhism. That seems very obvious—people wanted something to do, and they wanted a contemplative dimension to their lives. When they went back to their traditions they certainly discovered that these contemplative dimensions were there. They were there, and they're there intact. Many of the people who became involved in the meditative and contemplative traditions of Asia in the 1960s have gone back into Judaism and to Christianity and really worked to rekindle the more contemplative and mystical aspects of those traditions. If in three hundred years we look back and see that's what Buddhism did for this society, I think it would be fantastic.

52.

Many Deities, One God

Hinduism is probably the world's oldest religion. It is practiced by more than a billion people, most of them in India, with about one and a half million in the United States. To many Westerners, Hinduism may seem an unfamiliar but colorful, festival-filled polytheism. Hindus worship hundreds, perhaps thousands of deities in temples and at home, with prayer and such ceremonies as bathing their statues with milk and nutritious juices. But Hindus insist their gods and goddesses represent the many forms of one transcendent God, Brahman, who created the universe and is the ultimate reality with which Hindus want their souls to be united. When and whether such union happens depends on each person's karma, or righteousness. If in this life a person has built up great righteousness, his or her soul may be merged with Brahman after death. Otherwise, that soul is reincarnated in another life. Over the millennia Hindus have developed highly sophisticated disciplines—the several forms of yoga—to help them enhance their karma and thereby make union with Brahman more nearly possible. The oldest Hindu temple in the United States is in the multinational neighborhood of Flushing in Queens, New York. It is called the Hindu Temple Society of North America, and its president is Dr. Uma Mysorekar, a semiretired obstetrician and gynecologist who came to the United States from India more than thirty years ago. Seated in the board room of the temple office building in an elegant red sari, with a traditional red dot on her forehead, Mysorekar talked with Bob in 2006 about Hindu beliefs and her own everyday spiritual practices.

The word "Hinduism" came because of the river Sindhu, and the people who lived on the banks of the Sindhu. When the Persians came, over five thousand years ago, they could not pronounce the name Sindhu. They called it Hindu. Those who lived on the banks of the river then called themselves Hindus, and the religion they practiced became Hinduism.

It is not true that Hinduism has 330 million gods. It is true that when you walk into a temple you see lots of deities. But Hinduism has just one supreme god, and the many deities represent to us different forms of the same god. Each of the deities represents certain of our objectives [and needs], and we worship them in that fashion.

We develop a rapport with certain deities, just as we do with a friend. So we sit in front of the Lord and cry over the shoulders of the Lord. We sit and pray and continue to ask for his grace. We say this is my problem, that is my problem. And then when you meditate the Lord answers you. Suddenly, at the end of the meditation, something strikes you and you say, "My goodness, this is my solution." We strongly believe that intense faith in God, no matter which deity you worship and however you worship, brings the ultimate answer to all your problems.

When I was doing gynecology and obstetrics I had a patient who had just delivered and had massive bleeding. We had to open the belly immediately to see where the bleeding was coming from. She was close to death. It was impossible to think that I could stop that bleeding, and I almost gave up hope. But I prayed intensely, and I said, "God, we must not let this woman die. She's a young woman who just had a child. Please help me to do this." And, lo and behold, within a matter of a few minutes, whatever pressure I was putting on, it worked, and the bleeding stopped. I have had so many such experiences in my life.

Offerings and Vibrations

Rituals are important because they bring health, wealth, prosperity, and peace to the devotees. Our belief is that everything we do in life is an offering to God. That's the reason we pray first, before anything we do. When we go to the temple we take a bunch of flowers as an offering to God, thanking the Lord for whatever he has given us and asking for his continuing grace.

In one ritual, the priests bathe the Lord with milk, yogurt, fruit juices, and so on, pouring the nutrients on the deity. Almost all of these deities are stone, granite. People who sculpt the stone have enormous faith that they will be able to carve a particular deity in that stone. Then when the carved stones are brought into the temple, the belief is that the priests can instill real life into them through various rituals, such as mantras and chanting. The nutrients from what is poured over them enhance the power of the stone. Those who are standing in front feel the vibrations coming from them, and it is said the more rituals you do, the more power the temple has. And when there are strong vibrations people who come looking for peace are guaranteed that.

All these rituals are also done in our homes, where people have small altars and deities, and they pour milk or yogurt over them there. Some of the home altars are almost as good as the temples, except on a smaller scale.

When I get up in the morning I prostrate myself before the Lord and thank him for letting me get up yet again. Then I ask him to make sure there is use for me this day. And then after that, I take my bath and then go back to my *puja* [prayer] room, where the altar is. We always light a little oil lamp—sesame oil or mustard oil. In an area where there is darkness, when you light a lamp suddenly there is a glitter, a shining all around. But it also speaks about normal life. There is constant darkness in our lives, but the light reminds us of the sun shining. So now you sit and pray in front of God. I do this and then prostrate myself again before God and offer some more everyday prayers. It all takes about thirty minutes, and it's only after that that I think of taking anything to eat or drink.

Then, at the end of the day, I go home. We always leave our shoes outside, just like in the temple. We also wash our hands and feet at a faucet outside the house. Some of us take a bath again, and then we offer a small prayer again at the altar, and then have dinner. And before I go to bed, what I do is, sitting on my bed, I pray to God, thanking him for the day's events, especially if I've had the privilege to help somebody. And that ends my day.

The red mark on my forehead is called *tilaka*. Some people think it is only for married women, but that is not so. It simply represents that a woman is Hindu. But even that is misleading because it has become like a beauty mark. I see lots of non-Hindus wearing it. And there can be multiple colors, basically just to match their dresses.

We have at least ten major festivals each year, maybe more, and umpteen number of smaller festivals. I think God created them for two reasons. One is to intensify worship, increase your faith in God. It also brings the community together. Our biggest annual festival is the nine-day Ganesh Chaturthi festival [honoring the elephant-headed Lord Ganesha, the god of intellect, wisdom, and good fortune, invoked at the beginning of any trip or task.] Fifteen to twenty thousand people come here from all over the United States. It's extremely colorful. People dance and carry the Lord on their shoulders, and it's an event everybody looks forward to.

Hindus believe the ultimate reality is Brahman, who is both with and without form. There are three concepts, just like Christianity. Lord Brahman is believed to have created the universe. Lord Shiva destroys and re-creates. And Lord Vishnu is the protector of the universe. So it is the combination of the three, like the Trinity, that represents the ultimate universe.

Atman is Brahman within all of us. We believe that each of us is divine, so when I fold my hands and bow my head down I'm bowing to the divinity, the Atman within the other person. When God created all of us he created us as humans, but he was also in us. So we say don't hurt anybody because when you hurt someone you are also hurting the divine.

Nonviolence is one of Hinduism's major doctrines, not only in actions, but also in words. Mahatma Gandhi was a great proponent of nonviolence. But unfortunately politics infiltrate, and hatred brings out violence. In the name of religion people kill each other, and I think this is extremely sad and should be condemned. It most certainly doesn't speak of the teachings of Hinduism. Sitting across the table and talking is the best approach.

One of the doctrines of Hinduism is reincarnation. Reincarnation means rebirth. When a person dies, the firm belief is that the soul, Atman, migrates to different planes. Ultimately, it reaches the highest plane, and then it either merges with the ultimate reality, Brahman, if it has achieved righteousness, or it is reborn, and the capacity or shape or form of that rebirth depends entirely on the person's actions in the previous life.

God is so merciful and kind that he does not punish anybody. We do not believe in the concept of heaven or hell. What we believe is either you merge with God or you come back to this world of suffering. You could call this world hell and merging with God, heaven.

Somebody asked, "Does it mean that people who kill each other will be born as worms in the next life?" We don't know that. As humans, we can't ever know who will be born as what. But one thing we know for sure is that if we are to reach the ultimate goal as a Hindu—salvation, which is merging with the Lord—you've got to lead a most righteous life. Be most charitable, be kind, be compassionate. Help your people. Being selfish certainly doesn't help. If we build up our righteousness in this life, we are guaranteed that our suffering will decrease in the next life.

Whether the soul will be reborn or will merge with Brahman depends on the karma of that individual, what was done and not done in the previous life. Karma means righteousness, and your destiny in this life is determined by the karma of your acts in the past. Your previous karma now makes you do what you are doing.

Each one of us is responsible for our own actions, and our own actions and inactions will determine what our future will be. There is no doubt about that. God has been gracious to give us intellect, and therefore we are to use that intellect to decide what is right and what is wrong.

Let's say there are two classmates. They both studied and passed in the same way. But one is very successful, the other is not. One is very prosperous, the other is not. Somebody will say, "How can God be so unfair?" God is not unfair. It is just that individual's destiny under karma. It goes back to the karma of your actions in your past life, which now in this life we pay for in some fashion or another.

Your destiny is determined at the time of your birth. Can we change our destiny? The answer is we cannot change our destiny, but we can mitigate it. Number one, by intense faith and continuing to pray. Number two, by continuing to do good actions in many ways—community service, helping people, being charitable, and so on. Your bank balance [of good deeds] increases, and therefore you are guaranteed a good life in your next birth. Your suffering will decrease enormously. All our day-to-day activities should be geared toward karma.

We know what our karma is in this life. But, sad to say, despite the teachings that are so clear, the actions that are so clear, people still continue to do wrong things knowing full well that these cannot go away, that they'll have to pay for them at some time or other. But that's the way life is.

During everyday life here we are also guided by the various planets, and the combination of astronomy and astrology very often determines the future of individuals. So luck also has a role to play, but luck is based on a person's previous karma. It is because of that karma from a former life that he or she was destined or blessed with good or bad luck.

Real Yoga

The word "yoga" in the West usually refers to all those exercises. But the original Sanskrit means union with the ultimate, with the Lord. Yoga means yoke, to become yoked to, or united with, God. So yogic meditation is learning disciplines that will train your mind to concentrate on the superior being so you can merge with the Lord.

Lord Krishna says in the Bhagavad-Gita* that there are four different kinds of yoga.

There is Karma yoga, which emphasizes action, work, selfless service to others. That is a most important thing. There are people who get paid a million dollars and say, "I am also doing service." But that's not what it is. Selfless service without expecting any reward for it—that is the supreme form of yoga.

Bhati yoga is devotion. And what is devotion? Intense love of God. One should never be fearful of God, because God doesn't harm us. It is the intense love of God.

Then comes Jnana yoga, which means finding God through knowledge, knowledge of scriptures, so many things written by our ancestors.

Then it is Raja yoga, intense forms of community service, such as building temples, schools, hospitals.

Somebody asked me, "Can you follow just one [type of yoga]?" No, you've got to combine them.

---

* "Song of the Lord," one of Hinduism's most sacred texts.

I think in every faith there are differing, opposing ideas. But although we differ, ultimately we are all looking for the same thing, and that is God. That's our ultimate goal, whether one is Christian or Hindu or Buddhist. How you go to God depends on the way you have been trained. If I am trained as a Hindu, I will follow my path. At the same time I respect other faiths in whatever form they come because they, too, are seeking that ultimate same God. So why don't we look at the similarities instead of talking about the differences?

There was a great Indian philosopher, Swami Vivekananda, who addressed the World Parliament of Religions in Chicago, in 1893. He said Christianity, Hinduism, Buddhism, Judaism, Islam—they are all seeking the same thing. But I do it in my way, you do it in your way.

The goal is self-realization, which is God-realization [merging with the Lord]. We realize oneness with God, consciously. God-realization is infinitely higher than a mystical experience, and it is permanent.

You have to do your work without expecting any great reward for what you have done. I'm not here, the president of this temple, to get name or fame. I'm here only to achieve the goals of this institution. And if I continue to serve the temple and help achieve its goals, I think I will be able to reach God-realization.

CHAPTER 6

Paths Up the Mountain

On October 3, 1965, on Liberty Island in New York Harbor, underneath the Statue of Liberty, President Lyndon Johnson signed into law a radical change in U.S. immigration policy. No longer would people from northern and western Europe have priority over everyone else. The "golden door" would now be open to immigrants from all over the world.

At the time, hardly anyone foresaw the new law's consequences. But what happened turned out to be a human tsunami, one of the largest waves of legal immigration in American history, most of it from Asia and Latin America, plus a continuing inflow of the undocumented. And all the newcomers brought with them their languages, their customs, and their religions.

As a percentage of the total U.S. population, the number of Americans who are religious but not Christian is still small. But the variety and visibility of new immigrants who are Muslims, Buddhists, Hindus, Sikhs, and others have created what Diana Eck at Harvard calls "a new religious America."

This unexpected religious diversity tested the country's capacity for hospitality and challenged many people's theology.

Would there be inter-religious conflict, perhaps violence, as there had been with earlier immigrant groups?

Are all approaches to God, all paths up the mountain, equally useful? Or does only one go all the way to the top? Can believers explore other paths and still remain grounded in their own?

How should Americans resolve the apparent tension between the Bible's obligation to welcome the stranger and, on the other hand, an evangelical's duty to tell others about Jesus in the hope that they will convert to Christianity and thereby be saved? Is proselytizing one's neighbor disrespectful or an act of love?

Are the ideas and practices of Buddhism, Islam, or Hinduism in any way threatening to other faiths?

As things worked out, there was little cause for worry. As Alan Wolfe of Boston College and others have observed, hospitality—or, perhaps, indifference—trumped both fear and theological rivalry, and there has been remarkably little interfaith tension. Even after 9/11, although there were a few isolated hate crimes, the overwhelming majority of Americans remained quietly accepting of "other" religions and their practitioners. Many Americans urged Congress to change the law, again, to try to prevent illegal immigration, but the national debate that followed was not along religious lines.

Overseas, as Seyyed Hossein Nasr of George Washington University has noted, the United States invasion of Iraq seemed to many Muslims, from Morocco to Indonesia, part of a Western cultural assault on Islam, and religious differences continue to inflame conflicts over land and power, as between Israel and its neighbors.

But here in the United States, acceptance of religious diversity remains the rule overall.

At the same time, many students of diversity, such as Diana Eck, argue that mere tolerance is not enough. Tolerance, they say, means only "live and let live," with each group, perhaps, in its own "ghetto." What is needed, ultimately, say these observers, will be true pluralism, by which they mean engagement, dialogue, and a willingness to listen to and learn from each other. Tolerance, they plead, should lead to understanding, and understanding, to respect.

As Professor Nasr puts it, "There is no more crucial a problem for our day than to be able to cross religious frontiers while preserving our own integrity."

53.

The Measure of Diversity

In the early 1990s, Harvard professor Diana Eck began noticing among her students the same religious variety she had studied overseas. More and more of her students were Muslims, Hindus, Buddhists, and Sikhs, and Eck realized that most of them were the children of the people from Asia and the Middle East who had flocked to the United States after passage of the Immigration Act of 1965. With her students, Eck began documenting the country's growing and—for many—startling new religious diversity and considering its implications for theology and democracy. Bob spoke with her in 1997.

I grew up in Montana as a Methodist. I ended up traveling to India during my college years, living in the sacred city of Benares, and discovering a whole world of Hindu religiousness that I had never imagined before, a multitude of ways in which God is imaged and named. It helped me understand Christianity, my own faith, better.

I remembered those hymns I used to sing as a kid, you know, "There's a wideness in God's mercy like the wideness of the sea." Suddenly I'm here in Benares with people bathing in the River Ganges and saying their morning prayers. This was an example to me of the expansiveness of the one that I call God. I could not circle the wagons as if God were entirely the possession of the Christian tradition. I think that is a very deeply Christian insight, that Christians don't own God, that our very language of God reaches out toward all that is in heaven and on earth, the vastness and the multiplicity of God.

I had never seen anything like this when I first went to India and went to temples where one had images of God with four heads, for example, a multitude of eyes and arms. I looked at those, and I thought, "What is this?" And yet the way in which God is imaged as God in the Hindu tradition, the sense of the omnipotence of God in the form of Shiva, for example, was a real eye-opener. Also the idea that God could be seen in a visible form. We have such a taboo against it in the tradition that I come from, against what we call image or idol. And to come to understand through the Hindus that the consecration of these images is not to provide a container for God so one's vision stops there, but rather to provide a lens through which we see. They are sanctified in the same way that our bread and wine are sanctified to become the visible expressions of the divine in worship.

There are many ways of understanding the one that we call God. And what we need to be able to respond to is, "How do we think of those?" There is a wonderful story in a novel of Chaim Potok's about a rabbi who traveled in Japan during the Korean War and stopped at a Buddhist shrine and saw a man who was praying with his eyes so deeply closed, in deep concentration. The rabbi turned to his friend and said, "Do you think our God is listening? And the friend said, "I don't know. I've never thought about it." The rabbi said, "If not, why not? And if so, well, what are we all about?" That really is our question: if the one we call God, creator of heaven and earth, is not listening to the prayers of this man, what do we mean when we say "God?" And if God *is* listening, what do we mean when we say "we"—we as a group of people who have very often exclusively claimed the ear of God?

The Hindus are the ones who say, "God has many names. Three thousand names, 330 million forms." Which is really a way of saying that God is infinite. God is not limited by God's capacity to be present, but by our capacity to see. I think that is also at the heart of the Christian trinitarian understanding, that God has many faces, you might say.

Part of the question is: what does it mean for our tradition to be true? You can say with Gandhi, "All religions are true," or you can say, "All religions are true, and mine is the truest." Or you can say, "Only my religion is true, and all others are false." I think the moment that you actually meet people face-to-face, Muslims or Buddhists who are faithful in their own way, it is very difficult to come to the conclusion that all others' paths are false. When I go, as I have, to sit in the prayer room in a mosque, to sit with Muslim brothers and sisters as they are saying Friday prayers, it is very clear to me as a Christian, not simply as a scholar, that the one I call God is not a stranger to that place. Now I challenge people who are convinced that theirs is the only possible way of truth to enter into these places to discover the presence of the divine.

The experience of people who have come into deep dialogue with those of other faiths is that it more deeply enriches one's sense of oneself. We're not all asked to say that we're the same at the end of the day. Indeed, we are not all the same. But our encounter with people of other faiths is an encounter that is not premised on agreeing with them, but on knowing them.

One of the things that has been very powerful for me is the sense that God is present not only, you might say, in light and life, but in death and darkness as well. In some of the Hindu images of the divine, they have God carrying a skull in one hand, or maybe a little necklace of skulls, in the case of the goddess Kali. A lot of people are very put off by that. To me, it's a tremendous comfort. It's a comfort that I also see in the Gospel portrayals of Christ accompanying us in our suffering. But when my brother died, when my father died, the idea that God is present not only in the flowers on our altar, but in the skulls as well—that was an important realization. It's really at the heart of Christianity, but I discovered it more deeply by following my Hindu brothers and sisters into Hindu temples.

There is no word in the Gospels that occurs more frequently than "neighbor." These are our neighbors in the United States today—Muslim, Sikh, and Hindu neighbors. We don't have the option to say, "Oh, we don't want to get to know these people." This is part of Biblical theology, and we need to be bold enough to dare to do what the Gospel tells us: not only to know our neighbors, but to love them, as they are.

I had an elderly friend in India whom we called Uncle. He asked me once, quizzically, "Do you really believe that God came only once, so very long ago and to only one people?" And I searched my heart, and I thought, well, a lot of Christians do say that, but I actually don't believe that. The very idea, as Uncle would say, that God could be so stingy as to show up only once, to one people, in one part of the world exploded my understanding of incarnation.

The First Multireligious Democracy?

In simple terms, we have become the most religiously diverse nation on earth. We have multiple Buddhist traditions—for instance, Los Angeles is now really the most complex Buddhist city in the world. We have Hindus who have come not just from India, but from Trinidad and the Caribbean. We have Muslims who have come from the Middle East and from India and Pakistan and Africa and Indonesia.

If you drive down the interstate outside Toledo you might see a huge mosque rising from the farmlands. Or if you head out into the suburbs of Houston, you would see mosques and Hindu temples. If you turn off the little road on which the Boston Marathon starts outside Boston, there is a sign that points to the Hindu Temple of New England.

Pluralism really means what we do with all the diversity that is ours, how we engage with it, if we engage with it. It doesn't mean the ghettoization of diversity: here we all are, and we're all different from one another. It means engaging with that in some way. And that may be the engagement of parents of different children in the public schools. It may be the engagement of an interfaith council. It may be the engagement of an employer with the new diversity of the workplace. It means addressing diversity, trying to build bridges of communication.

In terms of my own faith, it has made me much clearer about the great mystery that is the divine truth and the humility that all of us need to comport ourselves with if we are to understand that mystery. We are not in the position of being the judges of others, nor in the position of being able to fully understand what, as we would put it, God is up to in the world. And I think our Hindu and Buddhist and Sikh and Muslim neighbors help us along that path of understanding.

Hospitality is one thing that people of many of these religious communities in the United States have developed to a high art. And I say that from personal experience, having dropped into a Sikh *gurdwara* [temple] in Fremont, California, or in some part of New Jersey and found that just about any time of the day I would be welcomed, I would be given a meal, I would have people to talk to who would tell me about their faith. It often makes me think about what the stranger who dropped into my United Methodist church on a Sunday morning might feel.

We live in the United States today in such close quarters with religious diversity that we really need to understand more of who we are when we say, "We, the people of the United States." That's a pretty big statement, and we need to be able to have some sense of who these neighbors are. The hate crimes, for example, are mostly generated out of the kind of half-baked, intolerant truths that we carry around with us in our heads.

Most Christians in the United States are ignorant about the religious traditions of the rest of the world.

I think the most important thing that people of different faiths can have in common is a real understanding of their differences. It's okay that we're not all the same. And, in fact, the building of relationship and coming to a clear understanding of who the other is may make us understand ourselves more deeply.

The obligation of a Christian is not only to witness to people of another religious tradition, but to listen to whatever witness they may have. And once you are speaking and listening you are already in the context of dialogue. I think the thing that many people who are not Christians feel about Christian evangelism and mission is that it's so one-way. It is so one-sided. It's all mouth, you might say, and no ears. And as a Christian, I would say that is a wrong understanding of what kind of relationship we should have with people of other faiths.

I think there are appropriate places for proselytization or for mission, but there are also inappropriate places. That does not mean that we should stop evangelizing either here or elsewhere, but it does mean that the attitude of relationship we need to have with neighbors of other faiths is something that requires a real seeking of dialogue and not the one-way process of mission.

One of the things that is most important about the United States is the cherishing of religious freedom. People have come to the United States from all over the world with the notion that religious freedom is something that this country supports. People who have come from parts of the world where religious freedom is not allowed are grateful for that. I think that is something that the United States has to contribute—a supportive environment to these new religious communities.

We have this challenge in the United States to do something that has really never been done before, which is to create a multireligious and democratic state. In fact, the multireligious America is an extension of our commitment to a constitutional democracy. We have an opportunity to create such a state in a world that has very few models for this kind of religious pluralism.

I rank [the chances of achieving that as] pretty high. We have a society that is very committed to a kind of neighborliness, maybe over and above everything. When we look at the way in which this has been expressed in the United States, even despite the new challenges of the last thirty years, I think we are looking at a very optimistic scene, indeed.

The Christian church does not have a corner on compassion and love and the virtues that are called in Saint Paul's letters to the Galatians the "fruits of the spirit." These are things that are widely shared, and we need to keep our eyes open for them wherever we find them.

One of the most startling things about the entire experience of Easter and Pentecost was that most of the people who came to call themselves Christians did not recognize what Christ was doing, did not recognize him when he was walking along the road side by side with them, didn't recognize him when he was standing on the bank of the lake, didn't recognize the outpouring of the Holy Spirit. I mean, these mysteries are things that the Christian church does not have locked up in its own treasure chest but are mysteries that we need to be alert to. I fully believe that people who have a very tidy view of Christianity, as if all the mysteries have been solved, need to open their eyes again to what God is doing in the world.

One of the stories I tell is that of a Vietnamese Buddhist temple in Boston, in the suburb of Roslindale, where the magnificent image outside of the bodhisattva of compassion, named Quan Yen, was smashed by neighborhood vandals, by boys in the projects next door, out of some kind of fear. In the course of deciding what to do when the vandals were caught, the Vietnamese Buddhists set an example of forgiveness for the whole city. They refused to bring the boys to court. They invited the entire neighborhood to a kind of festival of forgiveness. They had a picnic. They invited the vandals. They made them guardians of the temple. They basically displayed the kind of ethic of love and forgiveness that most Christian churches would cherish.

The boys went in and saw what happened in the temple, saw people at prayer. I remember talking with one of them. His name was Angelo. The president of the temple that very morning, when he welcomed Angelo and embraced him, had said, "Your name means angel, a guardian angel. We're going to make you the guardian angel of this Vietnamese Buddhist temple." When I talked to Angelo a little later, he said, "You know, if I had known anything about what went on inside this temple and about these people, I would never have done this." That is a lesson for all of us.

54.

Many Paths, Many Ways

Boston College political scientist Alan Wolfe believes that after decades of growing religious diversity in the United States, Americans by and large accept the validity of all paths to God. This is "the single biggest change in the way people think about religion," he told Bob in 2002.

———

I think the history here is instructive. We started out as an overwhelmingly Protestant country, although there were Catholics here, especially in Maryland, from the start. When we had the big Irish immigration and then the Polish and Italian and German immigration of Catholics to the United States in the latter part of the nineteenth century, it wasn't well received by the Protestant majority. We had the equivalent of religious wars in this country—vicious fights. I come from Boston, where the fights were probably more vicious than anywhere else. Boston had the largest Know-Nothing Party in the United States. And the Know-Nothings were as anti-Catholic as you could be. We're talking about Christians here. We're talking about Protestants and Catholics, both of whom believe in Jesus Christ. And yet, even though they both believed in Jesus Christ, you had this tremendous amount of hostility. Then Jews came. And they don't believe in Jesus Christ. But we got a little more tolerant here. We invented a new religion. We're very inventive people, so we invented one called the Judeo-Christian tradition, which actually never really existed. But we called it the Judeo-Christian tradition, and we managed to stretch our boundary a little bit more.

Even with all that, however, I don't think anyone back in the 1940s and 1950s could have predicted that there was going to be as much religious diversity as there is with so little conflict and so little violence associated with it. Given our history, it is absolutely remarkable, and it testifies to probably the single biggest change in the way people think about religion. There really was a time when saying, "I'm religious," meant, "My way is the only way." And that's not how people speak anymore. They recognize that there are many paths and many ways. We should congratulate ourselves for doing that, because so few countries really have done it. Even in countries with a long history of having more than one religion, it's often polarized, with each one having its own subculture. We have some of that here. It's not that your average Christian wants to walk into a mosque and see what's going on there. But there's more intermarriage. Especially with younger people, you're going to get much more of an intermixing. It's not going to be just each religion in its own ghetto anymore.

People are not confident about their truths anymore. Truth has taken a pretty severe blow. If you are a person who believes in a kind of absolute truth, this is one of the main problems you find with America these days. You look out and you say, "No one believes in the old truths anymore."

There's something positive to be said about being a little less confident that you have the truth and that everyone else doesn't. There's remarkable eclectic borrowing. Kids on college campuses these days who consider themselves religious will take a little bit of Thomas Merton, a little bit of Gandhi, a little bit of Mother Teresa, a little Elie Wiesel, Václav Havel, and they put it all into a mix. You say, "Hey, these are very different traditions." And they'll shrug their shoulders and say, "Well, maybe they are, but they speak to me." That's the important criterion.

55

Evangelizing by Deed

In 2000, Jimmy Carter broke his ties with the Southern Baptist Convention, citing what he called the SBC's "increasingly rigid" doctrines. But he remains an active member and Sunday school teacher at his local Baptist church in Plains, Georgia. The former president believes it is his duty to evangelize, as long as it can be done respectfully, especially by deed and example, and he sees no difficulty in respecting the truth of another religion while remaining committed to the truth of his own. In 1978, Carter put his sense of pluralism into practice when he brought together Egypt's Anwar Sadat and Israel's Menachem Begin for twelve days of secret negotiations that ended with the signing of the Camp David Accords, the first peace treaty between Israel and an Arab state. As he suggested in this conversation with Bob in 1999, Sadat and Begin found some religious common ground before they arrived at a political understanding.

———

I think I learned a lot at Camp David, where Begin, Sadat, and I spent the first three days together. They were so incompatible they spent the next ten days carefully kept apart. And one of the things that we did agree on is that we worshipped the same God. That is a tie that binds us. We worship a God of peace and a God of forgiveness and a God of accommodation. Sadat was the main spokesman for this premise, and he made it plain that all Muslims who followed the Koran must revere Christ as a prophet and on the same basis as Moses or Abraham and others. So I feel at ease with this proposition. I am pleased when I hear about Jewish conversions to Christianity. I do not have any doubt in my own mind that Christ is the son of God, that Christ is the expected messiah. At the same time, I do not feel that it is proper for me as a Christian to be judgmental. Jesus said, "Judge not that you be not judged." Why do you look at a speck in your brother's eye when you have a two-by-four in your own? And Paul taught that all people are equal at the foot of the cross. So I think God is the one to judge whether a person is lost through eternity or saved by a particular profession of faith.

I think there is a mandate from Christ himself for Christians to go into Judea and Samaria and other nations to spread the word of Christianity. And I try to do that, as a matter of fact. But I have restricted my own evangelical efforts to those who do not have any faith. I have never tried to target a devout Muslim or a devout Jew or a devout Hindu and say, "Your religion is wrong. Adopt mine as a superior religion," although I obviously think that Christianity is the religion that God mandates.

Let me give you one example. In the year that I was elected president, from our little, tiny church in Plains, there was another family of farmers, Jerome Etheridge and his wife, Joanne. He was not even a Sunday school teacher, but he felt the call to be a missionary. He went to Togo eventually, after learning French. He had never spoken any foreign language before. He was not and is still not eloquent at all. When he got to Togo, he assessed the area around where he was assigned. In an eighty-mile radius there were only five religious congregations—two Catholic and three Muslim. Jerome decided that he would do other things in the name of Christ. He got a North Carolina Baptist to give him a well-drilling outfit. He drilled 130 wells. He dug fish ponds. He built a bridge across a great river.

And Jerome will leave Togo this year. He will leave behind him eighty churches with five thousand Christians, because he actually did things for other people in the name of Christ. To me, that is the proper way to exhibit our faith, not just to try to convert people who have another, established faith in the same God.

56.

The Only Way to Heaven

Rev. James Merritt of Atlanta was president of the Southern Baptist Convention in 2001 and 2002. As his term ended, Bob interviewed him at the First Baptist Church of Snellville, Georgia, an Atlanta suburb, where he was senior pastor. He later became pastor of the Cross Pointe church in Gwinnett Center, Georgia.

I do believe that Southern Baptists, as evangelistic as we are, we're not nearly as evangelistic as we need to be. I think we need to be more attuned to a world that's lost and in need of the Gospel. I think we need to recapture even more of a passion to share that Gospel around the world. And even though we're doing, relatively speaking, a good job compared to maybe other groups, we're certainly not doing everything we're capable of doing.

Evangelism is the number-one task that God gave to the [Christian] church. In Jesus's Great Commission he said, "All thought has been given unto me" and "Go into all the world and make disciples of all the nations, baptizing them in the name of the Father, the Son, and the Holy Spirit." That is the raison d'être of the church. That's why we're here. General Motors is in the transportation business. Kroger, Publix, and Winn Dixie, they're in the food business. The church is in the evangelism business, and that's what really separates us from every other organization in the world.

I think the world's greatest problem, in a word, is sin. And the only solution to that problem is salvation through faith in Christ. So I don't think we can do anything that's more helpful to people in living a better life, in being better husbands, wives, mothers, et cetera, than to introduce them to a saving faith in Christ.

I'll give you a perfect illustration of what that means. I just got back from China, Japan, Cambodia, and Thailand. I was preaching in the University in Phnom Penh, Cambodia, to a group of more than a hundred students.

Half of them were Buddhists, half were Christians. And I made this statement to the Buddhists there. I said, "I want you to understand the difference between Buddhism and Christianity." I said, "Buddhism is a religion. Hinduism is a religion. Christianity is not a religion. Christianity is a personal relationship with God through Jesus Christ."

We are unapologetic in our belief that Christ is the only way to heaven. I know, in a day of political correctness, that sounds somewhat intolerant, but, you know, when I go to the doctor and he examines me, I want my doctor to be very intolerant. I want him to tell me exactly what the problem is and exactly what the solution is. We are not afraid to do that, as Southern Baptists, in the spiritual realm, as well.

Respect is mutual. I do respect the right of a Muslim to believe as he chooses to believe, and the Hindu. One of the great things about America is religious freedom, and I would die for the right of anyone to believe, or not to believe, in God.

Having said that, if we do believe that we have the truth about salvation, then, quite frankly, one of the most disrespectful things I could do is not to share that. I'll give you an analogy. If you had cancer and I had the pill that could cure any kind of cancer, and I knew it was empirically proven it could cure, I think I would have a responsibility to at least give you the option of accepting that cure.

If what I believe about Jesus Christ is true, not only am I obligated to share it—quite frankly, the news is too good for me to hold it in.

When you're willing to stand up in this day and age and say, "Jesus Christ is not a good way to heaven. He's not even the best way to heaven. He is the only way to heaven," you better believe the cannons of political correctness are going to be aimed right at your head.

Hopefully, our denomination will raise our work and effort and power another notch, another level in doing all that we can do to see to it that everyone on this planet has heard the gospel of Jesus Christ at least once.

57.

Is Every Truth True?

Robert Wuthnow, the Princeton sociologist of religion, thinks that most Americans don't care much about what others believe. At the same time, he thinks we should care and that we should also take fresh looks at our own beliefs, too. Bob spoke with him in 2001.

———

I would sum up Christians' reactions to other religions in one word: indifference. It really surprises me. You talk to people, you say, "Okay, your son's best friend in school is Hindu or Muslim. Your neighbor is a Buddhist or a Hindu. The building right across the street from your church is a Hindu temple. What are you doing about it? How do you think about this?" People have not thought about it. They sort of block out the religious identity and don't pay much attention to it.

You could call it tolerance, and people use the language of tolerance, because when you press them they'll say, "Well, of course, a Hindu, or a Muslim, or a Buddhist has every right to practice, just as we do." They flip into the language of civil rights, civil liberties. Push people, though, and say, "Well, but theologically, what do you think? They really believe something different from you." And it's sort of like, "Well, that's okay. That may be true for them. What I believe is true for me."

I think as a culture we are only beginning to face up to the sense of doubt that we have, within the Christian community especially, about "truth" as it has traditionally been defined. For many centuries Christians have thought that they had the truth and that other people did not have the truth in the same way. Now, Christians are not quite so sure of that. They are more likely to say, "This is true for me. I sort of know it from my experience, but I'm not willing to say anything about anybody else." That radically changes the

355

meaning of truth—when it's just true for you and not necessarily true for somebody else.

We did a survey in 2000, and one of the statements we asked people to agree or disagree with said, "Christianity is the best way to know God." About two-thirds of the public said, "Yes, we agree with that." Then, just a little bit later in the survey, we asked people to respond to another statement that said, "All religions are equally true." About two thirds agreed with that statement, too.

What that left me with was just a huge question mark about how much people are thinking deeply about the truth of their own religion, their belief in Christianity, and what they mean by other religions being true. I don't think a lot of people have really sorted that out, and I think that's going to be a big issue.

Evangelical Protestants I've talked with fall into two categories. There are those, often in leadership positions, who say, "Yes, as an organization, denomination, or church, we have that responsibility to proclaim the Christian Gospel." Then there are the others at the grass roots level who may be firm in their beliefs. But they say, "That's not really my role to get out there. I can live as a good Christian. Hopefully, they'll see something in my lifestyle. Or, perhaps, if they're really in need, they'll come to me. But I'm not going to go out of my way. That would be an intrusion on their rights. That would be a lack of respect. So all I can do is be an example and leave it at that."

It's hard to tell at this point what effects the new religions will have. One scenario, at least, that I think makes a lot of sense is that we will have a kind of leavening of the religious spirit in this country, meaning that there will be, on the one hand, more tolerance and acceptance, but on the other hand, more attempts to look back within our own religious traditions and say, "Well, what does it really teach? What do I really believe?"

I think the new diversity will probably make the society as a whole more religious than it is now and give us more ways of challenging the predominant secular tone. If you talk with Muslims, especially, they are concerned about the immorality of the society, what they see on television. They are very devout, they want something to be better, and they say, "We wish our Christian neighbors were more committed to their own faith." So, perhaps, that will happen.

58.

Our Great Challenge

Seyyed Hossein Nasr of George Washington University spoke with Bob in 2003, just before the U.S. invasion of Iraq, about "the profound battle afoot" between religious and nonreligious ways of looking at the world.

Modernism is always changing. I use the word "modernism" not simply as meaning contemporary, but meaning certain premises about the nature of the human being—rationalism, individualism, and, in a sense, rejection of the theomorphic nature of the human being, of the divine world over the human world, of the divine will over the human will, and so forth.

If you take modernism as a philosophical system, then Islam and modernism are incompatible philosophies in the same way that modernism was incompatible with Christianity and still is fighting, after five hundred years in many domains, with certain aspects of Christianity. Except that in the Christian case, modernism grew from the belly of a Christian civilization. Christianity has had five hundred years to deal with it. But for Islam, it comes from the world "out there."

I believe that the question isn't whether Islam can live with modernism. Why not ask the question, "Can modernism accommodate itself to live according to the truth of Islam, or Christianity, or Judaism?" I think there's a much more profound battle afoot. It isn't that modernism has won the day, and now everybody in the world has to conform to it. Modernism itself and its foundations are floundering. The crises it has brought about—of the environment, of the breakup of family relationships, of society, of the meaninglessness of life—have turned many people to try to seek something beyond its borders. That's why we now talk about postmodernism.

I think we are in a time when Islam as a value system, not only as a religion, has to be thought about as a contending way of looking at the universe. And Islam can live with modernism on a practical level. I mean, you can have a hospital and go to it if your wife gets sick. But the idea that modernism is reality, and everything else has to conform itself to it—that has to be challenged.

I think there's no more crucial a problem for our day than to be able to cross religious frontiers while preserving our own integrity. In fact, I think this is the only exciting intellectual adventure of our times.

Traditionally, human beings were created to live in a particular human world, which was also a religious world. They did not have to concern themselves with other worlds. You could not blame an Italian in the sixteenth century or an Englishman in a little village in the Middle Ages if they didn't think about Confucius or Hinduism or Islam or even Judaism.

Today, that world has changed. We have the interpenetration of, first of all, human communities and ideas, books, mass media, television. The great challenge is how to remain a good Muslim or a good Christian and at the same time have the empathy to be able to penetrate the world of the other without vilifying the other. That, I think, is our great challenge.

I believe that it can be done. There were throughout the history of both Christianity and Islam examples of great saints, of great sages who had the magnanimity, who had the vision to be able to see the truth on the other side.

On the Islamic side, we've had many, many great Sufi poets, for example, who were very pious Muslims and who at the same time spoke about the beauty of Christianity or Judaism or, when they went to India, of Hinduism. One of them said that anybody who reads the Bhagavad Gita realizes it is a book that has come from God. We have to learn from that, and it's a very great challenge. But I think it can be done.

I don't like the word "tolerance" very much, because you can also tolerate a toothache. There's enough spiritual substance, I think, within each religion to be able to see that God's creative power is not limited to just my religion or your religion. God is infinite, and he can manifest a truth outside our world into another world in the same way that he created the human species, other animals, the earth, and also other galaxies, other planets, other suns. We have to learn that. If we put our best foot forward now, it can be done.

59

The Passions of Jerusalem

David Hartman is an American-born Orthodox rabbi living in Jerusalem, where he founded and leads the Shalom Hartman Institute. Its purpose is to create understanding among people of different backgrounds in order to help make Jerusalem a place of safety and freedom for all three monotheistic faiths— Judaism, Christianity, and Islam. Herbert Kaplow spoke with him in 1998.

Jerusalem is a place which in some way generates fanaticism and generates the feeling of exclusive truth. I mean, the history of Jerusalem is the history of holy wars. Each group came and therefore had to destroy what the other group did in order to affirm its own dignity. You will notice that the mosque is built where they believe the temple is. You go into the old city, you get a feeling of geographic claustrophobia. Each group feels that its way is the only way: there is one God, therefore there has to be one truth. Christians built their story on the Jewish story and therefore feel they are the inheritors of Judaism. Muslims built their story on the Bible, and therefore they feel that they are the perfect expression of monotheism. Now, we've got to get out of each other's story. We can't feel that in order for me to tell my story, your story has to end.

A year later, on the eve of the new millennium, Hartman told Kim Lawton that after the Six-Day War in 1967, Jews in Jerusalem made a conscious choice not to punish those they had just defeated by destroying their holy sites in the city.

People decided not to create a conflict, not to have a return of the hurt, because when you live off revenge you never win. In other words, you have to decide how you want to live. And Jews have made a decision that they want all religions to feel secure in Jerusalem. Islam and Christianity are welcome. They are not aliens, they are not enemies. And that is a very important decision, that all three monotheistic faiths, which were in some way in conflict throughout history, can live in peace in Jerusalem. That is the very meaning of a holy Jerusalem, which in some way now teaches us that people of different beliefs need not see the other one as an enemy, need not see the other one as a threat. In other words, affirmation does not require that I demonize those who are different from me. I don't have to build conviction out of hate and fear.

Separation does not bother me. It is hate that bothers me. I am not asking everyone to love each other. I am just asking everyone to be decent to each other.

I believe that the fundamental mission of the Jewish people is to be a vision of pluralism and inclusiveness. They are meant to correct the mistakes of holy wars. Jerusalem is a city filled with blood in history. Each group in the Crusades was trying to conquer the other ones. Jews have come home to say that God does not want us to sing only one melody. It is beautiful to see on Friday Muslims in prayer, and on Shabbat Jews singing their prayers, and on Sunday the church bells ringing. There is different music in Jerusalem, and that is what I think we have to celebrate. The millennium is not the triumph of one faith. It is the triumph of sobriety. God is going to speak Latin or Arabic or Hebrew; he is multilingual. God can speak many languages and he can appreciate different music. This is what I hope Jerusalem will be for the world, and this is what I think Jews have to be a witness to.

That Jerusalem is the capital of Israel and will be forever is understandable. But in what way do we work out the geographic space so that others can feel a sense of dignity? The fact that Muslims or Arabs or Palestinians would feel that Jerusalem is holy for them does not take away my love for Jerusalem. Other people loving Jerusalem does not take away my love. And I have to learn to celebrate their love and at the same time not destroy my own national feelings. In other words, if, in the desire to accommodate, you deny your own feelings, that is a mistake. There are particular Jewish passions which have a right to live. But can they live and at the same time allow other people's passions to live as well? That is the hope for the future, that political sobriety and religious sobriety will reign.

CHAPTER 7

Lives Well Lived

Scott Neeson, a former top executive in the film industry, tells of when he received a life-altering telephone call from Los Angeles. Neeson was in Cambodia, pursuing what would become his vocation in life. His staff in Hollywood sent word that an unhappy actor was refusing to board a private jet bound for a publicity event because the jet didn't have all "the right amenities for him," in Neeson's words.

At the time, Neeson was shuttling between L.A. and Phnom Penh, reaching out to Cambodian street children who scavenge the garbage dumps outside the capital city. As he recalls in this chapter, he wanted to scream at the actor, "Come down here for a day and see what it's all about!" At that moment he realized that being a movie mogul with a sports car, yacht, and fabulous home wasn't who he was. He now lives permanently in Phnom Penh, and because of that, many children spend their days not at the dump, but in a classroom, and their nights under a roof.

Neeson arrived at a new grasp of what is real, of what it's all about. Many theologians believe that such an awareness of higher reality (they call it "ultimate reality") is the root of religion. Neeson and a few others in this chapter do not look at themselves as religious or very spiritual, for that matter, and yet each person in these pages has made a fresh encounter with what is, for them, the Really Real.

Such an encounter is felt more often than expressed and may not arrive neatly in conceptual packaging. Rajiv Vinnakota, who educates needy kids in Washington, DC, is not sure if his motivations can be bundled as religious or spiritual. "But I know what I know," he says, referring to what now feels, to him, like a calling.

Even some of the ablest articulators do not try to fully contain, in words, a sense of life and meaning that is uncontainable. "I don't find spiritual insight sitting around thinking 'thinky' thoughts about what it all means and who God is and who shot the Holy Ghost," the novelist Anne Lamott confesses. "I find God in the utter *dailyness* and mess of it all."

The people who have lent their voices to this book have a wonderful gift—an enlarged capacity to make meaning out of the "mess" of life. Those who are profiled in this chapter, and many others between these covers, have a particular gift of respond-ability (as styled here by the late William

Sloane Coffin). They have been able to make or remake their personal iden-
tities by responding to a broken world and to broken lives—in some cases,
their own.

By responding to this brokenness, our subjects in the pages that follow
have become heroes to those who know them, or knew them. But what they
have done is not so different from what millions of lesser-known Americans
do every day in their families, neighborhoods, and places of work and worship. They care for, write about, and speak out on behalf of the sick, the
handicapped, the hungry, the addicted, the weak, the confused, the poor—
all the "least of these."

Famous, controversial, or "just" quietly kind, they all help repair the
world.

60

Where the Weak and the Strong Dance Together

In the summer of 1964, Jean Vanier—a Canadian Royal Navy officer in World War II and the son of a French-Canadian diplomat—made what he would regard as a solid career move. He invited two mentally disabled men from a local asylum to come live with him at his home in a small French village north of Paris, and he named the little community L'Arche—French for "the ark," the biblical symbol of refuge and deliverance. Since then, L'Arche has blossomed into a federation of more than 130 communities in 33 countries on six continents, communities where the disabled people live with nondisabled people, who are able to pursue what Vanier sees as the opportunity of a lifetime—"to go down the social ladder, not up," as he explained to Bill when they first met in the mid-1980s. For many years, the conventional wisdom had been that mentally disabled people should learn how to live by themselves, hold down a job, "and go home at night to watch television and drink beer," as Vanier put it, but he felt that this view ignored "the greatest cry of handicapped people and all human beings—the cry for community."

A prolific writer whose books such as Becoming Human *and* Finding Peace *have appeared on international bestseller lists, Vanier often talks about the "fun" of living in such a community, but he does not mask the pain and the trials. When Bill profiled him for Religion News Service, he seemed worn out and a little weary of the praise he and other nondisabled helpers at L'Arche often hear for being so "heroic." Don't give us plaudits, he said, "give us community," by which he meant that these caregivers need the same friendship and fellowship from those outside the community that they give to the mentally disabled. That was two decades ago, and Vanier, a Roman Catholic layman, is still climbing down the social ladder, still discovering who he is in the community in Trosly, France. In 2006, Religion & Ethics NewsWeekly correspondent Judy Valente caught up with the then seventy-seven-year-old Vanier in Chicago, where he visited a L'Arche community and spoke with her about the paradoxes of power and friendship, and "how to live anguish." He began by looking at the side of life at L'Arche that is not so "fun."*

—

I think the greatest pain is when we lose the sense of why we are in community. When we lose the vision of community, what are we confronted with? People who are beautiful, but sometimes painful, conflicts in relationships, explosions, violence. We can be tired and start thinking, "let's get out of here and do something else." Yet, through all this suffering and pain and fatigue, we are seeing incredibly beautiful things: people are being transformed, and we ourselves are being transformed. Something has changed within us. We realize that we don't have to be in a world of power, rivalry, and competition in order to find our value; it's okay just to be ourselves. So we in L'Arche are continually in this paradox of pain, suffering, and resurrection.

Celebrations are one of the most beautiful things in L'Arche, when we all gather together to celebrate someone's birthday, or arrival, or departure, or twenty years in L'Arche, when we celebrate Christmas or Easter. We sing, dance, mime, laugh, and have fun together. There's something so beautiful that we know we are called to be there.

We become more human as we discover we are able to love people. And when I say "love people," I mean to see their value and their beauty, to love people who have been pushed aside, humiliated, seen as having no value. Then we see that they are gradually being changed. At the same time, sharing our lives in community with the weak and the poor, we come in touch with our own limits, pain, and brokenness. We realize that we, too, have our handicaps which are often around our need for power and the feeling that our value lies in being powerful—a power that frequently involves crushing other people. So we're confronted by two visions of society: a vision of the pyramid, where you have to have more and more power in order to get to the top, or a vision of *a body* where every person has a place.

Fundamentally, community living is about trust and growth in trust. You trust me, I trust you. You know that I'm not going to reject you or let you down. I know that you're not going to reject me or let me down. You can tell me your story, share your pain, and talk about the ways you have been hurt or felt rejected. You can talk about what happened in your family. We come together in truthfulness. Mother Teresa said something very beautiful and true: "When you meet someone in pain or dying, your first reaction can be repulsion. But if you get close to the person and take care of his or her body in pain, you touch compassion." And she went on, "If you go a little bit further in the relationship, you enter into wonderment." That wonderment is the heart-to-heart encounter, where you see and meet what is most beautiful in that person, which is the child of God. And at the same time you see and touch in yourself what is most beautiful and most truthful, which is also the child of God. And in that movement, that encounter, one to another, you sense the presence of God. It's what Martin Buber says in *I and Thou*: there is nothing more beautiful than when we come together, you and I, in a moment of wonderment.

Friendship is a beautiful reality. If it means, however, that we just spend our time flattering each other and thinking that other people outside "the group" are no good, friendship closes us up in ourselves. It becomes dangerous. Religions can also be dangerous when our religion makes us think that we are the best and that we have to impose our vision upon others whether they like it or not. In some way we're trying to free ourselves from guilt, pretending or living an illusion that we are the best.

The whole mystery of religion is that it brings us into the presence of God, opening up our whole being to something over and above the immediate. We can therefore rest and be open. That's what prayer is all about. It's about presence, to be present to God. As soon as there is a presence to God, there's wonderment, there's joy, there's peace. We can easily get caught up in the world of the finite, the contingent, in brokenness and suffering. Prayer is this opening of a door to something over and above and deeper, which gives meaning to all the pain of the finite. It is something that we can just rest in. I think that, fundamentally, prayer is rest.

Lost and Found

When I say that people in the West have "lost the meaning," I mean they've lost the zest for life. They've lost motivation. They are caught up in a very material reality, which essentially comes down to having more power, more comfort, and more wealth, instead of discovering that life is about transmitting life to others. The beauty of spiders is that they give birth to spiders, of elephants that they give birth to elephants, of roses that they give life to other roses. The beauty of human beings is in our capacity to give life to others, not only biological life, but to give life, hope, love, and meaning to others. But today we tend to fall into productivity; we think that our greatness and glory come from our ability to build or create new things and to have more money. We then lose the meaning of life, which is to transmit life to others. The beauty of communicating life is that we can't control other people. A mother cannot control the life of her children; she gives them life and helps them to grow to greater maturity and freedom. We are called to give life and help people discover who they are, so that they in turn can give life to others.

How do we get the meaning of life back? We often begin to discover what life is really about when we fall sick, when we feel closer to death—then we realize "I need you, I need people who trust me, I need people who love me." Most of the time, it is only in and through crises or breakdowns that we discover a new meaning to life.

Let me tell you an incredible story of an Israeli called Aaron whom I met when I was in Ireland for a festival of peace. Aaron gave us his testimony. He had two sons. Both of them were in the army. The youngest one was killed by Hamas. He told us what a beautiful boy he was and how he had suffered at his son's death. His eldest son was so disturbed by the death of his brother and by all that he himself had seen in the Gaza Strip that he became mentally sick. The father said, "I have lost my two sons." Then he went on to say that he met another Israeli man who had lost two sons in the army. Together, they decided to create an association of families for peace. They went to meet Palestinians who had lost their father, brother, or son, and with them they created an association, Families for Peace. If that man had not lost his two sons, he would have remained behind the barriers between Israel and Palestine. He had experienced great loss and pain but did not let himself be controlled or governed by that pain. He didn't remain locked up in anger, but went into a movement of transformation.

So where is the world going? On one side, it's going from empire to empire. Empires come and go, rise up and crash. Throughout the history of humankind there have been many great empires: the Roman Empire, the Spanish Empire, the Ottoman Empire, the British Empire, and now we have the American Empire. Today we are also seeing the rising of the Chinese Empire and a growing Indian Empire. The world changes and evolves, but there is this continual movement and struggle—people and nations wanting more and more power and domination, others wanting and calling for peace, nonviolence, and justice.

I always like to put things into context. The kingdom of God is a vision of peace. You can read about visions of peace, but where do we see peace? It's a world of conflict. The whole of the Roman reality was Pax Romana, an attempt to create universal peace through the armies of Rome. But a lot of people were angry with Rome; the peace was imposed upon them. There is another peace which comes from below, like the birth of the child bringing peace to the mother and to the father. The kingdom comes through the little ones, through the weakest ones. Weak people bring down our defense mechanisms; powerful people make us defend ourselves. To become human is to let our defense mechanisms come down so that we can be ourselves and be with others just as they are, so that we can touch the joy of togetherness, a togetherness in which weak people have an important gift because they call us together into a gradual birth of a body, not a pyramid. Together with them, we can let down the barriers and turn our backs on the need for power. We can discover that life is to be celebrated together, where the weak and the strong can sing and dance together.

Living Anguish

I'm not sure I could say I have "dedicated" my life to others. I've been pulled or attracted into something. That's very different. It's not a question of making a big choice in my life but more a feeling of being led or drawn into something which is a mystery. The difference between a mystery and a secret is that once you get close to the secret, nothing is left; but the more you get close to a mystery, the more it becomes mysterious, a place of wonderment. So my sense over these past forty-two years in L'Arche is that I have been called into a mystery, which is the discovery of the gospel message, of the kingdom, of how that togetherness with the little, the weak, and the fragile can help us build something beautiful together and celebrate life. I'd be crazy if I had regrets. That doesn't mean to say I haven't had to live through many difficulties and crises and much pain. But it also means that I see the meaning of what I am living and the joy of being together with those who are poor and vulnerable.

Loneliness brings you to anguish. And anguish can lead to a search for compensations—drink, drugs, even violence, and sexual encounters which have no fundamental meaning. But loneliness can also become a thirst, a thirst for meaning. It can even become a thirst for God. When you cry out, that cry says, "I need your presence because I feel too lonely, and I feel too much in this world of anguish and inner pain." I think one of the most fundamental and perhaps most complex realities is how to live anguish—not seeking compensations or superficial relationships, not filling ourselves up with television and the like, but somehow discovering that it is a cry for the infinite and for a presence. I believe that cry is at the heart of the incarnation: we yearn to discover and know a God who became flesh, not a God who came to manifest the power of God but rather to manifest God's love and togetherness and tenderness.

At the end of her interview with Jean Vanier, Judy Valente asked him, "What's left to be done with your life?" He said, "Ah, to die quietly."

61.

"Oh, Annie, Whatever"

Anne Lamott shatters many people's stereotypes of a successful spiritual writer. She's a dreadlock-wearing, left-wing, born-again Christian who uses edgy humor and salty language when speaking of her deeply held personal faith. Some readers are offended, but her books about her spiritual journey have become national best-sellers. "If Jesus doesn't have a sense of humor, I am so doomed that none of this matters anyway," says Lamott, who was raised by atheist parents in northern California, where she has lived all her life in Marin County. She writes expressly about her long struggles with addiction, sexual promiscuity, bulimia, and self-loathing—struggles that reached a crash point when she was thirty and in the throes of a hangover, just after having had an abortion. She felt what she grasped as the palpable presence of Jesus. A week later, she wandered into a Presbyterian vestibule, pulled in by the music, and began getting her life together, as Religion & Ethics NewsWeekly *managing editor Kim Lawton narrated in a February 2006 profile.*

Lamott's 1999 bestselling book Traveling Mercies *traces her turn to faith and her struggles living that faith as a writer and single mother to her son, Sam. She continues those reflections in her book* Plan B, *where she writes about dealing with Sam's arrival into adolescence and her own into menopause. Like her books that flout familiar genres (and which have not yet darkened the shelves of Christian bookstores), Lamott is hard to place, spiritually speaking. As Kim explains, "Her secular friends think she's a crazy Jesus freak . . . and many evangelicals are deeply uncomfortable with what they consider her loose theological views and her outspoken, obscenity-laden, pro-choice, pro-gay positions. . . . She's a Protestant who wears a Mary medallion around her neck and a red string blessed by the Dalai Lama around her wrist." In her writings as well as readings around the country, Lamott urges people to "mess up more" and "fall down more often," because that's when they will discover there are others nearby to pick them back up again.*

I don't think of myself as a spiritual writer. I think of myself as someone who writes a lot about faith and spiritual issues, but I actually think of myself as a novelist. The last several novels I've done have also concerned people of faith, but I need to be clear that I know that I really don't understand very much of these matters, and I don't want to sound like somebody who has an interesting theological understanding of the world, because I don't. I think of myself as someone who can be really funny on the page and can make people laugh, sometimes about very serious matters like God and faith and whatnot, and I do believe that laughter really is carbonated holiness. I think it's a form of spirituality. I'm good at humor and not so good at making sense of this whole spiritual mystery.

A lot of people who come hear me at readings or lectures or who buy my books—I'd say 94 percent—are Democrats or progressives, and many of them are people who were raised in spiritual, religious, often fundamentalist households, who just ran screaming for their cute little lives the second that they could, when they were old enough to, and never really thought they would go back to a church or back to the path or any path. Somehow in me they are able to find some sense of play or spaciousness, where the spirituality inside them doesn't feel so frightened to come forth.

A lot of people told me I'm the only Christian they can stand in the world, because Christians have such a bad reputation, which I think they deserve and I deserve also as one of them, for terrible judgmental behavior, terrible hypocrisy. There's a great line that my friend Tom, who's a Jesuit, said—you can tell that you created God in your own image when he hates all the same people that you do. I think that most people who are not part of a spiritual community see those of us who are believers, who are plugged in, as thinking we have the answer, we have the right God, that you really need to sign on the dotted line and really understand this stuff before you can be welcomed into the fold.

Most of my friends are secular, and most of them think I'm a little crazy. But almost all of them, almost everyone I know, has a spiritual part of their being. Everybody has a soul, I believe. Everyone has a part inside of them that is not available for rational thinking or for understanding much of anything, part of the spirit, or the soul, or whatever is touched so often by music or by the tragedies, say, in New Orleans, where people's hearts are broken. That's a good thing because the culture is so adamant that you keep your act together. People grow up and find that what they are left with is an act, and then something happens like a tragedy or just a piercingly beautiful piece of music, and something inside them comes fully to life. It's a relief for somebody like me who's not so strict in her beliefs to say that's what we are talking about. We are talking about feeding and nurturing the human spirit and bringing that forth into a world that is so thirsty and starving to death and battered.

I don't find spiritual insight sitting around thinking "thinky" thoughts about what it all means and who God is and who shot the Holy Ghost. I find God in the utter *dailyness* and mess of it all.

I was a very worried child. I'm a worried fifty-one-year-old now with a lot of faith. I was a watchful child in a typically screwed-up family. I paid attention, and my heart was always a big, open heart, and the world, my parents, my teachers, and the culture didn't succeed in closing that, for which I am deeply grateful. The places that were closed off were cracked back open by hardship, loss, and grief, and for that I'm deeply grateful. I love and often quote that wonderful Leonard Cohen song that says, "There are cracks, cracks in everything, that's how the light gets in." Any light that has come through me that I feel like communicating to my readers came through me in spite of everybody's efforts to keep me quiet and looking good and achieving more. In fact, that happens to be one of the messages that I carry: fail more, mess up more, screw up more, blow it, fall down more often. You usually fall about eighteen inches, and then you discover that there is someone nearby who is going to help you get up on your feet and dust off your butt and get you a glass of water and help you start walking again.

My faith is not a white paper—"I have a position paper on what it means to be a Christian." In fact, my faith has been so challenged by having America be under the thumb of fundamentalist Christians who, I believe, in my loving Christian and paranoid way, would love to see America be a theocracy, who think of America as a Christian nation. My faith has been so challenged because I feel, as an American, such a deep hatred of and sense of betrayal by the Bush administration. Yet Jesus said about four things that are absolutely the core of Christianity, and one of them is you really don't get to hate anyone. It doesn't say you don't get to hate anybody unless it's Dick Cheney. It's absolute that you break through this thing inside of yourself that thinks somebody is not welcomed at the table because you consider their behavior so reprehensible, so brutal. I went to church on a Sunday in this state of such discouragement and such rage, and we had a beautiful, beautiful sermon, and Martin Luther King was brought up and how he was adamant that you love the sinner as we ourselves are loved, and that you can hate the sin and do everything you can to overturn the people in charge of things if you believe their behavior is destructive, but you have to love them. That Sunday I happened to have a very spiritually evolved day, and I just felt like I could see who Bush was as a young boy and as a man—he's been a total screw-up at everything—and I had this feeling of tenderness for him. Maybe "tenderness" is stretching it a bit, but I had this feeling of not-hate for him, of softening, let's say. But the next day, I woke up and I was okay more or less, and I had a cup of coffee, still fine, and then read the paper and just went, "God! What are we doing?"

I'm an abject political animal. I'm politically plugged in. I do a lot of activism, I do a lot of benefits, I do a lot of marches, sort of freelance protest. I'm also a person of deep religious faith, and it's not my business to separate them so that my political readers will feel more comfortable and my readers who are more spiritual and creative won't feel uncomfortable because I'm so political. I can't start to censor myself to make anybody more comfortable.

A critic told somebody privately that he hated my simplistic faith, and it pierced me to the core. I thought for part of a day that I either really had to stop talking about it so much or come up with a more sophisticated, maybe a more East Coast kind of happening, intellectual faith. And then, I don't know, I took a nap or something, and that passed. I thought, all I can do is share what I think are the important stories of my life. There are a lot of Christians that can't stand me, which is just part of the territory.

Twenty years ago, I was still drinking. I was a drunk new Christian, and

I saw Jesus as my friend and companion whose presence I could feel all the time, much to my own horror in the beginning. I didn't want that to be the truth. I didn't want to be a Christian. I was raised to think Christians are idiots, and it's sort of like believing in pyramid power, and I mean no offense to the many pyramid power people who may hear this, but I was raised to think it was the opiate of people. I was raised by parents who were atheists, who worshiped at the temple of Miles Davis and who were culturally hip, bohemian types, and so this would have been horrifying to my father if he were still alive. He was raised by Presbyterian missionaries in Japan and hated Christians, especially Presbyterians, which is who I turned out to be, and he always called them God's frozen people, and I turned out to be one of them. I just have to release them—my parents, any critics.

My understanding of the kingdom of heaven, both as it is inside my heart, as Jesus said, and in the bigger world, is that it's a come-as-you-are party and that you are welcome to come to the table—people who are hungry and thirsty and needing rest. I understand that I'm welcome, and I'm accepted exactly the way I am. It's like that dumb bumper sticker that says, "You are loved exactly the way you are by God, but God loves you too much to let you stay like this." I'm definitely a work in progress, and I have a terrible time with Christian fundamentalists. Evangelical Christians and I can sit down and talk one-on-one about how much we love Jesus and how great it is to find this secret inside our own heart, and it not being a God of castigation and kicking you out, but a God of welcoming, caring, and nurturing, and yet I'm not carried in Christian bookstores. A typical Christian bookstore won't carry *Traveling Mercies* or *Plan B* because I'm irreverent, I have a very dark sense of humor, I swear, I have a very playful relationship with Jesus, I imagine. If Jesus doesn't have a sense of humor, I am so doomed that none of this matters anyway. But assuming that Jesus does and God does—that he or she does have a sense of humor—my relationship is reflective of that. I feel that presence of goodness, of holiness, and deep, sweet dearness kind of rolling its eyes.

Sometimes I can imagine God shaking his or her head going, "Oh, Annie, whatever." Other times, when I have been at my most awful, like I was this morning, most feeling cast out and lost and hopeless, I feel the love of a mother-father God. I feel loved like a baby would be. So evangelicals—we can talk one-on-one, but then, it's like that Dylan song "With God on Our Side." If you are not careful, you think you are right, and you are sure that your beliefs are the true beliefs. The opposite of faith is not doubt. The opposite of faith is certainty. I'm not certain about a lot, and I hope that gets me partial credit in heaven.

I'm so surrounded by love. I was born and raised in this county. I've lived here for fifty-one years. I go to church every Sunday, which is like going to the gas station once a week and filling up. I have a number of friends in recovery who are not Christians but are on profound spiritual paths, so our conversations are a lot about the restoration of ourselves from the kind of ruins of the children we were and the people we always tried to be. We thought the world would give us the stamp of approval if we just were good enough, or charming enough, or achieved enough, and it turned out it didn't. It turned out that it just left more holes than you had already managed to bear. Sam built this little cabin that I bought for him for a very good price, and I use it as a meditation room. It's quiet, it's peaceful. As you can tell, this house is very quiet. A lot of light flows through the windows, and I find that as spiritual as it gets. A lot of light and freshness and fresh air and silence, to me, are the components which go hand in hand with community and fellowship.

Writing itself is not really a very spiritual experience for me, except in the sense that I get a great deal of guidance and help from forces that you wouldn't be able to see, because they come from the deepest part of me and from some sort of field of spiritual companionship around me. I don't actually like to write that much. I would really rather be doing almost anything else. Luckily, if you're a writer, you also get credit if you're reading stuff—that counts for study, and if you go someplace where there is either material or details that are useful, or if you're talking with people on the phone in a way that might throw a little light on the material that you're working on right then.

I write terrible first drafts. I have to write things over and over and over again, and people say, "You write just like you talk." I write four or five drafts of everything. I give up hope a lot. But I have a number of spiritual tools, and they are not dazzling, beautiful things to look at. It's a kind of cruddy old wooden toolbox with these slightly bent or rusty tools in it, and they are the wisdom to stop sometimes, just stop when all else fails and follow instructions. For me the instructions are: just stop. Do something else, take the dog for a walk, breathe, go outside to the little shed. Also, no matter what I do, I carry a pen with me. My skin is very fair, and I can write notes on it if I have to. I know to watch, I know to pay attention, which is also another thing which is as spiritual as you can get. Anything that can bring you into the now and into the breath and into the present moment—that's why they call it a present, because it's the present. So I am able to rein myself in from tripping out on how poorly the story's going.

My writing problems are not particularly different than my problems of being a human and a mother and a member of community. They are about living in the past, living in the present. They are about having equal proportions of terrible self-esteem and grandiosity, being a raging narcissist who really isn't sure if my voice is an interesting voice or if my talent is a particularly big one. So the struggles of being a Sunday school teacher* are not all that different from being a writer.

Another part of life is that you get to ask people for help. I think that the American way of doing things is that you should do it alone and not enjoy it very much, but be sure you're doing the right thing—like Bush and Iraq, that we can go it alone. But the truth is that we are people of community, tribal people. I have people who help me with my work, who read it and who listen to me. There are a lot of writers I help with their work, and I'll listen to them.

It's the same thing I do at my Sunday school. I listen. It's the same thing when I'm in a bad mood. I'll go out, and I will flirt with old people at the health food store, and if people need me, I will listen. I will bring them water, and I will listen, and that's basically what Jesus did. Jesus didn't say, "I'm going to take away your problems," or "I'm just going to fill your head with a Dictaphone recording of your next spiritual piece." Jesus said, "I will keep you company, and I will be here if you need me." That's what I try to be in the world, and some days go better than others.

---

* Yes, Anne Lamott teaches Sunday school.

I wrote [in *Plan B*] about all of my jewelry because I do wear stuff to remind me not about who I am, but whose I am, because I have really turned my will, my life, and my days over to the care of God. I'm a Protestant, and Protestants are not that big on Mary. It's always surprising to people that I wear a Mary [medallion], but I just love Mary. She's been so sweet and good to me my whole life. When I was in the worst of my drug and alcohol days, I would sing the Beatles song "Let It Be," where "Mother Mary comes to me speaking words of wisdom" and just says the greatest spiritual advice anyone has ever given another, which is just "let it be." So I love Mary, and, in the midst of this terrible hurricane and flooding and aftermath in New Orleans, I knew exactly what Mary would do, which is that she'd cry, and she would bring people water, and she would sit with people, and Mary would see the world in that shape, whether or not there's a specific catastrophe to be addressed. That's how Mary sees all of us, I know—as AIDS babies. When I don't know what to do, I just touch this Mary. It's my touchstone, and I remember we are all AIDS babies, we are all going to die, and it's all very scary. It's a dramatic thing to have to live with.

I wear a red cord, because my cherished friend Jack Kornfield gave it to me. He's the founder and director of Spirit Rock,* and it's blessed by the Dalai Lama, who I think is utterly one of the most fabulous people on earth, and he [Kornfield] blessed it before he tied it around my wrist. You'll see that Sam is wearing one also, that Jack has also blessed, and he blesses them with the courage to be who we are and the courage to be honest and to remember that we are made up of kindness, love, and compassion, and to act that way. That surprises people, and then they think it's kabbalah, or Buddhist, but I think there is only one God and that we can't really know very much about that God. For me, that God came and presented himself to me in the form of Jesus, who literally was about eighth on the list of spiritual deities that I had wanted to hear from. I just said, "I give up" when Jesus came to me. But I love the path of Buddhism on this earth, and I'm proud to wear something from a very beloved, cherished Buddhist teacher. It reminds me, "Oh, right, breathe. Oh, right, now I remember, breathe."

---

* A Buddhist meditation center in California.

62.

No Return

"Scott Neeson found most of his kids at this mountain of garbage outside Cambodia's capital city of Phnom Penh. Pictures alone don't do it justice—don't reveal the stench, the filth, maggots, the chemical waste, and sharp, jagged objects." That is how correspondent Lucky Severson began surveying the world of a former Hollywood movie magnate who climbed down the corporate ladder to help some of the poorest children on earth. His Hollywood friends recall that Neeson always took interesting vacations, and it was on a backpacking trip to Cambodia in 2003 that he saw the street children begging for handouts and trolling in the dumps for anything they could sell. He gave them money and paid for their schooling, but within days their parents had spent the money and pulled their kids out of school so they could work, as Lucky reported in February 2006. At the time, Neeson had left his position as president of 20th Century Fox International and taken a senior job at Sony Pictures. For a while he engaged in shuttle philanthropy, honoring his Sony commitment while returning often to Phnom Penh, where he established the Cambodian Children's Fund, which is both a school and, for many of the kids, home. Neeson has financed these works mostly out of his own resources, which are waning, and has gotten some help from his old Hollywood buddies.

"He represents what so many of us would aspire to," Fox Filmed Entertainment co-chairman Jim Gianopoulos told Lucky. "The notion that you can give up this life and the cars and the houses and the glamour and all the trappings of success—particularly in this industry—to just give it all up and do something really meaningful for people who really need it is, I think, something that all of us feel that we, hopefully, have the nobility and capability of doing. But few of us actually do it. In fact, I don't know anybody [who's] doing what Scott's done." What has delivered Neeson to this embodiment of the meaningful life is not religious inspiration as such, although he has affinities with Buddhism. Rather, it is the sheer pull of the human spirit, which he finds overflowing among Cambodians who, materially, have just about nothing. Here, Neeson describes the moment when he decided to move to Cambodia permanently, after getting an "emergency" call from Los Angeles.

The phone rang and it was my office. The actor who was on tour was having quite a serious meltdown because the private jet didn't have the right amenities for him, and he didn't want to get on the jet. The whole tour was in jeopardy, and the quote was that their life wasn't meant to be this difficult. That's what his staff said to me on the phone. And I thought: I don't want this to be my world. Here we've got this jet sitting on the tarmac, and I'm sitting with these dying children, and I just wanted to scream into the phone, "Come down here for a day and see what it's all about!"

At the time there were a lot of rumors and suspicions in Hollywood that it was all a strategy on my part—that I was going to another studio and this move to Cambodia was the only way I could get out of my contract. It was all about position, and I would magically turn up three months later in a more senior position with a better salary. Those suspicions have diminished now.

There's not much more I could have had materially. It was everything: a five-bedroom house in Brentwood which just sold for many millions of dollars, a yacht that I could take out on weekends with friends, a wonderful sports car, and I was traveling the world first class. All that made it far more difficult for me to give it up. It was quite frightening. It's particularly so when people constantly say, "Man, you're so lucky, you've got the best life."

I sort of enjoyed it, but I wasn't particularly happy. It was always eating away at me. At some level I was always just a little bit discontented. I could never quite put my finger on it, but it didn't seem like it was me. I had no idea I would be led to this other extreme.

The thing that just amazes me—everywhere I turn I see these kids that come from such a horrible life, and they all have such huge smiles. I sound like my father, but it really matters if the child has a mother and father, how well she's looked after at home. No matter what the conditions, she's loved by her mother, her mother worries about her. She's got a mom and a dad, and they care for her even though they can't afford her.

The kids are amazing. You give them the opportunity to learn, and they just soak it up like sponges. It's such a treat for them to be taught.

My pet peeve is people saying, "Well, it's just a drop in the bucket." But how do you sit with these kids and say they're just a drop in the bucket? They're not. Every drop is a child's life, and it's those drops that make up society. There's a certain amazement on my part as to how easy it was to help change a child's life completely. It wasn't thousands of dollars, it was a hundred dollars.

On the Up Side, No TVs at the Dump

The family values here are remarkable, even among the homeless families. You see the children beg on the streets during the day, but when they go home at night, they get together. I've been down there with the families, and they talk about what they've done during the day and how their day has been and, indirectly, about their feelings and what's good and what's bad and how the mothers and fathers are proud of their children. They're sleeping outside, but they've got such a sense of family values.

If these kids had TVs it would be difficult. There would definitely be a breakdown in the closeness with the parents which without doubt to me is what gets them through the day. When they're working at the rubbish dump, when they're begging on the streets, it's knowing that when they come home they have loving parents who want to know how they're doing, want to know how they're feeling, want to hear their problems.

The one thing it's really taught me, even more than spirituality, is the resilience of the human spirit. What these kids have been through is remarkable, and you come and they have a sense of real happiness. They have some issues, but they're happy and they're appreciative.

Speaking of spirituality, the basis of Buddhism is that life is suffering, that things will go wrong. When you understand that and let go trying to change things, let go feeling that you deserve better, that this is unfair, then I think it helps you get through. It makes you more accepting of the circumstance.

When I first came here I had nightmares, I had terrible dreams for a week or two afterward. Some of the things I've seen here are horrendous. I don't know how I'd adjust back to our version of civilization. It would be hard to readjust. The values changed so much. This feels so much more like reality than what I was doing before.

There is no home anymore. I've sold everything. There is no house, no car. I'm going back for a visit with no place to stay, and I'm trying to find a friend with a spare room. When I'm back in the States and I see people having minor tantrums over certain things, whether it's at a coffee shop and the coffee is not right, or they don't have the organic cereal they're after and it's a major trauma in their lives, it's somewhat entertaining and somewhat sad. I can't really judge because I was one of those people. I was exactly the same way.

If I have children of my own, I would want them to understand the full spectrum of human life, not just West Los Angeles or an exclusive, wealthy upbringing.

I get asked all the time when I'm coming back. But what happens here if I go home? One thing that didn't quite click—it's such an obvious thing, but it didn't occur to me at the time—was, there's no going back. What would happen here with 170–180 children who are going through the process of changing their lives? It may sound rather pretentious, but they're off the garbage dump, they've got vocational training, they've got an education, they've got a safe place to sleep, and they are really pumping along. They're trying their best. How can you just walk away from that? How can you put them back on the streets? I didn't realize the permanency of what I'd started here until relatively recently.

I've never been happier in my life. Every day is an emotional roller coaster, but I get up early in the morning, and I can't wait to get into work. How many people in the world can say that?

63

Changing Your Social Footprint

Rajiv Vinnakota is a tall, likable educator in his mid thirties. His parents, both teachers who emigrated from India, raised him in Wisconsin. He studied molecular biology at Princeton and then became a management consultant. But he decided when he was twenty-five that the work he was doing was unlikely to create the social footprint he wanted to leave. So he and a friend, Eric Adler, who was also looking for a more meaningful vocation, turned their attention to the educational problems of inner-city children in Washington, DC. They concluded that what many of them needed was rigorous instruction, with good role models, in a safe environment. Although neither Vinnakota nor Adler is wealthy, they raised $26 million and opened The SEED School in one of the poorest parts of DC in 1998. It is the country's first public, charter, college preparatory boarding school for grades seven to twelve. Each new seventh grader is chosen by lottery. Ninety-nine percent are African-American, and 80 percent are below the poverty line and from a single- or no-parent home. The average new seventh grader arrives at SEED two or three grades behind. Because their families move away or for academic or behavioral reasons, about half of the students who enter do not stay on to graduate from SEED. But of those who do, since 2004, 97 percent have gone on to colleges and universities, and 81 percent of them are still there. Largely because SEED is a boarding school, the cost per pupil is $32,500 per year—two and a half times the cost per pupil in the regular DC public schools. Vinnakota is not ready to prescribe school reform for the whole country or for every child, but he insists, for SEED students, "This model works." Bob spoke with Vinnakota in 2004 and again in 2006.

My grandfather was a farmer in a town of six hundred people in backwoods India. He earned thirty rupees a month and spent twenty-four of them making sure his four sons and two daughters got an education. All of them ended up getting college degrees, most of them got professional degrees, and all of them moved here to the United States. They are now safe, secure, and stable and really value education because of what it did for them.

My mother is a teacher in the Milwaukee public school system, and my father is a professor at Marquette University. They are not only educators, but the greatest advocates for education. It changed their lives.

I can think of no higher calling than being in the education field. So after being a management consultant for three and a half years I thought, "You know what, that's not the social footprint that I want to leave, so let's start looking at where I can really add value." I immediately went to issues in urban education, started talking with friends and one of us said, "Why aren't there boarding schools for some of these students in the inner city? Why aren't there schools that provide a safe, supportive 24-hour environment, along with a rigorous academic curriculum and constant access to role models?"

I took a leave of absence and spent two months studying this idea, and Eric and I left our jobs in early 1997 and started working full time.

I did not leave management consulting or start SEED for religious reasons, but somewhere in that first year this became a calling. I have no doubt that this is where I need to be and that the role I play—helping lead this institution—is the reason I'm here. Whether or not that's religious or spiritual is up for debate, but I know what I know. This is what I like to do, what I can do well, and I get up every morning knowing I'm doing the right thing.

The reason we have an urban public college prep boarding school is because there's a group of students that need it. We have to acknowledge that we're losing a group of children who have all the potential in the world, and unless we do everything necessary, they're not going to be successful. Society needs to step up and say, "Yes, we will make the investment to leave no child behind. And if that investment requires three times as much money, we will make that investment, because it is necessary."

I decided to work in urban education because I wanted to change the system, but one of the things I learned is that you can only do it one child at a time. So the SEED School is working with three hundred students, and we hope to start ten more SEED schools in the next ten years.

We get a cross section of the city, especially those parts that we target. We go and actively look for those students who might need additional help. Eighty percent of our students come from below the poverty line and from single- or no-parent homes. Ninety-three percent don't know anyone who has attended college. They come to SEED on average two to three grade levels behind. We're not skimming off the cream.

For many of the students and their mothers, they send their children here because they see this as a safe environment. That's the number one criterion. Then it's up to us as an institution to also get them to engage academically and socially.

We are trying to build a culture here around the expectation of getting ready for college and everything that entails. It doesn't only involve academics. It means understanding risky behaviors and making sure to curtail them. It means knowing what kinds of things you need to do outside of the school day in order to be a good student. That can mean everything from health, nutrition, and wellness, to how to study for two hours a day and make sure you get your homework done. It means when I go to college can I actually make my bed and be able to live with roommates? Finally it means, how do you act in social settings? We have an etiquette class for our students, which includes everything from how to sit at a table and eat, to how to welcome and thank adults, how to look them in the eye, and how to shake their hand.

There is a great multiplier effect to being able to send students to college. When our students graduate and attend college, there's a 76 percent likelihood that their children will go to college, versus only a 17 percent chance for those who just have a high school diploma. So the impact of this school is not only with the students that we serve, their families, and communities, but it's over generations.

Two years later, in 2006, Bob interviewed Vinnakota again. He spoke of some of the unexpected problems he has encountered, of the lessons learned, and of his determination to create a second SEED school in Washington, DC, and others all over the country.

I've been both heartened and dismayed by my experience. The challenges are so great. Things are so intertwined. It's about employment, it's about housing, it's about health care, it's about healthy living, it's about opportunities, it's about education, it's about faith and hope. It's about race and it's about class. I am dismayed because it is such a complex web. However, I am heartened because I see hope in a number of places. I see programs that really work, that do an amazing job. It tells me that if the will is there, if the understanding of what success looks like is there, and if we're willing to invest both time and resources, we can make it happen.

There's a lot that needs to be overcome. When you talk about being behind one, two, three, four grade levels when you enter our school, that's a lot of catching up to do. A lot of social factors play into that. We have four mental health counselors whose portfolios are completely overwhelmed with the time that they need to spend with our students. We have one of the best special education departments in the city. Somewhere between 10 and 15 percent of our kids have special needs. For many of them, we're the first time society has acknowledged the fact that they have special needs.

I got into this business because I had a simple hypothesis that said if you provide them with an academic environment and a safe boarding environment, that would do it. What I've learned is it's actually a lot harder than that. The school needs all kinds of support services—mental health, special ed, nurses on the health side, and role models, adults who are on campus and can't just walk away at 4:00 p.m.

One thing we have talked about integrating into our program is the interaction between the classes. I don't mean math and physics, but rather between low income, middle income, and high income—getting our students to be comfortable around people of wealth.

One of our graduates is at an Ivy League school, and she had a very rough first year. She was put in a quad with three other young ladies, two of whom were phenomenally well off. The culture clash of class was tough, seeing one of the girls, for instance, ordering lip liner over the Internet that cost $40, using it once, not liking it, and then throwing it away.

The message came through most loudly from our students who are attending historically black colleges and universities. They had some level of comfort around the idea that "I'm poor black. There are rich white people and there are rich Asian people. They're rich and they might not understand me, but I'm going to have to deal with it." But the idea that there would be rich black people who would look upon them the same way they'd expect from someone who was white, and in many ways look upon them even in a worse way, was really tough. I think there are things we as an institution can do to help. But we are still trying to work this out.

[As for recommending what other schools and school districts can do,] we are not there yet. We have to prove to ourselves that we can do it more than once. I have to prove that to myself. My hypothesis is that this is replicable, but I've got to prove it. That's number one. Number two is that for all of our successes, I continue to be worried about the retention of males in the school. We still have a phenomenally higher retention rate than the public school system, but we lose boys at a much faster clip than we lose girls. I think that figuring that out is going to be very important to whatever advocacy we want to voice.

There is a lot of research suggesting that there is an anti-intellectual bent, especially for African-American boys, and that the culture of anti-intellectualism is undermining society's ability to educate them. It's fairly complex because at times our students can't say why they are leaving. Many boys are so far behind academically, more so than our girls, that they get frustrated in class, and they act out. So they have to be disciplined, over and over again. You think the reason for them leaving is a discipline issue, when in fact the underlying issue is that they are academically so far behind they can't get up to speed.

This issue of creating a positive intellectual environment exhibits itself most explicitly through our ninth grade gate. We require that students be on grade level in order to enter ninth grade. That means we have to keep back 40 percent of our students for a growth year sometime in their first two years. But we find that many of our boys would rather leave and continue to be socially promoted at some other school. There's a pride issue. Once our kids get into ninth grade the retention rate between the boys and girls is fairly the same. But, roughly speaking, for every girl that we lose, we lose almost two boys. We're still trying to figure this out.

Here is what I can say: Our school, The SEED School of Washington, DC, is not marginally, but *orders of magnitude* better than the regular DC public schools in getting kids off to four-year colleges and doing this with the exact same population as the regular schools.

That's because we have small class sizes, we have a twenty-four-hour environment, adult role models, a rigorous academic culture, people who care, and because we're willing to spend the money to make sure our students get support—academic, study hall, mental health, special ed, regular health support, meals, uniforms, athletic programs, art program. Because we are willing to do all those things, this model works. That I can tell you.

My wife and I have a nine-month-old daughter. That gives me perspective and balance. It's also given me a very clear understanding of why I do what I do in my vocation. Annabelle, our daughter, has someone who is taking care of her all the time, who has been reading to her since the first week she was born. I was sitting there reading to her when her only interest was in chewing on the book. I know she's getting her booster shots, her immunizations. I know she's growing in a very healthy way, and if there are any issues with her diet, we can take care of them. I know that we have a very strong set of systems and support, so she is affirmed all the time and she's a happy child. I know this will continue going forward. I know that my wife and I will do everything possible to get her into the best educational setting, and we have every option available.

I want this for everyone else. Everyone else deserves exactly what Annabelle is getting. If they're not getting it, then, shame on us.

64

Healing Body and Spirit

Rev. Scott Morris, MD, says he knew when he was a teenager in Atlanta that he wanted to become a minister and a doctor, and take care of poor people. He did just that and settled, in the 1980s, in Memphis, because that city then had the highest percentage of poor people of any major city in the country. Morris became an associate pastor at St. John's United Methodist Church and set out to create what became the Church Health Center. He communicated his vision to 150 of the city's churches and synagogues, and to its medical and philanthropic communities, and opened the Center in 1987 with a staff of one, himself, and twelve patients. Today, the Church Health Center sees forty-five thousand patients a year, most of them uninsured working poor who, as Morris puts it, "shine others' shoes, cook their food, and will one day dig their graves."

Morris leads a paid staff of 200, assisted by 600 doctors, nurses, and dentists who volunteer part time, and another 1,000 volunteers who are not medical professionals. The annual budget is $11 million, with no support from government. The money comes from churches and synagogues, foundations and—most of it—from private donors. All patients except the homeless pay a small fee; the average charge for an office visit is twenty dollars. As a companion to the Church Health Center clinic, Morris has also created a huge $7 million Hope and Healing Center, where patients can exercise and learn how to live more healthy lives. One of the patients, Margaret Warren, said, "They don't know what race or color is, they don't know anything what age or beauty or ugly is. They just know human beings and a patient that needs them. And that's why I love coming here." Bob and Morris spoke in 2000 about why the Center works and about Morris's larger goals of reforming both how his patients take care of themselves and the practice of medicine itself.

—◆—

The mission of the Church Health Center is to reclaim the [Christian] church's biblical and historical commitment to care for the poor who are sick. It is about people of faith rising up and doing what we are called to do: care for the body and the spirit. The government cannot do the work of the church, and neither should we ask them to. There is a role for the government in solving the problem of health care for the poor and uninsured, but that's not what we are about. We are about calling the church to task, to take seriously, from the Judeo-Christian point of view, the ways we are to care for the poor.

The most effective argument for recruiting volunteers is that this is the right thing to do. We also take away a lot of the excuses some people might use to prevent them from living out their own sense of mission. For example, in asking a doctor to volunteer, all we really ask for is their time. They don't have to worry about who is going to pay for the CAT scan or if someone has to be admitted to the hospital. We worry about all that. We basically only ask doctors or nurses or dentists to come for a four-hour shift once every two or three months. That's something they can sustain for thirty years. So far, there has not been anybody who has stopped coming because we were asking too much. For the most part, somebody comes to me and says, "I would like to do it. Do you have a place for me?"

Every little piece of what we do can be reproduced, the whole of it or every little part. You don't need Scott Morris, who is a physician and a pastor, to do this. What you do need is one person who lives and breathes the idea, who has the commitment and the passion to make it happen. It's not something that just a volunteer board can pull together.

The secret of making the Church Health Center happen is, number one, a sense of Providence, of God truly looking out for what we are doing. The second point is we take seriously the spiritual dimension in everybody's lives. Just giving people pills for what ails them isn't going to solve the problem. Fifty percent of all the people who come to a primary care doctor have no medical problem. They come because their life is falling apart. I can't fix that with a fifteen-minute office visit. I can't tell you how many people I've seen over the years who came saying, "My back hurts," when, in reality, it's because their heart hurts. They have a broken heart. I can't fix that with all the things that allopathic [conventional] medicine has given me. A spiritual problem requires a spiritual solution. We are always aware of that.

A woman who immediately comes to mind first came to see me because she had a pain in her rectum. She had had three operations on her rectum before. She thought that there was one more thing back there that needed to be taken out. After talking to her the first time, I finally got around to asking her the one question that nobody had ever asked before: "Have you ever been sexually abused?" The answer, of course, was yes. First by her father. She was taken out of that home, put into a foster home. It happened again. She did not need another operation. I cannot sit here and tell you that everything is all fine and dandy. It's not. But at least now she sees our pastoral counselor, and we are dealing with the real issues, those things having to do with her broken spirit and heart.

I have a patient who recently almost died. The woman had had both her legs amputated in a terrible situation years before. She came to see me and was in pain. Before she left that day, she wanted me to pray for her, which I did. Twenty-four hours later, she was in the intensive care unit, and she almost died at that point. She subsequently came back to see me and asked me, "Do you remember what we did the last time I saw you?"

I said, "Yes, ma'am, I do." I remembered that prayer and was thinking, "She's thinking, 'Oh my God, what kind of God is this that would lead me to the verge of death?'" Instead, her response was, "What would have happened had we not had that prayer?"

That happens to me over and over, every day with patients. The person comes with a very physical complaint, and yet, both of us, by the time we finish the interview, have connected in some spiritual way that sustains us, that helps us both grow. I'm able to see that partly because I totally get rid of the idea that "I'm the doctor and you're the patient." Instead, I try to adopt a viewpoint that we're in this life and world together. I think patients do sense that from me.

God has told us that the body is the temple of the Lord, and it is within our purview to take care of the body and the spirit. But somehow we've come to think the only way we relate to God is from the neck up. That is not right. This body is part of the wonderful gift that God has given, and we must find ways to care for the body as well as the spirit or else we are not doing what we're called to do.

The Hope and Healing Center came to be because I realized that two-thirds of the problems we see could be prevented if—these are really big "ifs"—we were either smart enough to know how or could intervene early enough. Preventive medicine is what this is about.

People are still going to break their arms, people are still going to get real sick. The clinic piece of what we are doing is not going away. But we are trying to find a way, primarily motivated by faith, that we can practice true preventive medicine. To do that we have created the Hope and Healing Center, and it has two main arms. One arm is to create in churches health care ministries that work, that are effective. We've created a whole menu of ideas. One is something we call "Walk and Talk." Every day I see patients and encourage them to get more exercise. I'll say, "Why don't you walk?" The answer I'll get is, "I'd love to walk, but my neighborhood's not safe." With "Walk and Talk," fifty people, twenty people, meet at the church. They go for a walk through their neighborhood. In the process, they've made the neighborhood safe. The talk part is you talk about something of the spirit—a passage of scripture, it doesn't matter. What matters is finding body and spirit.

We identify "congregational health promoters," women in our patients' churches who already give out health care advice—sometimes good, sometimes not so good. We go to them, get them to come to an eight-week training session where we teach them about high blood pressure, diabetes, the importance of prenatal care. They go back to their congregation and look for people who have medical problems that are going untreated. Also, we are trying to develop the means to have a healthy church supper. The least healthy meal anybody could eat every week is at your church. Now, we're not trying to get churches to eat tofu, but we ought to be able to take off the first layer of grease.

The second arm of Hope and Healing is to train young doctors to write a "prescription for health." Right now, we have a health care system that is really based on disease. We wait until your body is sick, ravaged with disease, and then expect the doctor to play the white knight and rescue you from the jaws of death. Wouldn't it be better if we had a health care system where the doctor's role was to try to keep you healthy rather than wait until your body is broken?

I really do feel that poverty is a spiritual disease. Poverty drives people to lose hope and to lose a sense of who they are. Children who are born in poverty never see adults who are going to work, who are loving life, unless it's somebody who has risen above that. But there are so many people who have lost their direction, and it is infectious. For a child to see that day in and day out—it leads to children who are hopeless. In many ways the Church Health Center is much more in the hope business now than we are in the healing business, because if you can't take children and help them see that their life has meaning and value, and that they can succeed and rise up and be a child of God—unless we can help them do that, they are going to live a life that ends in despair.

My own personal need and drive is to be a doctor and be in contact with the people who come to our door. When you are poor, life has oftentimes taken away all those material gifts that are distracting to us. Many people that we see, who don't have material wealth, substitute for that with an incredible spiritual drive and a spiritual wealth that is overwhelming to me. Every day I see people who struggle through life, and I wonder whether I could have done that myself. Yet they show me. They teach me. They help me understand how to better deal with my own problems. And they are doing it on a shoestring. It is a powerful experience for me every day that I come to work, and I would never give that up.

I'm a great believer in what the Apostle Paul has called us to do, which is to "pray ceaselessly." I say the Jesus Prayer* in my head ten thousand times a day. I can talk to you right now and be saying the Jesus Prayer.

I am very much attracted to the concept of being a disciple. I don't think it's easy to be a disciple. It requires us to really believe that God is in charge. It requires us to act in the world as though the kingdom of God were here now. And that sort of action is day in and day out, for your whole life.

I get called from time to time and offered jobs here or there. But nobody needs to call me for another job. This is what I am going to do. I am going to do this until I draw my last breath.

In addition to the Church Health Center and the Hope and Healing Center, Dr. Morris has developed an insurance program for those with low-paying jobs, and he is now developing a service, also for the working poor, to provide low-cost prescription drugs.

---

* "Lord Jesus Christ, Son of God, have mercy on me, a sinner."

65.

The Cathedral of Charity

Billy Shore, once a top aide in the U.S. Senate, is pioneering a new way to raise money for charity. Instead of relying primarily on rich people and foundations for gifts and grants, Shore has discovered how to invite talented people to contribute their skills, and then to create fund-raising events that combine those skills with corporate partnerships. The result, over the past twenty-plus years, has been the raising of more than $200 million to help fight hunger in the United States and abroad. Most recently, Shore has turned his own considerable skills to the goal of ensuring that within the next twenty years the nearly fourteen million American children who face hunger will have access to nutritious food. Bob spoke with Shore in 2002 in his office at Share Our Strength, the antihunger organization he founded and leads, just two blocks from the White House.

When I have tried to think about my commitment, a lot of it has to do with my parents and the way they raised me. My father was active in community service and in public service. He was the administrative assistant to a congressman in Pittsburgh, and in those days members of Congress didn't come back to their districts very often, so my dad was almost like the surrogate congressman. Probably my most vivid memories are walking three blocks to go get a pizza with him and it taking maybe three hours because so many people would come up to him and say, "Mr. Shore, my Social Security check didn't come in the mail. Can you do something about that?" Or, "My father needs to get into the Veterans Administration hospital. Can you help us do that?"

My father would make mental notes of all these things and go home and make some calls, and that would all get fixed. He was not preachy about it, but my day-to-day observance gave me the sense that the reason we are here is to help and serve others.

My mother reinforced that. We grew up in a nonobservant household of the Jewish faith. I remember I lived in a very Jewish area and was not being bar mitzvahed, and that was borderline scandalous. There was a lot of stigma attached to not being bar mitzvahed. I remember my parents said to me, "We are going to teach you to be a good neighbor and to serve others, and if you understand both of those things, you'll know the major principles of every religion in the world." It didn't mean anything at the time, but it did stick, and I thought about it a lot afterward.

In Washington, working in the Senate for thirteen years, my passion was trying to change public policy and trying to create social change through government action. One of the things I learned was that government alone could not do the job. It really takes all of us. The other thing I learned is that money alone is not enough. It takes more than money. It takes mentoring, it takes working with people, it takes coaching. It takes that type of personal exchange to really turn someone's life around.

In 1984, I read a story on the front page of the *Washington Post*, below the fold, kind of in the corner, under a very small headline that said, "200,000 to Die This Summer in Ethiopia." I was just shocked by that figure. It seemed to be an enormous number. I started to think, "What would I do about it?" So we started Share Our Strength based on that, and we funded relief efforts in Ethiopia.

We also have a lot of Americans who are hungry in this country. We are sitting a block from McPherson Square, which is also one block from the White House. Every night, fifty, sixty, seventy, a hundred people line up there for sandwiches and soup and food assistance. It's not for the same reasons that people are hungry in the rest of the world, which is usually famine or war or drought. Here it's because of an economy that just has not brought everybody into it fully.

We're all familiar with people who panhandle for money at a subway stop or in the park. Many of them have substance abuse problems, mental health problems. But they really mask what the real issue is. Millions of Americans, many of whom are in families where one person is employed, are not making enough to be able to pay the rent, support the transportation costs, and also feed the family. I guess there are not people hungry in America in the sense that they are starving to death. There is a place for them to go. But they had to go there because they were hungry and because they were out of resources.

The idea of Share Our Strength—which is fundamentally, I think, a very spiritual idea—is that everybody has a strength to share, everybody has been given a gift of some type, and if we can tap into that, if we can create vehicles in which people can contribute whatever their unique talent or gift is, then that can change the world.

When we thought about how we could most effectively fight hunger, what group or community of people would most respond to giving of their strength and giving of their gift that way, we thought of chefs and restauranteurs. So we started to very methodically ask them to contribute to the fight against hunger—not by writing us a check, not even by donating food, but by sharing their strength, doing what they do best, which is cook. We structured these food and wine events called Taste of the Nation. The chefs get good visibility and an opportunity to be part of the community. People who come get great value for their dollar—they get to sample the best dishes of the best chefs. Our corporate sponsors build relationships with their customers, who are the chefs. It's a win-win situation. Taste of the Nation raises about $4.5 million a year now, 100 percent of which is donated.

In spite of all the efforts to fight hunger, poverty and hunger have gotten worse. But there is one aspect of this that has become much better, a major unsung victory. There is a network today of food banks and emergency feeding assistance programs that did not exist twenty-five years ago. There is a place for every hungry American today to get food assistance. There are 185 large food banks, and they supply sixty-five thousand church basements and soup pantries and trucks that deliver food to homeless men and women. So stage one of the battle has been won. Stage two is to make sure that people are in a position where they don't have to apply for food assistance in the first place, and we are still far from winning that one.

Ending hunger is really a matter of political will more than anything else.

Doing Good, Feeling Good

When we started Share Our Strength we wanted to be a grant maker to all of the most effective antihunger and antipoverty organizations. We made this unorthodox decision that we would not take government money, we would not apply to foundations, we would not have direct mail. We did not want to be fighting just for our share of the charitable pie. We wanted to make that pie grow. One of the reasons we started to work with chefs and restauranteurs and so many other businesses is that we saw an opportunity to not just redistribute wealth, but actually to create it. About two-thirds of our revenues come from cause-related marketing, contracts, and corporate partnerships, and that puts us in a very advantageous position, because we ended up not competing with our brother and sister organizations. And there are no strings attached to the dollars that come in.

This idea of creating wealth became very important to us, and we realize that most nonprofit organizations have developed assets in the course of executing their mission that can be leveraged into revenue generation. This is vital to their long-term success and sustainability. In fact, at Share Our Strength we own a for-profit consulting firm called Community Wealth Ventures, and we pay taxes on it.

When I created Share Our Strength, I realized that as public service oriented as it appeared to be, it was also fulfilling a deep-seated need that I had. My need is to be involved in the community in ways that are fulfilling, to serve others. I resist the notion that that is an altruistic thing to do because I know why I do it. It makes me feel good.

Fundamentally, I think this idea of really being in touch with yourself and what gifts you were given, and trying to understand where they came from and what opportunities you had to nurture them—to me, that's a very contemplative, spiritual, almost religious experience, although not in a formal religious sense. Most religions have some sense or some teachings about the inside and the outside person being one. Some state of grace really exists when you know who you are in the world is who you really are inside. I think this idea of being in touch with your strengths and your gifts gets you pretty close to that.

We can eliminate hunger in America. That will happen. I would like to think it will happen in my lifetime. I certainly think it will happen in my children's. Overseas, we may never see the end to world hunger, certainly not in our lifetimes. It's that vast and complicated a problem.

Just by chance one day I walked into the Cathedral of St. John the Divine in New York, and I thought it was a remarkable building. I started to study cathedrals, and I realized that they took hundreds and hundreds of years to build. One that I went to visit was the cathedral in Milan, which took 513 years to build—tens of thousands of people worked on the cathedral and almost all of them could have known one thing for sure, which is that they would not see their work finished in their lifetime. That did not detract from their commitment or their craftsmanship. It actually enhanced it.

An issue like hunger is very much the same. As hard as we work, we are not going to see the end of *world* hunger in our lifetimes. But we are, in effect, building a cathedral. We're building a foundation on which others can work. We know that whether we have the gratification of seeing our work finished or not, we're making a difference every day. We're adding to that cathedral.

66.

Listen to Your Life

Frederick Buechner is an ordained Presbyterian minister, but has never pastored a church and rarely attends one. His ministry is his writing: thirty-two novels and memoirs so far, and a slew of sermons he has given as a guest preacher, many of which are collected in his book Secrets in the Dark. *Buechner (pronounced BEEK-ner) lives with his wife on a hilltop in Vermont in what he calls "fathomless obscurity," and yet for many Christians and other seekers, he's a celebrity. His eloquence, insight, humor and honesty have made him a hero in the eyes of many who admire both his faith and his doubt. In a 2006 interview, Bob reminded Buechner that he had once described himself as a "skeptical old believer and a believing old skeptic."*

———

What makes me a believer is that from time to time, going back almost as far as my memory will go back, I've had glimpses of things that made me suspect the presence of something extraordinary and beyond the realm of the immediate. I think that in a lot of my writing and preaching, I've been trying to listen to that voice again, to see those moments again. I wrote a book called *The Sacred Journey*, the title meaning each one of us could describe his or her life as a sacred journey. And what makes it sacred is that in the process of this journey you encounter the holy in various forms, and unless you have your eyes open you might not even notice; they're so subtle and so elusive. That's what I've spent my life trying to track.

The skepticism comes from having a mind. There is a lot of horror in the world—sadness and brokenness and disappointment—and you cannot help but say, if you're honest with yourself, "Well, maybe this whole holy business is just a lot of hogwash. How do I know I'm not just trying to keep my spirits up? How do I know I'm not just inventing it for my own comfort?" But I never came out on that side. I've never given up this conviction, faith, profound sense that all ultimately is well. Beneath the worst the world can do there is always the glimmer of the best.

And what do I say to those who can't come out as I do? I say: You might be right. You might be right. But don't write it off too easily. Don't write off the possibility of the holy too easily. Listen to your life. Pay attention. Observe. That wonderful phrase, "religious observance," means observe religiously. Observe deeply. Don't just get through your life, as all of us are inclined to do, on automatic pilot, not much noticing anything. Listen. Maybe nothing much will come of that but maybe the secret of all secrets you need to hear may come through some event, something that happens or fails to happen.

That's really been my life. I've been a listener in that sense all my life. I'm trying to listen to my past, listen to what is going on most deeply inside myself. It's not as if I know answers that I'm going to set down in the form of a novel or a memoir or a sermon. Rather, I'm going to search myself for what I might have to say. And what I like to think is that I'm in some sense hearing the mystery itself, what William James called "the More," with a capital M, hearing, maybe feeling, being in touch with something vastly beyond my own power to express or to seize.

You can't pretend suffering does not exist. I think you simply have to say it exists in spite of faith. I remember that great remark of Tillich's,* "Doubt is not the opposite of faith. It's an element of faith." But how do you hold together belief in an all-powerful, all-loving God, and the shadow side, the horrors that are going on in the world? My answer to myself is: Don't give up hope. God is greater than all those things. The holy transcends all the wretchedness.

There's a quotation from a novel I wrote, *Godrick*, that is told in the voice of an eleventh century English monk and mystic named Godrick. At the end of his days, he speaks words that I in a sense put into his mouth, but which I, in another sense, heard from his mouth, which is part of the mystery of

---

* The late theologian and Christian existentialist philosopher, Paul Tillich. He was one of Buechner's professors at Union Theological Seminary in New York in the 1950s.

creating a character. As an old, old man who'd lost almost everything, he said, "What's lost is nothing to what's found. And all the death that ever was set next to life would scarcely fill a cup." The other day, in the way people who are approaching their eightieth birthday do, I was thinking about funerals and all the last business. And I thought: If anything were to be inscribed on my tombstone, let it be that. "What's lost is nothing to what's found."

Beyond Belief

[Formal adherence to traditional beliefs] is not what matters most. What's important is to carry in your heart some sense of what the word God means, and at least to me, it means a loving, creating, everlastingly renewing presence deeply concerned with the well-being of the earth and all its creatures. And you can do that whether you believe anything about anything. Marcus Borg* makes the point that the word "believe" comes from the same root as the German *beliebten*. To believe is to belove. To believe is not to give intellectual assent—"Yes, I believe in Jesus. I will sign my name to the creed. I believe it all"—which you could do and it would have no effect on who you were or what you did. It is rather to give your heart. To believe in God is to give your heart to God. To believe in Christ is to give your heart to Christ.

Is one religion more true than the others? I'm not sure what the word "true" would mean in that sentence. The religion that is for me the closest to being "true" would be the one which seems to speak most eloquently, most vividly in images, most meaningfully about what I take to be the heart of reality. And that is, ultimately, love.

I don't go to church all that regularly. And one reason I don't is, very often when I go, I am bored out of my wits. I find myself being addressed by men and women, mostly men—preachers who I assume were led by some initial passion for Christ, for the truth, for God, for "the More." But that has gotten buried under all the debris of having to run a church. It comes through to me as something that simply has no living conviction to it anymore. They're not

---

* A bestselling liberal religious author.

telling me anything I haven't heard before. They're not moving my heart. They're not touching me. And I think, what am I doing here?

A lot of people who say "I believe in God," and I'm one of them, are people whose belief doesn't go down deep enough to change the way they conduct their lives most of the time. I believe in God with the best of who I am, but I sometimes think if anybody would watch me alongside somebody who didn't believe a damn thing, they'd have a very hard time deciding which of us is which.

I do not have an ordered prayer life. My prayer is spasmodic, occasional, desperate, not out of the most religious part of me, but the most anxious part of me, the most desperately loving, fearing part of me. I pray for the well-being of my children, I pray for people I love who are sick. Things like that. But at another level I think writing is a kind of praying in the sense that in both writing and in praying what I'm really doing is listening, listening to the deepest level of myself for what of truth, for what of hope, for what of beauty, for what of meaning may be there. So in that sense I like to think that despite this ragged, inadequate, ludicrous non-prayer life, I somehow or other spend a great deal of time at it.

Years ago, before I had any notion that I was going to be a minister, I went to a church where the great George Buttrick* was preaching. And he spoke of how Jesus was offered a crown by Satan, and said no. Despite that, Jesus is crowned again and again in the hearts of people who believe in him, amidst confession and tears and other predictable things, but he is also crowned, Buttrick said, with "great laughter." And that phrase "great laughter" was my Damascus road. I think part of the laughter is the laughter of incredulity. Can it be true? Can it be true that there really is a God and that he was in Jesus and loves us and forgives us and will make all things right again? Can that be true? I can only laugh. Or maybe the laughter is relief: "Oh, my God. After everything, it's true." I can weep at the absurdity and beauty of its truth.

Just the other day a man came to me in some sort of a crisis and said, "I

---

* An English-born minister who served as a Presbyterian pastor in New York and was considered one of the great preachers of the twentieth century.

don't feel I'm being what I ought to be." And I said, "Well, what makes you happiest? That's the clue." I struck him dumb. He said, "I never thought that." What makes me happy? I think he was thinking what makes me useful, what makes me religious. No, no, no, what makes you in the deepest sense of the word happy? That's what you should be doing.

And the vocation for you is the one in which your deep gladness and the world's deep need meet. When you are doing something you are happiest doing it must also be something that the world needs to have done.

For me, writing is what makes me happiest, whether it be spoken in a sermon or read in a book. And I can only hope that the world needs me to do it. I've never been a great bestseller, but I get enough letters from people saying in one way or another "you saved my life" that I have to take them seriously. Always with tremendous embarrassment, because I don't know how to save my own life, so I can't take responsibility for anything they have found in what I've written that saved theirs. But something I touched upon—something that's touched me and, through me, them—has saved their life. And that's something I love more than anything else to do. I mean, the world needs people who save lives.

67.

Raging against Boredom

During what have been called the "days of rage" in the United States, Rev. William Sloane Coffin became variously known, celebrated, and repudiated as a liberal Christian stalwart, emerging at the forefront of the civil rights and anti-war movements in the 1960s and 1970s. For much of that time he served as Yale University's chaplain, before becoming pastor of the interdenominational Riverside Church in New York City during the 1980s, when he returned to the spotlight as the leader of the nationwide nuclear freeze movement. It was an unlikely passion for someone who had once been a dedicated Cold War warrior, having served in the Central Intelligence Agency during the early 1950s before growing disenchanted with the agency's interventions around the globe. All through his activist life, Coffin carried on what he calls a lover's quarrel with America, railing at neglect of the poor, military policies, discrimination in all its guises, and other social injustices. In his latter days, Coffin condemned what he saw as America's self-righteousness, and yet he did not come close to losing hope, because to do so would be to commit a pitiable sin, the sin of being "bored and . . . boring." Those were his words in the summer of 2004, when Bob interviewed him in the little town of Strafford, Vermont, where Coffin had retired, living on the village green, with his wife, Randy, and their terrier, Rosie. Two strokes had slurred his speech. He couldn't walk much, and he had to give up playing the piano, of which he had been a master. But his beliefs were as stout as ever, and his passions were centered in a hard-earned and resilient spirituality of gratitude and hope. "I'm convinced that gratitude is the most important religious emotion," he explained. "When you're grateful for the undeserved beauty of a cloudless sky, you're praying."

⁓

I understand that people want to be safe, polite, obedient, comfortable, but that's not being alive. Irenaeus, the great early church father, said the glory of God is a human being fully alive. Now, if you back off from every little controversy in your life you're not alive, and what's more, you're boring. It's a terrible thing that we settle for so much less.

The greatest pleasure for me was being with black civil rights leaders and followers, because they were so alive. You can be more alive in pain than in complacency. These often very poor blacks in Alabama, Mississippi, and Georgia, were so wonderfully alive, so cheerful, so courageous. It was inspiring. I felt from the get-go that the so-called "black problem," as it was called in those days, was the white folks' problem, because we were the ones discriminating against black folk. While it was right to have the civil rights movement led by leaders like Martin Luther King, Fred Shuttlesworth, Ralph Abernathy, all the wonderful black leaders, whites were necessary—to bail them out of jail. The NAACP's Legal Defense Fund did that well, and whites were necessary to raise money, and the Jewish community in New York City was generous to a fault. It was very moving to see that. The rest of us who weren't lawyers and who didn't have money—we could go to jail with our black brothers and sisters.

It's clear to me that almost every square inch of the earth's surface is soaked with the tears and blood of the innocent, and it's not God's doing, it's our doing. That's human malpractice. Don't chalk it up to God. Every time people lift their eyes to heaven and say, when they see the innocent suffering, "God, how could you let this happen?" it is well to remember that at that exact moment God is asking exactly that same question of us: "How could *you* let it happen?" You have to take responsibility, and then you have to say with the poet, "We're always undefeated because we keep on trying." You have to keep the faith despite the evidence, knowing that only in so doing has the evidence any chance of changing. You hang in there, and not to hang in there is to abdicate and to get bored and be boring, and it's important to be engaged in the right way.

For instance, I think the great trouble now is self-righteousness. Self-righteousness is the bane of all human relations—interpersonal, international, interfaith. Self-righteousness destroys our capacity for self-criticism. But it's very hard for me to war against the self-righteousness of my beloved nation without engaging a little bit in self-righteousness. I have to watch that all the time, because the quality of the engagement is very important. Abraham Joshua Heschel* always had a wonderful sense of humor about him. King wasn't exactly a barrel of fun, but still he had a kind of ability to step back and not run himself into the ground. Humor is very important. Faith is important for the ultimate dilemmas of life; humor can take care of the immediate ones rather nicely. I have a wonderful son, David, who keeps me in good jokes, and a joke a day keeps the doctor away. I'm a great believer in that. Then you have to have moments when you let it go. Often I work with one crowd and drink with another, because the drinking crowd is a little bit more fun, but I wouldn't want to work with them.

The bedrock of my faith—mind you, I didn't get to it easily—is that we are loved by God. He loves us as we are, but too much to leave us that way. We are loved by God, and that's what gives us value. We don't achieve value. It's not because we have value that we're loved by God, but because we're loved by God that we have value. Our value as human beings is not an achievement, it's a gift. We don't have to prove ourselves. All that is taken care of. What we have to do is express ourselves, return God's love with our own. What a world of difference there is between proving yourself and expressing yourself.

That's the core basis of my faith. Of course, Jesus is primary. God is not confined to Christ, but to Christians God is most essentially defined by Christ. In other words, when we see Christ empowering the poor, scorning the powerful, healing the world's hurt, we are seeing transparently the power of God at work. How do we know what to pray? "Through Jesus Christ our Lord"—that's why all Christian prayers end that way. We are confident about the things we pray for through Jesus Christ our Lord. That's not to say that Rabbi Heschel, who was a great mentor in my life, didn't see the same things about God from the perspective of the Talmud and the Torah and incredible Jewish literature throughout the ages.

I'm convinced that gratitude is the most important religious emotion. Duty calls only when gratitude fails to prompt. When you're grateful for the undeserved beauty of a cloudless sky, you're praying. You're saying, "Thank

---

* The great Jewish theologian who blended mysticism and social action, and became a fighter for civil rights and peace in the 1960s.

you, Lord," praying all the time about the beauty of nature, the beauty of the deeds some people do. In World War II, occasionally a soldier fell on a grenade there was no time to throw back. Well, you could be absolutely appalled by their deaths, but you could be struck by the beauty of selfless courage.

I feel grateful all the time, so my prayers of thanksgiving are very full. I don't tell God what to do, but thinking about other people and trying to think what God would think about them is a way of directing my thoughts to other people. I pray for world peace, but not, "Grant us peace in our time, O Lord." God must say, "Oh, come off it. What are *you* going to do for peace, for heaven's sake?" It's not enough to pray for it; you have to think for it, you have to suffer for it, and you have to endure a lot for it. Don't just pray about it. A lot of people think their prayers aren't answered. They are answered; the answer is no, and they haven't heard it. I don't think you have to be self-conscious about your prayer life. You can just live in wonder and gratitude and with a sense of wanting to respond—responsible means "respond-able," able to respond. If you're able to respond to the beauty of nature, you'll be an environmentalist. If you're able to respond to human beings' basic right to peace, you'll be a peacenik. It's a matter of being full of wonder, thanksgiving, and praying for strength to respond to all the wonder and beauty there is in human life.

One World at a Time

With age, you should step aside. Let other people take over, and maybe the next generation or the one after that will do something much better than we did. Besides, as the great French writer Albert Camus once suggested, there is in the world beauty, and there are the humiliated, and we must strive, hard as it is, not to be unfaithful either to the one or to the other. Blessed as I am living in Vermont, it's easy to be loyal to beauty. If I get too down on our failure to deal with the humiliated, I can always say, "God was good. The creation hasn't totally been corrupted yet."

Hope needs to be understood as a reflection of the state of your soul, not a reflection of the circumstances that surround your days. So I remain hopeful.

The opposite of hope is despair, not pessimism. As a very convinced Christian, I say to myself, "Come on, Coffin, if Christ never allowed his soul to be cornered into despair, and his was the greatest miscarriage of justice, maybe, in the world, who the hell am I to say I'm going to despair a bit?" Besides, when I addressed people as I used to frequently in the peace movement, there would be, in the last ten years, always somebody saying, "I am so disillusioned." Well, being old now, I can be forthright and say, "Who the hell gave you the right to have illusions in the first place?" We have no right to have illusions. So we have only ourselves to chastise when we feel disillusioned.

The moments of great satisfaction in my life are many, for which I'm deeply grateful, most of all because I'm a pastor and my pastoral relations have been some of the most satisfying experiences of my life. After all, when I was at Yale for eighteen years, I spent most of the time just counseling students, one-on-one. People who invite you into the garden of their soul are really wonderful people. They're never boring. I don't bear fools' company gladly, but people who are deeply personal and willing to air their conflicts—that's very satisfying. I must say, you feel a sense of undeserved integrity when you're in the right fight—against segregation, against the war in Vietnam, against the stupid and cruel discrimination against gays and lesbians—these are the right fights, I feel very deeply. The sense of self-fulfillment which comes with being in the right fight is a wonderful thing.

Lastly, only because I'm mentioning it last, is my family. I was too busy when I was younger to really appreciate the incredible ties I have with the family, with my children and two stepchildren also, and with a wife without whom, I think, I would not be sitting here now. When you get older, friendship obviously runs deeper and deeper. I would add, nature gets more interesting the nearer you get to joining it and also more beautiful. I can sit on the front porch here and just watch the sun coming in through the maple leaves. You know, God is good.

Regrets? Well, I don't say this to excuse myself, but I think it's basically a myth that people who are so devoted on public fronts have a wonderful relationship with their families. They're kidding themselves. My regret is that when my children were growing up, I was there for them but not in the way that a father ought to be there for them.

After my son died, I preached a sermon, and the part that many people appreciated was when I said I have no comfort in thinking that it was the will of God that Alex die.* My comfort lies in feeling that of all hearts to break, God's was the first as the wave closed over the sinking car. God is not too hard to believe in; God is too good to believe in, we being strangers to such goodness. The love of God is, to me, absolutely overwhelming. It was an awful tragedy, and you have to go into the depths of pain, and grief is experienced often as the absence of God: "My God, my God, why hast thou forsaken me?" said Jesus from the cross. But those are the first words of the Twenty-second Psalm, and the end of the psalm is in praise of God. It's always in the depths of hell that heaven is found and affirmed and praised.

I'd just as soon live a little bit longer, but when you're eighty you can't complain. To quote Franklin Delano Roosevelt in his inaugural address, "We have nothing to fear but fear itself." Fear of death is what is insidious, and once the fear is behind you, then it is only the physical death which is ahead of you. If we didn't die, we'd be immortal, like the Greek gods, and perhaps up to their same dumb tricks. It's a very good thing we die. In fact, it's death which brings us to life. But we need to be scared to life, not scared to death. I await death with no protest. "Do not go gentle into that good night, rage, rage against the dying of the light": I'm sorry, Dylan Thomas, but that's not always the case. You *can* go gentle into that good night. Stop complaining. Remember that, as old Hamlet said, "The readiness is all." Basically, when I said I don't think much about death, I was really thinking, I don't think much about what comes next because I believe our lives run from God, in God, to God again. And that's enough. We might want to know more, but we don't need to know more, and demanding that I know more about the afterlife somehow demeans my faith. One world at a time, I think.

On April 12, 2006, William Sloane Coffin died at age eighty-one.

---

* Alexander Coffin was twenty-four years old when his car slipped into Boston Harbor on a rainy night in 1983.

Photo Credits

WILLIAM ABERNETHY: courtesy of William Abernethy; **RANDALL BALMER**: courtesy of Randall Balmer; **DIANA BUTLER BASS**: Courtesy of *Religion & Ethics NewsWeekly*; **ROCHEL BERMAN**: George Berman; **TINA BROWN**: Courtesy of *Religion & Ethics NewsWeekly*; **FREDERICK BUECHNER**: Courtesy of *Religion & Ethics NewsWeekly*; **JIMMY CARTER**: Courtesy of *Religion & Ethics NewsWeekly*; **WILLIAM SLOANE COFFIN**: Courtesy of *Religion & Ethics NewsWeekly*; **FRANCIS COLLINS**: courtesy of Francis Collins; **DALAI LAMA**: Courtesy of *Religion & Ethics NewsWeekly*; **MENACHEM DAUM**: Moshe Gutman; **EILEEN DURKIN**: John Goebelbecker; **DIANA ECK**: courtesy of Diana Eck; **TILDEN EDWARDS**: Mary Edwards; **ROBERT FRANKLIN**: Myron Cloyd; **ANDREW GREELEY**: Jack Lane; **BLU GREENBERG**: courtesy of Blu Greenberg; **IRVING GREENBERG**: Courtesy of *Religion & Ethics NewsWeekly*; **THICH NHAT HANH**: courtesy of Thich Nhat Hanh; **DAVID HARTMAN**: Kobi Gideon; **STANLEY HAUERWAS**: courtesy of Duke Divinity School; **CHRIS HEDGES**: Kim Hedges; **RUSHWORTH KIDDER**: Carol M. Miller Photography; **ELLWOOD KIESER**: courtesy of Paulist Press, Inc., from *The Spiritual Journey of a Showbusiness Priest* by Ellwood E. Kieser © 1991, 1996; **HAROLD KUSHNER**: Arielle Kushner Haber; **MADELINE L'ENGLE**: courtesy of Madeline L'Engle; **ANNE LAMOTT**: Mark Richards; **RICHARD LAND**: courtesy of Richard Land; **ALAN LEW**: Bernie Hirschbein; **EDWARD LINENTHAL**: courtesy of Edward Linenthal; **ABRAHAM LUBIN**: courtesy of Abraham Lubin; **THOMAS LYNCH**: Alan Benson; **MARTIN MARTY**: Courtesy of *Religion & Ethics NewsWeekly*; **FREDERICA MATHEWES-GREENE**: Mary Taber-Lind; **MARILYN MCGUIRE**: Susan Osborn; **JAMES MERRITT**: Smith Studios; **SCOTT MORRIS**: Marvin Stockwell; **ABDUL ALIM MUBARAK**: Courtesy of *Religion & Ethics*

Index of Contributors

About the Editors

Bob Abernethy is the executive editor and host of *Religion & Ethics NewsWeekly*, which he developed and created for PBS in 1997. For many years he was a correspondent for NBC News in Washington, London, Los Angeles, and Moscow.

William Bole is a freelance writer and editor whose articles have appeared in the *Washington Post*, *Commonweal* magazine, and other outlets. He is also a research fellow of the Woodstock Theological Center at Georgetown University and an editorial consultant at Boston College.